Praise for the First Edition

"[*Degunking Windows* is] a great new book that explains why computers lose their vigor over time. It offers easy-to-follow instructions for cleaning out your hard drive, tweaking programs, eliminating spyware, sorting e-mail, and updating your system."

—*Parade Magazine*

"Do you own a PC or Mac computer and use it regularly? Then, it has gunk. Gunk is all the unnecessary junk on your computer that can slow down performance and ultimately cause system malfunction. It's those fuzzy photos that never got tossed, e-mail you've filed and forgotten, old programs you never use, hidden programs you don't want, and too many programs that launch at startup. I found very useful advice from...*Degunking Windows* by Joli Ballew and Jeff Duntemann."

—*Seattle Times*

"I once wrote a four-part series in *InfoWorld* about correcting what I called 'Windows arthritis.' This is a lethargy that seems to overtake the operating system as little as six months after it's installed...Now Joli Ballew and Jeff Duntemann have compiled an entire book [*Degunking Windows*] on the subject, and it's a good one."

—Brian Livingston

"After all the worm news these days, when something goes wrong, users will often jump to the not-necessarily accurate conclusion that they have a virus or something like that. Maybe they do, but it's not usually the only problem they have. Joli Ballew and Jeff Duntemann have beaten me to a great idea for a book on this: *Degunking Windows*...I really wish I'd thought of it first."

—Larry Seltzer in *eWeek*

"The information found in *Degunking Windows* is exactly what the doctor ordered. Joli Ballew and Jeff Duntemann do an excellent job of helping you to find the things that are slowing down and cluttering up your system. They explain in plain English what you need to know to remove unwanted programs and optimize your Windows machine for maximum performance."

—*About.com*

"I am impressed. [*Degunking Windows*] makes a very useful companion for step-by-step computer maintenance...My copy is filled with highlighter marks and 3M page markers."

—Memphis PC Users Group

D0564930

"I thought I knew my way around a PC until I bought this book...I can heartily recommend Degunking Windows to any PC user and only wish it had been published sooner. Now I have uncovered many ideas, solutions, and practical hints that I was totally unaware of."

—Bits & Bytes

"When explaining network security to your users, have on hand *Degunking Windows* by Joli Ballew and Jeff Duntemann. Chapters explain file cleanup and organization, spyware, spam, cookies, and setting up a Windows XP Internet Connection firewall."

—Network World

"Only one word is needed to summarize [*Degunking Windows*]: terrific! The authors display an awesome knowledge of Windows XP and its workings, and tell us how to use them to good advantage. The information provided in the book is comprehensive and detailed, yet highly readable."

—Sierra Vista IBM PC Users Group

"The authors in nontechnical language can help you keep the registry clean, back up your critical files, organize your file systems, clean up your desktop, keep your hard drives from working too hard, clean up your e-mail program, work with the taskbar, remove spyware, prevent spam, and a great deal more. Even if you never want to touch your computer in a maintenance kind of way, this book will help you understand why you should."

—Billings Gazette

"Just follow this book [*Degunking Windows*] chapter by chapter and you'll be amazed at how you can improve your PC. The targeted audience in this extremely valuable book includes all serious Windows users who are tired of the common gunked up result that is just what happens in a Windows machine, and who are willing to take charge of their machine and take control over those gunking aspects. While most all extant PC technicians are likely already to be savvy to many of these super suggestions, I bet most all will also find some ideas in this book they have not yet heard of."

—Golden Triangle PC Club

DEGUNKING WINDOWS 7

Joli Ballew

New York   Chicago   San Francisco   Lisbon
London   Madrid   Mexico City   Milan   New Delhi
San Juan   Seoul   Singapore   Sydney   Toronto

The McGraw·Hill Companies

Library of Congress Cataloging-in-Publication Data

Ballew, Joli.
    Degunking Windows 7 / Joli Ballew.
        p.   cm.
    ISBN 978-0-07-176005-8 (alk. paper)
      1. Microsoft Windows (Computer file)   2. Hard disk management.
3. Software maintenance. I. Title.
    QA76.76.O6335924234   2011
    005.4'46—dc22   2011000076

McGraw-Hill books are available at special quantity discounts to use as premiums and sales promotions, or for use in corporate training programs. To contact a representative, please e-mail us at bulksales@mcgraw-hill.com.

Degunking Windows® 7

1234567890 QFR QFR 10987654321

ISBN   978-0-07-176005-8
MHID   0-07-176005-9

Sponsoring Editor Roger Stewart	**Copy Editor** William McManus	**Illustration** Glyph International
Editorial Supervisor Janet Walden	**Proofreader** Madhu Prasher	**Art Director, Cover** Jeff Weeks
Project Manager Tania Andrabi, Glyph International	**Indexer** Jack Lewis	**Cover Designer** Ty Nowicki
Acquisitions Coordinator Joya Anthony	**Production Supervisor** Jean Bodeaux	
Technical Editor Greg Kettell	**Composition** Glyph International	

Contents at a Glance

For my agent Neil Salkind, Ph.D. Thank you for ten years of friendship, service, and support.

About the Author

Joli Ballew (Dallas, Texas) is a technical author, a technology trainer, and web site manager. She holds several certifications, including MCSE, MCTS, and MCDST. Joli is also a Microsoft MVP (four years running), and attends the Microsoft Summit as well as CES every year to stay on top of the latest technology and trends. In addition to writing, she teaches computer classes at the local junior college, and works as a network administrator and web designer for North Texas Graphics. She's written over three dozen books, including many in McGraw-Hill's How to Do Everything™ series. In her free time, she enjoys golfing, yard work, exercising at the local gym, and teaching her cats, Pico and Lucy, tricks.

About the Technical Editor

Greg Kettell is a professional software engineer with a diverse career that has covered everything from game programming to enterprise business applications. He has written and contributed to several books about software applications, web design, and programming. Greg, his wife, Jennifer, and their two children currently reside in upstate New York.

Contents

x   Contents

Foreword

I am both honored and excited to write the foreword for Joli Ballew's latest book, *Degunking Windows 7*. I was a huge fan of its predecessor, *Degunking Windows*, back in 2004, and I had Joli and her co-author, Jeff Duntemann, on my radio show several times. Degunking Windows was a hot topic for my listeners back then (as it is today), and I always had a large audience anytime either Joli or Jeff was on the air with me.

Now we have Windows 7, and thank goodness we have this new book to deal with the gunk we'll acquire and the performance degradation that's bound to occur eventually. *Degunking Windows 7* covers the gunk we had back then, of course, like too much media, unwanted programs, spam, and the like, but it also tackles the new gunk we have now, such as cell phone gunk, networking gunk, and duplicate copies of media on our home networks. We have unsigned drivers, difficult-to-diagnose performance issues, phishing, and multiple user accounts complete with passwords, sharing, permissions, and other things that cause us headaches. We have lots of devices to sync, including multiple i-devices, phones, MP3 players, and more. Yes, we still have some spam, but our e-mail problems stem from keeping too much e-mail—including attachments that are much larger than they used to be—and not understanding how to organize it all (much less back it up).

I got off the purpose at hand; I get so excited about degunking that I forget what I'm supposed to be doing here. What I'd like to say is this: I love Joli's work, and especially her writing style. It's informative but brief, funny, intuitive, and, at times, a bit sassy. This makes it a great read, but also makes it a great a reference. It's written for everyone, from novices to professionals. It's easy to understand, and anyone can use it to degunk a PC, but if you want to dig deeper into topics like improving performance or deleting every last unnecessary item on your PC, Joli shows you how to do that too.

It works like this: You read the book from start to finish and work through the, yes, proven 12-step program, and you relish in the results you get. You brag. You prove that your computer is performing better than it was through performance monitors and Task Manager. Then, you leave the book on your desk, and every time you have a free minute, half hour, or half day, you simply refer to the section "Degunking with Time Limitations" (see page xxii) to do a little cleaning. Everything is right there for you.

Finally I'd like to say this: In my eight years with the *Computer Outlook Talk Show*, nothing has generated as much interest as the topics around making your computer perform better, and degunking is right there in the middle of it. So keep your eyes and ears open, faithful readers (soon to become faithful listeners, hopefully): you can rest assured that Joli will be on the show again very soon!

—John Iasiuolo
Host of *Computer Outlook Talk Show*

Preface

For a long time, what I'm calling *Windows Gunk* was The Problem That Had No Name. People knew that Windows got slow and weird over time, but they could never quite put their finger on what was going wrong. When *Degunking Windows* was first published in 2004, people said "Yeah, that's it! It's Gunk!"

Suddenly, everyone understood the problem with their PC, and the original *Degunking Windows* book became an instant sensation. It wasn't just the name or the cover. We had dared to assemble a 12-step program to help people recover from Windows gunk, and it just worked: "Hello. My name is Windows, and I'm a gunk magnet. I need help." We saved a *lot* of old PCs from the curb.

Not long after the first book's release, I and my coauthor, Jeff Duntemann, were both in demand for radio shows, and scant weeks later we were often back on the same shows, explaining the ways that Windows bogs down and offering tips on how to make things work again. Reviewers began to rave. The *Chicago Tribune* said "The advice is elegantly presented with superb hand-holding from coauthors Joli Ballew and Jeff Duntemann," and the reviews climaxed on July 4th, 2004 with an exceptional review in *Parade Magazine* and a listing as a "Best Bet" for books. That landed *Degunking Windows* on Amazon's Bestseller list, just below Bill Clinton's *My Life* and Dan Brown's *The Da Vinci Code*. We followed up these books with *Degunking Your PC*, *Degunking Your Mac*, and others. Sadly, Paraglyph Press folded a couple of years later, and the Degunking series' reign ended. Now, I've obtained the rights to the original book and have rewritten it for Windows 7.

Degunking Windows 7 is a much different task than degunking older versions of Windows. We barely talked about *network gunk* back then, and now, we have homegroups, workgroups, Wi-Fi networks, Ethernet networks, and all kinds of things that connect, sync, and cause us headaches. Back then we spent a lot of time discussing how to organize data because people tended to put data everywhere, even on their root drives, but now we have "libraries" to help us stay organized automatically. Back then, believe it or not, we didn't have iPods. I'm not even sure I had a cell phone, but if I did, it was not capable of retrieving my e-mail and letting me surf the Web, and I certainly didn't sync it with my computer. Thus, we didn't talk at all about cell phones, iPods, iPads, digital cameras, and the gunk that comes along with them—syncing issues, unwanted software and pop-ups for software updates, and duplicate files—and now that's a big part of where gunk comes from.

We also have a lot more media than we had back then, and it's hogging up our hard drive space. Luckily for us, though, these days we often have plenty of hard drive space to work with. Thus, while our gunk from media can come from its size, it more often comes in the form of duplicate files, unwanted files, files that won't play, and files that won't sync. Along those same lines, the ability to record TV and movies has caused us a lot of gunk, too. The default settings for Media Center are to record all instances of a program, not just new ones, and this can fill up a hard drive fast. One day you're minding your own business, the next you get a message you have no hard drive space left! And, of course, those pictures! Pictures with awful names like IMG_0012456.png; what is all that about? Something needs to be done.

In addition, as it has been forever, I suppose we'll always have a problem with spam, but my spam is not nearly as bad as it was back in 2004, and yours probably isn't either. ISPs and e-mail providers are getting a good handle on that. While I will address spam, our e-mail gunk often comes from keeping too much e-mail, having unorganized e-mail, mismanaging attachments, and backing up e-mail. I'm betting that most readers have no idea how to back up e-mail messages.

There's so much more to degunking, though, including securing your PC with user accounts, installing and configuring antivirus software, incorporating Windows Defender, and really, truly *using* the new Action Center. You have to protect your network with passwords and encryption to keep others out, too. There's a new Internet Explorer and lots of new security settings and features. Heck, there are new browsers! There are programs that run in the background that you may not even know about, much less want. The Start menu and Taskbar can become cluttered. There are error messages to resolve, drivers to update, data to back up, and "crapware" to delete. (Crapware is all of that stuff that comes installed on a new PC, like trial versions of software.)

Don't worry; although you may feel overwhelmed now, you can manage it. In this book, I'll walk you through cleaning it all up and keeping it in order. I've had many years' experience in this area, and have been writing about Windows, operating systems, computers, and even Microsoft Office programs for a decade. You'll get through it with step-by-step hand-holding and encouragement, and you'll see results immediately. Yes, there is such a thing as instant gratification!

Acknowledgments

The people from McGraw-Hill and I go way back. I believe our first book together was *Hardcore Windows XP*, published in 2005. That was a long time ago, but the same people are still there to thank. Roger Stewart is one of them. He's very particular about what makes the cut and what doesn't with regard to what books get the go-ahead nod, so I'm always thankful when they pick up a book I've proposed or choose me to write one they have designed. They do high-quality work at McGraw-Hill, and I'm proud to be a part of their team. We've done a lot of books together since 2005, including the extremely popular *How to Do Everything: iPad*, and I'm always impressed with McGraw-Hill's editorial team and the people they choose to act as technical editors.

For this book, Joya Anthony was my acquisitions coordinator, and was awesome at it. She kept me on track and within my page count, and was supportive every step of the way. My technical editor was Greg Kettell, a highly organized, superbly trained, very intelligent man. He had a few things to say about my work technically, as all editors do, but more to say about other things we could include to make the book better and more informative. He was a great help and easy to work with. There were a few other people on this project, roll the Oscar fade out music ...My project manager at Glyph International was Tania Andrabi, who managed the schedule, the freelancers, and my tendency to want to use "we" instead of "I." When you have had a coauthor as awesome as Jeff Duntemann, it's hard to get the word "we" out of your head. The copy editor was Bill McManus, who did the moving around of text when the need arose and who was kind enough to not only suggest that specific sentences be reworded, but also offered the entire sentence up (in case I simply wanted to copy and paste his words) to speed up the editorial process. I did that in almost all cases. My production supervisor was Jean Bodeaux, who worked with Roger Stewart and the composition team at Glyph to develop a design that fit "degunking." I'm lucky to have such wonderful people to work with.

I'd be remiss if I did not say something about the original team that helped me write and publish the original *Degunking Windows* books back in 2004 and 2005. Those books were a raving success, and the first edition of *Degunking Windows* was featured in *Parade Magazine* as a "Best Bet" for books in 2004. It was named Best Computer Book of the Year by IPPY in 2005. Critics raved, and we were extremely excited for months on end. We later extended the series to *Degunking Your PC* and *Degunking*

Your Mac, both successes in their own right, and both of which I wrote as well. Unfortunately, Paraglyph Press, the publisher of these fine books, didn't make it in the long term and is now out of business, but McGraw-Hill has picked up the series to bring you this book. The members of the original team included Jeff Duntemann, my coauthor; Ben Sawyer, Cynthia Caldwell, and Kim Eoff; and of course the founders of Paraglyph Press, Keith Weiskamp and Steven Sayre.

I have a family to thank, too: Dad, Jennifer, Cosmo, Andrew, Garth, Theresa, Doug, and Laura. There are some others, too, including my cousin Lindy, Uncle Bradley and Doris, and Nathan. I lost my mom in 2009, which, although expected, hit me pretty hard. I continue to think of her daily and dream about her at night. I hope someday I get to see her again. I have lots of good friends to support me, too, including Mindy, Bryan, Pam, Jan, Jerry, Charley, Brenda, and a few others. I might have a small group of family and friends, but we're strong.

Finally, I'd like to thank Studio B and the Salkind Literary Agency. My agent is Neil Salkind, and this year will be our 10-year *anniversary*. Over those years we've published over 40 books in 10+ languages, and we've had best sellers and duds. I'd have no career without him and appreciate his service, support, and friendship over all of these years. He's a good friend. Thanks, Neil.

And for you, dear reader, please feel free to contact me anytime with your thoughts, concerns, suggestions, praise, or questions. I'd have nothing at all if I did not have you. I'd love to hear from you at Joli_Ballew@Hotmail.com.

Introduction

Your brand new PC was awesome when you took it out of the box. You were in heaven. You told everyone how great Windows 7 was, how sleek Internet Explorer was, and how much faster your Internet connection seemed. You could find files easily, you could save files in their proper places, and you had no problems whatsoever installing hardware and software.

You started to notice you had a lot of stuff you weren't using, though. Some people refer to it as "crapware." That's the stuff like a 60-day trial of antivirus or office software, photo editing software, music programs, DVD burning programs, and the like. You don't want it. You don't need it. So you spend a little time trying to uninstall it, only to find yourself either bored or uneasy with the entire thing and stopping before the task is complete.

And *then* you noticed that while there was a lot of stuff you had but did not want, there were also a few things missing. There was no e-mail program, no Microsoft photo editing program, and no Microsoft messaging program. There may have not been any movie-making program, and no antivirus program short of a trial from Norton or McAfee. Perhaps you downloaded, purchased, installed, or tried out various programs to resolve these problems. Maybe you found something that seemed to work but didn't, or perhaps you installed programs that caused the system to become buggy or unstable.

Then you used the computer for a while. You installed toolbars and add-ons for Internet Explorer, you disabled some of the controls so that you could avoid pop-ups and warnings from Windows, and you may have even disabled updates for fear of getting one that was buggy. You copied data from other computers, tried to share data with others, and haphazardly added your new Windows 7 machine to an existing network. You probably copied lots of data to your new PC you now wish you hadn't, especially if you used Windows Easy Transfer to do the job.

A few short months later, you're no longer in heaven and you're no longer touting how great Windows 7 is. Your computer is slow, your Internet connection is slow, you can't find your files or they are unorganized, and you have duplicate data everywhere. There's also all kinds of software on your PC you don't want. What a pain. How did you get here? Why did this happen? What can you do?

Why You Need This Book

Without proper and regular maintenance and careful work habits, all PCs running Windows will bog down and get gunked up over time. You probably collected your own gunk when you set up the PC, too; you undoubtedly installed various programs, transferred data you don't need, or copied the gunk you already had (like that long, unruly list of Internet Explorer Favorites or all of your unorganized contacts). Thus, the goal of this book is to show you how to rid your PC of the gunk you have now and keep additional gunk from piling up.

The Degunking Windows Approach

Degunking Windows 7 uses a unique approach that can save you countless hours of valuable time, and a bundle of money on software and hardware you don't need. For instance, you shouldn't bother messing around with third-party mail and photo editing programs when Windows Live Essentials is free; uninstall the rest and get on with your life! Since the "Live" programs are created by Microsoft, you know they'll play well with Windows. This book includes information on this and more; here are a few more unique features of this book:

- An easy-to-follow 12-step degunking process that you can put to work immediately
- Explanations, in everyday terms, of how to fix common problems that create gunk on your PC
- Information on how to improve your PC with free utilities and programs
- GunkBuster's Notebook sidebars in every chapter to help you solve specific problems while reducing clutter on your PC
- Instructions on how to degunk your e-mail
- Advice on how to work smart to keep your PC from gunking up in the future

I also include instructions on how to drastically improve the performance of your Windows 7 PC; specifically, I explain how to

- Stop processes and programs from running in the background that hog system resources without your knowledge
- Rid the computer of unnecessary data, programs, e-mail gunk, media gunk, trial software, and temporary files that can make the computer slow down and make it hard to manage
- Improve the speed of Internet surfing
- Keep the computer free of adware, spyware, viruses, and unwanted pop-ups from web sites, instant messaging software, and Skype, among others
- Stay organized and keep the computer running efficiently so you can enjoy it for years to come

How to Use This Book

Degunking Windows 7 is structured around the order of the degunking process that you should follow. The book starts off by explaining the importance of degunking and why operating systems like Windows 7 require degunking and regular maintenance. Each subsequent chapter describes an important degunking task, explained in plain English with step-by-step instructions.

NOTE It's important to work through the book in order, from start to finish. This will result in the most benefit from the time you spend degunking.

Once you've completely degunked your PC, you should then perform different degunking operations at different times, depending on your needs, to keep your PC in tip-top shape. Keep *Degunking Windows 7* on your desk or your bookshelf and within easy reach; I expect you'll access it often!

Degunking Earlier Versions of Windows

The degunking tasks presented in this book were written to work with Windows 7. There are several tools detailed in the book that are only available in Windows 7, such as homegroups, the Action Center, Jump Lists, and others. You simply won't find these tools in pre-Windows 7 machines. However, you can use the book to help you degunk the other computers you own; in fact, *most* of the techniques can be applied to computers running Windows Vista, Windows XP, and even Windows 2000. For instance, you can use Control Panel in any Windows computer to uninstall programs you no longer use, noting that the way you do it won't be exactly as outlined here (but similar). The concept is the same, though. Some features are practically exactly the same. The command msconfig.exe is one of those. No matter what operating system you use, you can type that command to control what boots when Windows does.

Here are some of the more general (and less version-specific) tasks you can perform, regardless of the version of Windows you have:

- Getting rid of files that shouldn't be there
- Uninstalling programs you don't need and tweaking those you do
- Organizing remaining files and folders
- Tweaking the Start menu, Desktop, and Taskbar
- Preventing e-mail gunk
- Optimizing your hard drive
- Resolving syncing issues, network issues, and error messages
- Backing up data
- Staying gunk-free in the long term

The Degunking Mindset

The more you learn about degunking your PC, the more you'll realize that degunking is a mindset, not just a set of technical skills. Degunking is mostly psychology, and only some technology. Degunking involves a disciplined approach to setting up and managing your computer and organizing your work habits. If you follow the basic steps outlined in this book on a regular basis, you'll provide yourself a sort of Windows insurance policy and save yourself a lot of aggravation down the road. I also believe that *Degunking Windows 7* will make time on your PC more time efficient, more productive, and maybe even more enjoyable. Windows can be fun, especially with Windows 7's Play To feature, Media Player and Media Center, and Games. With a little care and attention to detail, your PC can be just as much fun three or four years down the road as it was the day you took it out of the box!

The Degunking 12-Step Program

Here is the basic 12-step degunking process that you will follow while working through this book to fully degunk your PC. Once you've worked through these steps, repeat them as necessary to keep your PC in tip-top shape for years to come.

1. Get rid of files and programs you don't need.
2. Organize your remaining files and folders.
3. Clean up your Desktop, Start menu, and Taskbar.
4. Optimize your hard drive and limit the programs that run in the background.
5. Clean up and secure Internet Explorer and consider alternative web browsers.
6. Reduce your e-mail spam, learn how to back up e-mail, and organize your mail.
7. Install Windows updates and/or reconfigure antivirus, antimalware, and antiadware programs.
8. Clean up your network and create a homegroup.
9. Fix problems with media, including duplicate files, files that won't play, and files that are taking up hard drive space unnecessarily.
10. Optimize syncing with cell phones, music players, iPads, iPhones, netbooks, and laptops.
11. Get rid of errors for hardware, the operating system, and third-party programs.
12. Create a working, reliable, and fool-proof backup system.

Degunking with Time Limitations

To get the full benefits of degunking, I highly recommend that you complete all of the main degunking tasks in the order that they are presented in this book. Performing all of these tasks will require a bit of time, though. If your time is limited, the following sections offer some suggestions for valuable degunking tasks you can perform in the time you *do* have—whether it's ten minutes, an hour, or a half a day.

Ten-Minute Degunking

If you have a very short amount of time—less than half an hour, say—you can still degunk something. In fact, degunking in ten-minute spurts may be perfect for those of you who have trouble staying focused!

- Delete e-mail from your Inbox that doesn't *have* to be there.
- Delete everything but the last two or three months of e-mails from your Sent Items folder in your e-mail program, and then repeat for your Deleted Items folder.
- Empty the Recycle Bin on your Desktop to free up space on your hard drive.
- Download and install the free Microsoft Security Essentials if your computer is not protected with another antivirus program.
- Delete shortcuts on your Desktop for programs you do not use.
- Move files saved to your desktop to the Deleted Items bin or an appropriate folder (Documents, Pictures, Videos, etc.).
- Use a dry, soft, dust-free cloth to clean smudges and fingerprints off of your computer monitor.
- Disconnect and store peripherals you aren't using, including iPads, iPods, and digital cameras.
- Look at the System Tray and scan the icons on it. If you see that "updates are ready to install," install them only if you trust the publisher and want to keep and use the related program.
- Unplug or turn off peripherals you aren't using (such as printers and scanners) to save energy and reduce wear and tear.
- Drag the items in your Documents, Pictures, Videos, Music, and other "main" folders to an external hard drive to back up the data.
- Run Disk Cleanup to remove temporary files.

Thirty-Minute Degunking

If you only have 30 minutes or so, there are plenty of degunking tasks you can complete. I suggest focusing on getting rid of programs you don't use, checking for and installing updates, and resolving problems that the Action Center has found. You can also work on that ever-expanding Inbox of e-mails.

- In Control Panel, review the list of installed programs and uninstall any program you haven't used in a year or more.
- In Documents, delete documents you no longer need. Next time, repeat with your Pictures, Videos, Games, and Music folders.
- Open Windows Update and install any critical updates. Review the available optional updates and install if desired.
- Verify your antivirus software is running and the definitions are up to date. Install updates if necessary and configure updates to install automatically, each day.
- Reply to the e-mails in your Inbox that need attention, and then delete them.
- Open the Action Center and resolve any problems listed. (The solution may take more than a half hour to complete, but you can get started on it anyway.)

- Create a subfolder in your Pictures folder and move related photos to it.
- Look for updates to software you use with cell phones, iPods, iPhones, and the like. If you use iTunes, for instance, open it, click Help, and Check for Updates.
- Create e-mail rules to move e-mail from a user group, e-mail list, or specific sender (noreply@facebook.com, for instance) to a specific folder as it comes in. This will allow you to stay focused on what you're doing without being interrupted by e-mail that is not of immediate importance.
- Turn off all of your hardware and all computers. Then, reboot in this order: cable, DSL, or satellite modem first (wait two minutes), wireless or Ethernet router second (wait two minutes), all computers, and then hardware you use often, including printers and scanners. (I suggest leaving the latter turned off until you need them, though.)
- Name a batch of your favorite photos descriptively and get away from the naming conventions you likely use now (IMG100425.jpg, for instance).
- Run msconfig.exe to limit what programs start when your computer boots. If you aren't sure what a program name represents, research it on the Internet.

One-Hour Degunking

If you have an hour to devote to degunking, you can go a little deeper and make some serious progress toward a totally degunked PC.

- If the PC tower is in a "cubby" or small area, turn off the PC, disconnect all hardware, and reposition the PC so that it has enough room to "breathe." Reconnect the hardware, turn on the PC, and verify the keyboard, mouse, and other peripherals work.
- Check obscure places on your hard drive for orphaned files, misplaced files, and missing files. Check (C:\), which is your root drive, and also look at any partitions your PC may have. Delete unwanted compressed files, look for duplicate files in Public and shared folders, and clean the nooks and crannies of your PC.
- Search for programs you didn't even know you had and uninstall them. This may require you to scour the All Programs menu, the root drive, and areas other than Control Panel.
- Open Network and verify you can access data on each networked device. If you can't, apply passwords to the computers you can't access and configure sharing settings on them.
- If you have a new Windows 7 PC, download and install Windows Live Essentials. At least get Live Mail, Live Photo Gallery, and Live Messenger. Make sure to get a Live account too.
- If you use Windows Movie Maker or another movie-making program, delete unnecessary files related to them. Once you've created the movie and burned it to a DVD, you may only need the movie file and nothing else.
- Fine-tune programs you use often to improve their performance.
- Clean up and personalize the Start menu or Taskbar.

- Recheck the System Tray. Note what's running. Open each program and configure it to open only on your command, not automatically, as applicable. (Leave antivirus software and the like running.)
- Set up a backup program to run automatically and on a schedule. If you don't have a backup program, consider Windows Backup and Restore.
- Rename, move, delete, and organize data folders on your PC. Move (don't copy) data you want to share with others on your network to the Public folders.
- Open the computer's case and use canned air to blow out dust and pet hair. (Don't touch anything inside the case.)

Half-Day Degunking

If you're ready to spend a half a day degunking, you have a long attention span! Here are some ideas for really making your computer and network shine.

- Work through an entire chapter of this book, starting where you last left off.
- Reposition your wireless router so that it is located as closely to the center of the house as possible. This will likely involve turning off all computers, the cable or satellite modem, and the router, moving the hardware, and then turning them all back on (modem first, router second, computers third). You may even have to run to the store for additional cables, extenders, or surge-protecting power strips.
- Look at what's plugged in all the time. Reposition your hardware and surge-protecting power strips so that all nonessential hardware plugs into a single strip. Then, you can disconnect power to nonessential components quickly (printers, scanners, camera and cell phone chargers, and so on) to reduce your energy bills. (When the hardware and its related software aren't running, your computer will run faster and better, too, because you've freed up resources.)
- Research any error messages you see when you boot the PC, plug in a peripheral, or run a specific program. Locate the solution and employ it. If no solution exists, unplug the device, uninstall its related software, and replace the device with one that is Windows compatible.
- Set up a stand-alone spam filtering utility, install and configure a new web browser, and/or reassess security settings, add-ons, and toolbars to improve Internet functionality.
- Go through all of your pictures, create folders and subfolders, and move images to their proper folders. Repeat with music and videos.
- Call your Internet service provider and ask if they'll come out and test your Internet connection for speed, errors, and functionality. Many will do so for free. If errors are found, have the company resolve them.
- Verify that all of your data is in a folder that is automatically backed up by your backup program. If you can't move a specific folder, add it to the "watch" list for the appropriate library.
- If you have other Windows 7 machines, create a homegroup. Configure the other machines to join. Then, search for Windows 7–compliant devices on your network and add them. Try out the feature Play To in Windows Media Player once you're finished.

- Move off of your computer data that you haven't accessed in two years or more. Put that data on a network drive, external drive, or DVDs. Make sure to rename the data so that it's easily recognizable, should you ever need to access it.
- Replace your aging wireless router with a newer, faster router (provided your computer supports the faster speed). Use the Network and Sharing Center to configure sharing settings exactly the way you want, test all connections, and access all shared data, to completely degunk your network.
- Start degunking another PC in your home or office.

Spare-Moment Degunking

There may be times when you are doing something at your computer and you discover that you have a few minutes to spare. Perhaps you're waiting for a response to an e-mail or a phone call. To this end, here is a list of 20 things you can do with only a few clicks of the mouse to further degunk your PC. These tasks do not need to be performed in any order, and you can perform them often to keep a degunked PC, well, degunked!

- Delete unwanted icons from your Desktop.
- Empty the Recycle Bin.
- Delete two or more items in your e-mail Inbox.
- Add or remove default icons on your Desktop.
- Remove a program from the Start menu.
- Pin a program to the Start menu or Taskbar.
- Check your e-mail program's Junk E-mail folder.
- Empty the Deleted Items folder in your e-mail program.
- Unsubscribe from an e-mail newsletter you no longer want to receive.
- Physically clean your keyboard or computer screen.
- Check Internet Explorer's Security options to verify you're protected.
- Make sure your antivirus program is running and has recently performed a scan.
- Make sure your backup program is set to back up data automatically and that a backup has been performed in the last week.
- Search for the largest files on your PC and consider deleting them. Make sure to check the Videos folder and all folders related to Media Center.
- Check Virtual Memory settings and make sure they are optimally configured.
- Create a subfolder and move data into it.
- Create a folder on the Desktop to hold files you're working on now.
- Rename a few pictures.
- Uninstall a program you no longer use.
- Configure Internet Explorer to better manage cookies.

1

Why Is My Computer All Gunked Up?

Degunking Checklist:

- ☑ Understand the four basic processes involved in degunking Windows 7
- ☑ Learn that how and where you save files can gunk up your machine
- ☑ Understand why you need a strategy for dealing with files, both wanted and unwanted
- ☑ Learn that you can develop a plan to combat e-mail gunk
- ☑ Understand why installing too much software and hardware can really gunk up your machine
- ☑ See how your Desktop, Taskbar, Start menu, and menu system are places where gunk can build up
- ☑ Understand how unorganized web favorites can gunk up your machine
- ☑ Understand that connected devices use system resources

Because you've picked up this book, chances are you fall into one of three categories: You have a Windows 7 machine whose performance you are unhappy with; your mom or dad recently asked you why their Windows 7 machine doesn't function as well as it used to and asked you to fix it; or you're a help-desk clerk trying to show people how to save their Windows 7 machines from oblivion. Whatever the case, you're the victim of a fairly common problem—you have a gunked-up computer that you need to keep from falling apart (and driving you crazy).

Don't worry; I'm going to straighten it all out in this book. In this first chapter, you'll learn how and why Windows machines get gunked up. That's pretty important. You have to understand and admit you have a problem before you can really do something about it! With that knowledge, you can then work through my 12-step program to degunk it. That's what this entire book is about, degunking! Let's look first at why you are here.

You Are Here! (But, Why?)

You may know about or have some of the most common gunk-symptoms: Your computer's hard drive works way too hard when you're editing pictures or rendering videos, and the process takes longer than it used to. You get errors when you sync devices, but don't know how to resolve them; worse, sometimes nothing syncs at all. Internet Explorer hangs up, programs freeze, or your mouse stops working in your word processing program (although it works elsewhere), and the only way to resolve the problem is to reboot the computer. Speaking of rebooting, the bootup process takes a lot longer than it used to, adding to the list of grievances you have with your Windows 7 PC.

When you start getting frustrated, your mind may wander to thoughts of reformatting your computer's hard drive and starting from scratch, or, buying a brand new hard drive. Maybe you just need more RAM or a bigger hard drive! Surely, that would solve these problems and they'd never occur again! (Now, you have to know this isn't the best solution—you'd just have more room to accumulate gunk or you'd have a newly formatted computer all prepared for your making the same mistakes again!) When you feel that your computer is ready to be handed down to one of the kids, or worse, put out to pasture, you're likely also to ask yourself, "What the heck happened? Where did I go wrong?"

You may have gotten off track from the very beginning if you had gunk on an older PC and transferred all of it to your new computer. That's a very common mistake. If you had duplicate files on your old PC, you have those same duplicates on this one. If your pictures were not named or organized effectively before, they won't be now either. In a worst-case scenario, you could have actually moved infected data, the result of a latent virus, adware, or spyware. But wait, there's more!

This gunk now on your new PC may have been exacerbated by a combination of internal factors too (forgetting to back up your hard drive, not closely watching what programs were installed, subscribing to too many e-mail newsletters, and so on). In addition, there are external factors (spam, Internet viruses, and unexpected power outages) that can cause a number of issues. The gunk that comes from power outages, among other external factors you can't control, certainly isn't your fault, though.

GunkBuster's Notebook: Don't Buy Another PC Until You Read This!

Don't let computer enthusiasts, friends, relatives, or salespeople at the big-box stores convince you that your computer needs to be replaced just because it's slowed down, is running low on hard drive space, or produces errors. Salespeople want you to buy a new machine every year, and your kids have no qualms (no matter what they say, believe me!) about accepting your "broken" machine and fixing it up for their own use. The truth is, you probably don't need a new computer at all. You just need a little experience, a little time, some degunking insight, and a copy of this book.

Additionally, because you continue to acquire music, movies, video footage, data, and applications that aren't easily deleted or organized, gunk just keeps piling up. It's hard to delete music you never listen to (and music you paid for at some point but don't like). It's equally difficult to delete raw footage of an event even after you've edited it, created a movie, burned a DVD, and backed it all up to an external drive. Believe me, I understand. It's equally difficult to delete programs you've purchased, even if you've never used them. There are things you just can't bring yourself to delete (although you could move them off the computer to a DVD or external drive).

It's important that you don't feel like all this gunk is *entirely* your fault, though. After a while (no matter who you are or how meticulous you keep your computer), with normal wear and tear, every computer will start to slow down. The hard drive spins longer, programs take longer to load, programs crash more frequently, and in general, the computer becomes harder to use. PCs don't last forever. The bright, shiny packaging and five-star reviews make saying no to software downloads difficult too; and the hardware—there are so many totally cool gadgets you just have to have, all of which come with their own software! Everything you install causes processes to run and monopolizes resources. You have to install updates and service packs as well, and system-hogging programs and their own updates use more and more valuable resources every year. After a while, your computer simply can't keep up with the demands placed on it. "Getting gunked" happens to everyone; you are not alone.

So while it's hard to pinpoint *exactly* what caused *your specific gunk problem*, it is certainly possible to make the gunk buildup stop, clean it up, and keep it from happening again. That's great news; there are solutions to overcoming the common factors that create gunk on every PC. In this book, I'll identify common PC gunk creators, explain how to get rid of them, and show you how to manage your degunked computer so that it keeps running quickly and efficiently.

What the Experts Know

Hardcore Windows users and those geeky guys you hear on Sunday afternoon radio shows know how to keep their machines working well. And the good news is that most people can learn how to do this too; you just need all the important degunking information in an easy-to-follow book. To that end, this book organizes your degunking efforts into four areas of focus:

- **Basic computer housekeeping 101**   Here you'll focus on how to get everything back in its place and rid yourself of all the gunk. (Just think about how good it feels to clean out your closet and throw away all the stuff you don't need.) You'll start with data, such as files, pictures, videos, and music, and continue with applications and programs and services that run unnecessarily and hinder your PC's performance. You'll then spend some time organizing what you want to keep and personalizing Windows to suit your preferences.

- **Repairing common problems**   Once you've culled down the programs and files on your machine, you'll repair some rudimentary and common problems. You can think of this as a basic tune-up of your system, and it can be the capstone to a core cleaning and improvement process. Here's where you'll resolve errors, problems with hardware and software, and syncing issues.
- **Improving preferences and settings to maintain things better**   Once you've officially degunked your machine, you'll want to tweak the operating system and key programs so you don't end up back where you started. This can involve scheduling tasks (such as when virus updates are acquired), adding commands you use often to toolbars, or personalizing menu systems such as the Start menu and Taskbar.
- **Improving security and backup**   In this area, you will take steps to further improve the security of your PC with user accounts, Windows Defender, the Action Center, and similar features, and learn ways to back up your data so you'll always feel safe.

Understand How You Got So Gunked Up

You understand now that it is common for your system to run more slowly than it once did. That's the nature of things; computers don't last forever, and before they completely give up the ghost, they start to run a little slower and have a few more aches and pains (just like us). You may have, by now, conceded that you may have played a role in the amassment of gunk too. You may have installed software you don't use and hardware that's not on the "Plays Well With Windows" list. You may have never taken the time to organize the data on your computer or manage what you record on TV. And you may have aggravated existing problems by failing to maintain the computer with updates and antivirus software, by being reluctant to delete unwanted data and files, and by being lax in running adware and antimalware scans. So although you probably, by now anyway, have a general idea of what might be wrong and what you can start to do about it, let's go ahead and review how *most users* end up with a gunked-up PC; just so you know.

Files Are Stored Everywhere

Novice users, and even some savvy ones, will have document files, downloaded program files, and other data saved in many different places on their hard drive. This scattering of files and data happens all the time. For example, a program that is used to open an attachment from an e-mail program may lead a person to save the file in a temporary directory in the Windows directory system or an obscure folder that that program has created. If the user doesn't notice this and doesn't decisively save the file in their Documents folder, a subfolder they've created, the Public Documents folder, or the Documents Library, the document will remain in the wrong place. This is an example of gunk.

FIGURE 1-1   Although saving files to the Desktop can be handy, it can also end up looking like this.

Some users will also casually save stuff to their Desktop or the C: root directory of their hard drive without giving it much thought at all. Although they can find the file using Windows 7's Start Search window, it's still *gunky* because it's simply not stored in the proper place where it'll get backed up automatically by backup software. Storing to the Desktop is fine in the short term, but many people never take the time to clean up the data they save there, and later become overwhelmed with it, as is the case with the Desktop shown in Figure 1-1. It's ultimately better to take the extra couple of seconds it requires to save the file in its appropriate folder, which I'll harp on again and again in this book.

Many people collect gunk in their e-mail Inboxes too, and when they think about where files are stored and where gunk may be collecting, their e-mail program may not come to mind. It's important to know when to throw e-mail away, how to filter what arrives, and how to create folders and subfolders to handle the mail one wants to keep. People can overdo this too, though; and some eventually create an e-mail folder system that's difficult to manage. See Figure 1-2.

Temporary Files Aren't So Temporary

Windows keeps a lot of temporary files. When computers crash, programs crash or freeze, or files are "automatically" saved by the operating system, temp files hang around and gunk up the system. Internet Explorer keeps loads of temporary files too, for the purpose of making web sites load faster, and to remember usernames and passwords, among other things. Unfortunately, these temporary files are often

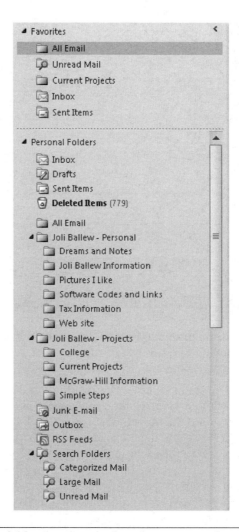

FIGURE 1-2   When a folder system is so big that you use the scroll bars to view the data, it can start to look and feel like gunk.

like temporary tax hikes—they somehow become permanent fixtures, even if they started out with good intentions of remaining temporary. The result is that there are hundreds, if not thousands, of files stuck in obscure places, with obscure filenames, throughout the hard drive. To make matters worse, some of these files can't even be located unless one really understands how to find them. Getting these files off of a hard drive is not always easy.

Of course, there are third-party automated utilities that can locate and delete temporary files, but they don't typically clean out all the temporary files. I have a hard time trusting most software created by third-party publishers that offer these kinds of services anyway. Windows offers Disk Cleanup, to get rid of the temporary files manually, but Disk Cleanup doesn't run automatically or on a schedule by default.

Even with Disk Cleanup, there will still be a need to resort to some hand-cleaning to get rid of all the temporary files on your hard drive. Thus, it helps to know where files hide and how they get there in the first place.

Spam, Spam, Eggs, Bacon, and Spam!

I'm sure you've gotten your share of spam; I think it's safe to say everyone has been spammed. *Spam* is junk e-mail, and is difficult to deal with. Spam adds gunk to already bloated hard drives and fills up Inboxes and Deleted Items folders quickly. Spam can also be a common source of viruses and worms on ordinary people's PCs.

Internet service providers (ISPs) and companies that provide web-based e-mail services have gotten a pretty good handle on spam, though. They filter the mail that comes through their servers, and catch a lot of unwanted e-mail before it hits e-mail client Inboxes. Some spam will still get through, though, and there are ways to deal with it. There's no need to throw in the towel when it comes to spam. A more proactive approach, including using different e-mail addresses, setting up spam filters, using different e-mail clients, and avoiding activities that trigger spam in the first place, could really help reduce it.

Unwanted Software and Trialware

New computers come with all kinds of software and trialware. New manufacturers often install music programs, DVD burning programs, video editing programs, and trials for office programs and antivirus applications. I'm always shocked to see all the "crapware" that comes preinstalled on a new PC. The first thing I do, and the first thing anyone should do, is uninstall all the applications and programs that aren't warranted, are trials, or are not desired.

People install their own array of programs and trialware too, though. There are cool utilities, gadgets, screen savers, and font subscription services, and neat games to keep the kids occupied. There are also media and music programs, instant messaging programs, and even "Registry-cleaning" programs (that claim to make your computer run faster and smarter). People tend to install any program they have acquired on CDs too, like mapping software, printer software, scanner software, and digital camera software. Chances are most of it could now be uninstalled.

The unfortunate part about having all these programs is that some of them run in the background all the time, using system resources required to do other things, like burn a DVD or run a resource-intensive program like Photoshop. They also use hard drive space and may have created their own folders and subfolders that require hard drive space and perhaps another "bad" place to save files. Just because programs aren't being used doesn't mean they aren't playing a role in the gunk problem.

NOTE   When a program is installed, more is happening than just copying files to the hard drive. Programs can and often do make actual changes to the Windows operating system, including something called the *Registry*, which is sort of like a street map or rulebook on how programs work in Windows. Gum up the Registry and it can be like driving in New York City without the traffic lights working.

The Menu System Is Overrun

When programs are installed, they add program icons to the All Programs menu and, often, the Desktop. Eventually, given enough time and lack of upkeep, a person ends up with tons of separate folder entries on the Start menu, making it unmanageable. Worse yet, some of the icons might not even work anymore. Their system is probably still functional, but it's possible to make Windows quicker to load and easier to use by cleaning up the Start menu.

Low Hard Drive Space

Windows utilizes the hard drive to keep the operating system running, to keep open programs running, and to perform basic tasks, in addition to storing temporary files, running scheduled operations, and handling a myriad of other tasks. Windows also uses the hard drive to serve as an extension of working memory and to perform other core operating system functions. Thus, if a hard drive is too full, Windows may crash more frequently or slow waaaaay down. This is less of a problem nowadays because people have machines with gigantic hard drives and loads of memory. However, with the inevitable increase in the number of video files, music files, recorded TV, big Internet downloads, and digital photographs, the hard drive is likely to fill up really fast. See Figure 1-3.

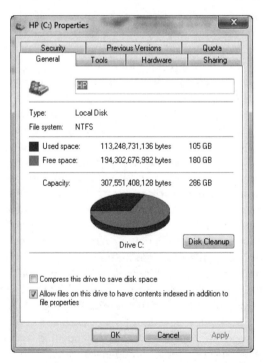

FIGURE 1-3   Check your hard drive often to verify you have plenty of hard drive space.

GunkBuster's Notebook: A Note About Cookies

Cookies are not programs, and generally they aren't bad. They're basically tiny pieces of text data that web sites place in a special directory on a computer. For example, a site like Yahoo! might place a small cookie on a machine with the contents "xu44$@dncsdlk3," which is a unique string of characters that it uses to recognize the user and computer. Unless a person is logged in to Yahoo!, that string doesn't serve any purpose; it is used only by Yahoo! to recognize a logged in user.

Overall, cookies are fairly harmless. They hardly require any hard drive space, and they usually don't give a site much information other than that the user has visited before. However, many people like to get rid of them because, after a while, there may be a few thousand of them, and about 99 percent of them are useless. In addition, when a person accidentally stumbles onto a gambling or porn site, cookies from the site might be stored from it, which can be disconcerting for some people. Imagine searching for all text files and seeing a small 1KB file named cookie:www.tripleXfunland.net.txt!

It's possible to set a browser to avoid accepting cookies altogether, but some very legitimate sites use cookies to make the web experience better and more customized. (Ever wonder how Amazon recognizes you when you visit? Cookies.) Disabling cookies can sometimes lead a person to throw the baby out with the bathwater, so to speak. It can prevent a person from accessing a web site that requires it.

Unorganized Data Files

Computers get gunked up because they're flooded with new files all the time. The gunk isn't limited to just text documents, presentations, pictures, and a few spreadsheets. It's MP3 files, audiobooks, videos, entire CD collections ripped to the hard drive, digital photos and videos uploaded by the hundreds, PDFs and PowerPoint presentations, JPEGs and GIFs, and Photoshop collages. It's an Inbox bursting at the seams and a Media Center full of recorded TV shows and movies. Most people tend to just dump this stuff in folders and hope for the best. Unfortunately, this isn't a good solution; one has to learn to move some data off of the computer and onto DVDs and external drives, get rid of files they don't need, and locate and delete duplicate files. Additionally, there's no reason to store this data on multiple PCs; it's OK to put it in Public folders to share with everyone on the network.

Unorganized Web Favorites

Web surfers often amass a long list of Internet favorites. (If you've discovered the keyboard shortcut for saving favorites, which is CTRL-D in Internet Explorer, you may have an even longer list than most.) Although it's possible to organize them, it's difficult to keep them organized, and there are always additional favorites hanging around the bottom of the list. It's hard to find what you want in a long list, and this type of gunk adds frustration to computing and surfing. See Figure 1-4.

Spyware, Adware, and Viruses

Spyware is a catchall name for products that, once installed, essentially report back information on a person's web surfing habits or helps bombard them with pop-up

FIGURE 1-4 Organize your Favorites list to simplify your life.

ads and other advertising, including spam. Spyware has also become synonymous with installed programs that don't show up in your installed programs directory. This makes them hard to find, hard to deal with, and, worst of all, hard to uninstall. In truth, some spyware is pretty harmless—it won't raid a hard drive or report the balance of a bank account to hackers—but some is not so harmless. Spyware these days can track keystrokes and thus potentially steal passwords and account numbers. Either way, since these programs can eat up available memory or resources, slow down your machine, and/or interfere with other programs, it's imperative to get rid of them.

Configured Service Packs and Updates

I'll preach throughout this book that everyone should always get the latest fixes, patches, updates, and upgrades for their system, noting all the while that some can cause problems. Some are simply buggy (this is rare), and third-party updates can wreak havoc, especially antivirus software updates. So, part of degunking is not only getting updates but managing them. It's important to know how to view updates, opt for what updates to install, how to uninstall a buggy update, and perform similar tasks. Although what you see in Figure 1-5 *looks* like gunk, it's not.

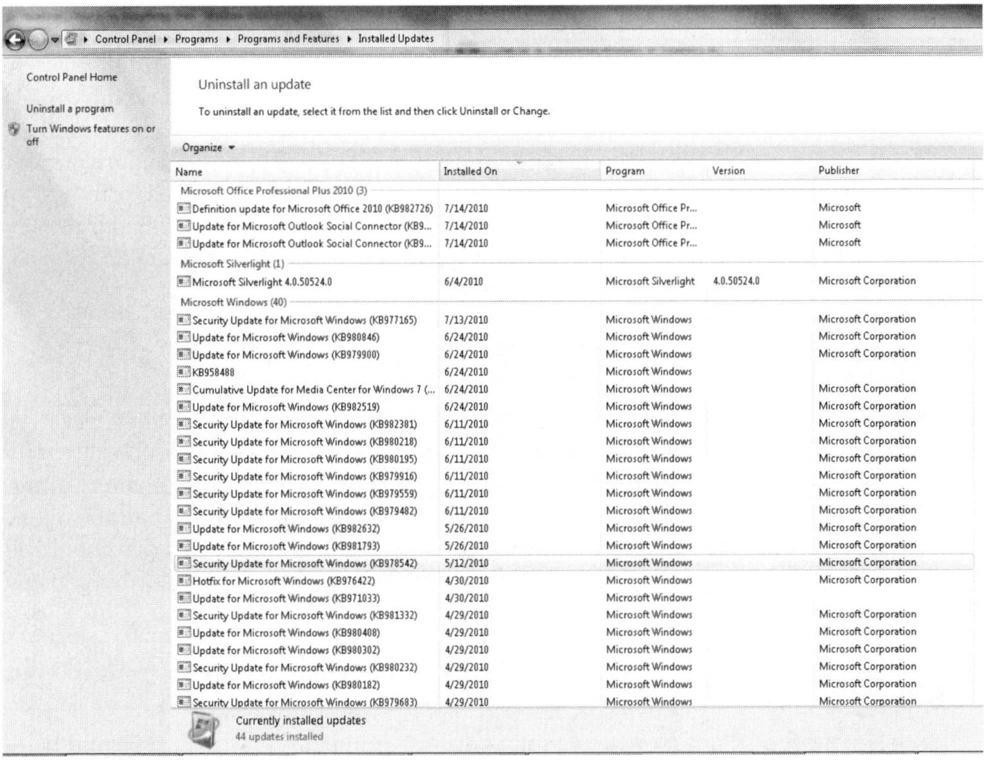

FIGURE 1-5   You can review the Microsoft updates you've installed in Control Panel.

Too Much Music, Photos, Media, and TV

I've harped long enough already about how music, photos, video, recorded TV, and other media can bog down and fill up a hard drive. Hopefully, every reader will now be more than happy to delete the media they don't want and organize the rest. But there's more to it than that. It's possible to convert media that won't play to a format in which it will play (or delete it), find missing media files, change recording settings in Media Center and learn how long it will take (at the current rate) to fill up a hard drive, and understand how to "authorize" a computer or device to play media files. Media has overtaken spam, documents, and unwanted programs as the main gunk culprit for the modern computer, and it's vital to take control now!

Too Many Connected Devices

Every time a new piece of hardware is connected to a computer, *something* is installed. It may only be a very small driver file (necessary), or it may be an elaborate printing, sharing, and photo-editing program (perhaps not so necessary). In some instances, connecting a device causes a program to open and sync automatically, as is the case with an iPad, iPod, or iPhone, or any of hundreds of other devices such as MP3 players, smartphones, or PDAs. Devices can also charge while connected. All these things require system resources. I think it's best to disconnect from the computer any devices that aren't being used, such as cameras, cell phones, scanners, iPads and iPods, and similar hardware, and I will encourage everyone to do so as well.

It's equally important, if not more important, for people to take inventory of the devices they use and own (two different things). Phones, cameras, printers, and the like that have been retired probably still have their software installed on the computer. It's important to understand that this software can now be uninstalled.

Are You Gunked Up?

Chances are that if you can relate to some of this gunk and how people get it, you can probably relate to all of it. If you don't have every ounce of the gunk listed here *yet*, you likely will in the future unless you intervene now. All is not lost. If you commit yourself to degunking, you can get most or all of your computer programs and the operating system itself back running the way it used to. The problems I just discussed will only get worse with time, and that's why your entire computer can get so bogged down.

Ready for Degunking?

The most difficult part of getting your machine back to where it should be involves dedicating a little time. As you move forward and begin to look at the different degunking techniques, remember to perform the tasks in the order that will likely get you the most results in the shortest amount of time. The *Degunking Windows 7* approach will show you not only how to fix things, but how to get yourself on a maintenance program so that your computer *always* runs well. If you're new to the world of degunking, don't worry. It's much easier than you think. It's more psychology than technology!

Summing Up

Yes, you have gunk. Yes, some of it is your doing, but some of it comes with the territory. You can take control of it though, by understanding first from where it comes, second, knowing that you can stop any more from accumulating, and third, learning how to get rid of the gunk you have. You're off to a good start here, and you're ready to move forward with degunking!

2

The Degunking 12-Step Program

Degunking Checklist:

- ☑ Understand that the best degunking results can be obtained by performing cleanup tasks in a specific order
- ☑ Learn why file management is a critical aspect of degunking Windows
- ☑ Learn about hard drive optimization and how limiting what runs in the background reduces gunk
- ☑ Learn why protecting your PC with updates and antivirus software is imperative and how to do it effectively
- ☑ Uncover network gunk and learn how user accounts, sharing, and Public folders can help
- ☑ Learn that media causes the most problems for most users
- ☑ Understand how connecting and syncing cell phones, MP3 players, iPads, iPhones, netbooks, notebooks, and laptops all contribute to gunk
- ☑ Learn that errors, adware, spyware, and lack of a working backup system all work against both you and your computer
- ☑ Understand the 12 steps you'll take to degunk your PC

The purpose of this chapter is to introduce the proven 12-step degunking program. Following this program will surely help you improve the performance of your PC. But to get there, you'll need to understand the strategy behind the degunking process; you need to understand the steps in the 12-step program.

The most important thing to understand about the degunking process is that you will get the best results if you follow the processes outlined in this book in order, from start to finish. So, while you might feel tempted to skip around, understand that if you do, you probably won't see the best results. Of course, there are some processes that can be performed at any time to solve specific problems, but it's best to have an organized strategy the first time you do a "major degunk" so that you get the best results.

The Strategy Behind Degunking

The strategy behind degunking is based on how Windows operates in the first place. To fully understand how the 12-step program works, you must first understand

- How Windows stores certain types of files in specific folders and libraries
- How Windows provides default folders for specific types of files
- How data is stored and retrieved on your hard drive
- How programs and utilities automatically load when you start Windows
- How Windows uses an internal database, called the *Registry*, to store critical information about your computer
- How basic services such as e-mail, security, and data backups work
- How the Windows recovery features, such as System Restore or the Repair option on the Windows 7 DVD, can be used to repair your system when things go wrong

Windows needs lots of free memory and system resources. Windows also needs lots of hard drive space. Most Windows computers nowadays have ample amounts of both. More and more, new computers come with dual processors too, maximizing the available resources. The biggest challenge with Windows 7, then, is that there are so many components, such as files, programs, and system utilities, aggressively competing for the available resources, even the most elaborate systems can gunk up. When too many resources get used up, your machine really starts to bog down. You have to configure your PC so that as many resources as possible are ready when Windows needs them.

Your basic degunking and ongoing maintenance strategy is to ensure that the resources you have are used wisely, even if it appears you have enough resources available. If you have too many files on your hard drive because you never remove any, your computer will slow down over time. If you have too many programs installed on your computer (or you try to run too many at the same time), your computer will take a long time to start up and will run very slowly. Of course, you can add more memory to your computer and increase the size of your hard drive, but you'll eventually run out of resources (again) unless you monitor what you have and regularly get rid of the things you don't need.

As you'll learn in this book, the more you understand about the basics of how Windows operates, the better you'll get at degunking and improving the performance of your PC. Of course, you don't need to be an expert on operating systems to make your machine run better. A little bit of knowledge and common sense goes a long way.

Important Questions to Ask Yourself

To further make the point about the 12-step program and the usefulness of degunking, ask yourself some of the following questions:

- Does my computer seem to be running slower and slower with each passing month?
- Do I put a lot of new files on my computer but rarely remove any old ones?

- How often do I look at my personal data folders and libraries to see if I'm storing files I don't need or keeping my system organized?
- Do I really need all the programs on my computer? (When was the last time you even looked at all the programs you have installed?)
- Do I use all the programs and utilities that load automatically when Windows starts up? And by the way, what programs *do* start up when Windows boots?
- When was the last time I went through my e-mail and deleted the messages I no longer need?
- When was the last time I ran Disk Cleanup to remove the temporary files on my hard drive?
- Is Disk Defragmenter set to run on a schedule?
- Do I have third-party software set up to keep viruses, adware, spyware, and other nasty programs from gunking up my machine?
- Is my PC secure?
- Do I know what to do if something goes wrong with my machine because it has gotten really gunked up?

Let's continue now by exploring the important system-level components of Windows and the features available to you for staying organized and degunked. Once you are familiar with how Windows works, you'll be able to see how the 12-step degunking program will help improve the speed and performance of your computer.

The Hard Disk and Default Folders

Data is stored in folders and libraries on your PC's hard drive. Windows is fully aware of these folders and looks in them first when you search for a file. You'll go to these folders first too. Backup programs come preconfigured to back up these folders and libraries automatically as well, so if you're saving files where you should be saving them, you're on the right track already. If you're saving "outside" of the normal parameters, it may take Windows longer to find what you're looking for, and the data may not be backed up when you run your backup program. Figure 2-1 shows the Public folders, available on all Windows 7 machines.

It's highly likely that you are using your computer for storing lots of personal files you don't want or need. Personal data files take up a lot of space, and if you have too much data, your computer can get to a point where Windows won't have enough free hard drive space to run as well as it should. Most of the time, the hard drive-hogging culprits are media files, including, but not limited to, videos, movies, recorded TV, duplicate files, and pictures. (The movie *Avatar*, on my computer, takes up over 2GB of hard drive space. Imagine if you had a collection of movies coupled with the entire series of four or five TV shows.)

Even if Windows has enough hard drive space to function properly, though, if the files are fragmented (not stored contiguously on the hard disk), it'll take Windows much longer to find them and offer them up to you when you ask for them (the hard drive has to spin longer to gather all the parts of the file you need).

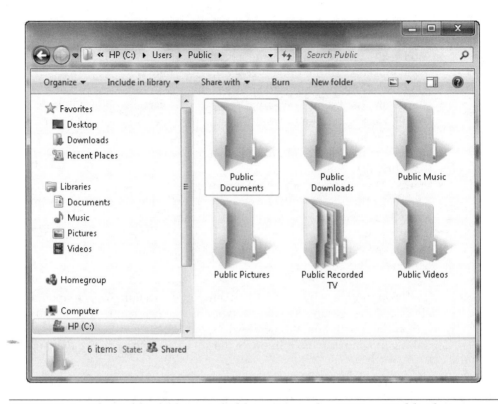

FIGURE 2-1 The Public folders are hidden away under C:\Users\Public, but are worth the search.

Although defragmenting should be occurring automatically and on a schedule, you still need to verify that it's happening.

Let's say those two things aren't a problem, though; you have a huge hard drive and you've checked that your computer is defragmented. You still have to work around all the unwanted files and muddle through them to find the files you want. Finding the picture file IMG10045.jpg is going to take three times as long as finding one that's named WeddingLimo or JenniferGraduation. Think about how much time you could save if all of this was organized. So, degunking your hard drive isn't just about the computer; it involves you too.

NOTE   Disorganization also affects your backups. If your file system is unorganized, your backups will be unorganized as well. You don't want to waste your resources by backing up your unwanted, unplayable, duplicate, and unorganized data.

Programs and Services

Microsoft applications, Windows features (like Windows Defender and the Action Center), third-party software, and software that runs when you connect devices (like the iPad's iTunes) run in the background and use system resources. Some of this is warranted; you certainly need your antivirus software to run all the time, and the Action Center is only protecting your best interests when it automatically looks for solutions to problems your computer has experienced. You keep your e-mail program and Internet Explorer open and running all the time because you want to. All of this is "good" gunk.

Unfortunately, there are lots of programs that run all the time when you don't want them to, and this is bad gunk. These are generally music sharing programs, PDF readers, communications programs like Skype, instant messaging programs like Live Messenger or AIM, and others. With all of these things running alongside the programs you want and need to run, it should come as no surprise that, over time and as more and more programs are added, your computer will slow down. If your system takes a very long time to boot up, you can bet you have more than a handful of programs to degunk.

There's also the matter of the Registry. The Registry is a part of the Windows operating system that I recommend you do not mess around with, but it is important to note that as you add and remove programs, items are added and deleted from the Registry. The more programs you can uninstall, the cleaner the Registry will be (theoretically, at least). If, after working through this entire book, you want to invest in a tried and true Registry cleaning program, I won't try to persuade you not to. A good Registry cleaner can really spiff up a machine's performance. However, I won't recommend one since I haven't tried them all. That part of degunking will be up to you.

CAUTION   Editing the Registry manually should only be attempted by advanced users!

NOTE   The Registry holds information about your entire computer and the applications, users, and hardware configured for it. It's hierarchical, and stores settings for everything: your preferences for a screen saver, the preferred device driver for your digital camera, how you want Windows services to run, information about your user profile, and more.

E-Mail

E-mail programs store e-mail in a relatively similar fashion to how Windows stores other data; that is, all e-mail is stored in a database that consists of folders and subfolders, and those folders are stored in a specific place on the hard drive. If you work within the norms of these programs, data can be backed up fairly easily, although it will probably require quite a few more steps than you're used to. In addition, as with "regular" data, you can create your own folders and subfolders inside your e-mail program to manage the e-mail you need to keep.

Of course, there's the matter of spam, or junk e-mail. Spam exists because people want you to buy their products, send them money, or give them personal information so that they can steal your identity. There are always bad people in the world, and most spam exists because of them. Most e-mail programs offer assistance in controlling spam, and you'll want to explore those options. There are other options outside of that, though; you can create a "disposable" e-mail address for making purchases online or joining newsgroups, and you can create rules to send incoming e-mail to specific folders to keep it out of your way until you're ready to view it.

Unfortunately for us, each e-mail program stores its data in a different database system, so this bit of degunking is not a one-size-fits-all situation. The good news is that no matter what e-mail program you use, you can apply some general principles to manage your e-mail better, reduce the amount of spam you receive, and better organize the e-mail you receive and send out.

Updates

During the degunking process, you'll be encouraged to upgrade the software on your machine and patch up the programs you use most often. This can benefit you in two ways. First, it reduces exposure to bugs that could crash the program. Crashes are often indications of the need for degunking, but they can also contribute to adding more gunk. Second, it reduces exposure to viruses and security problems (leaks). If your software isn't fully up to date, nasty viruses can get into your machine and attack your computer when you least expect it. Viruses and security leaks are the bane of diligent degunkers.

CAUTION   Microsoft releases patches (fixes) for all its programs, including Windows and Office. However, the savviest users, despite wanting to keep their systems up to date, usually wait to update their machines. This happens because some newly issued patches and service packs actually do more harm than good. What I recommend is that you upgrade minor patches and security patches quickly, when you're notified of them. Conversely, you should wait a month or so to upgrade with larger, all-encompassing service packs.

Security

Security is a key degunking issue, and that's why I've devoted so many pages to it throughout the book. Without proper security on your machine, you're at serious risk of getting viruses and other menacing programs that can be directly harmful or take up power and resources. This could cause your computer to run slower or crash more often. You may have also left yourself open to snooping neighbors, siblings, or kids, if you don't have the proper usernames, passwords, and security settings in place and if you don't log off your PC when you're finished using it. There are also more than a few Windows components to help you secure your machine, such as Windows Defender and the Network and Sharing Center. Thus, a good security plan has several pieces:

- **Antivirus/antispyware software**   This software helps prevent malicious computer programs from getting installed or otherwise affecting your system.
- **Firewall**   Activation of a firewall will protect your computer from unwanted intrusion by hackers or programs.
- **Usernames and passwords**   Using these helps prevent unwanted visitors to your computer, such as coworkers, spouses, kids, or visitors.
- **Guest account**   The Guest account can be enabled so visitors can get online but cannot cause harm to your computer or view your private data.
- **Network and Sharing Center**   This allows you to create a private home network, home group, and configure sharing options, among other things. Figure 2-2 shows this.

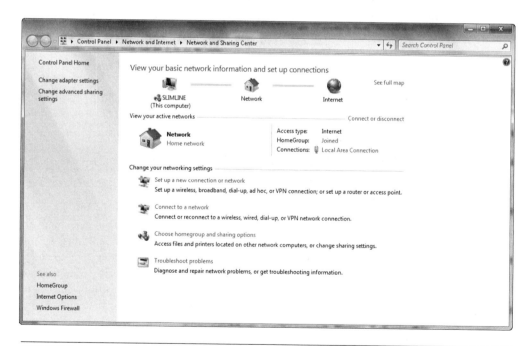

FIGURE 2-2   The Network and Sharing Center is new to Windows 7 and offers lots of sharing and security options.

Backups

A backup is a copy of your important data. This includes documents, pictures, videos, presentations, spreadsheets, e-mail, contacts, and the like. You can back up in various ways, by using backup software or by simply dragging and dropping data from your computer to an external or network drive. You can even burn data to DVDs or save data to SD memory cards or USB flash drives. I prefer a combination of backing up using backup software (once a week) and dragging and dropping (every day).

Developing a regular backup procedure with backup software is a must, not only because it will keep you from losing valuable data but because it will save you from losing all the setup information and critical programs that are essential to the operation of your computer. As you'll learn in this book, creating backups on a regular basis using proper procedures will allow you to quickly get your machine back up and running in the event you suffer a major setback, such as a hard drive crash.

Recovery Tools

Windows 7 comes with various recovery options to use when your computer encounters problems. There's System Restore, which can be used to restore your computer to an earlier time (such as just before you installed that buggy software update), the Repair option on the Windows 7 DVD (to copy system files to recover from system error messages), Device Driver Rollback (to uninstall a new driver that didn't work), and more. All of these features come with Windows, and it's important you understand their usefulness.

GunkBuster's Notebook: What to Do When Nothing Works

The best part about degunking is that you can easily extend the life of your PC by performing the set of tasks presented in this book. But there may come a time when your PC simply won't respond to the basic degunking operations. As a last resort, you can either format the drive and reinstall Windows or give up completely and get a new machine.

Whatever option turns out to be the best one for your situation, you'll want to proceed carefully and apply a smart approach to help save time and money. For example, if you decide to sell your computer and purchase a new PC, there are procedures you should follow to safely move all of your personal data and applications over to the new PC. If you purchase a new machine, you'll need to degunk it before you even start using it. Of course, you'll also want to create a backup program, make sure your Internet and e-mail settings are secure, get antivirus software, and more. If you're planning on getting a new PC, spend some time with it and this book to degunk it.

The Degunking 12-Step Program

Here is the basic 12-step degunking process that you'll follow in this book:

1. Get rid of files and programs you don't need.
2. Organize your remaining files and folders.
3. Clean up your Desktop, Start menu, and Taskbar.
4. Optimize your hard drive and limit the programs that run in the background.
5. Clean up and secure Internet Explorer and consider alternative web browsers.
6. Reduce your e-mail spam, learn how to back up e-mail, and organize your mail.
7. Install Windows updates and/or reconfigure antivirus, antimalware, and antiadware programs.
8. Clean up your network and create a homegroup.
9. Fix problems with media, including duplicate files, files that won't play, and orphaned files.
10. Optimize syncing with cell phones, music players, iPads, iPhones, netbooks, and laptops.
11. Get rid of errors for hardware, the operating system, and third-party programs.
12. Create a working, reliable, and fool-proof backup system.

Summing Up

If you follow the degunking process in the way that's described in this book and you perform certain tasks on a regular basis, you'll be surprised at how your PC will respond. You may think your computer is ready for the trash heap, but I'll show you that (in most cases) you can squeeze more life out of it. So don't throw in the towel too soon. Just take the time to perform the tasks that are outlined here and you'll begin to see results almost immediately.

3

Remove Unwanted Data and Programs

Degunking Checklist:

☑ Remove the excessive junk in your default folders, shared folders, and libraries

☑ Remove the files you don't need from your root directory (C:\)

☑ Remove elusive, unnecessary files from other parts of your computer

☑ Uninstall programs you don't use, including software for hardware and gadgets you no longer own

☑ Remove extraneous Windows components from Control Panel

☑ Run Disk Cleanup

☑ Empty the Recycle Bin

☑ Delete unwanted user accounts and related data, if applicable

Welcome to Basic Housekeeping 101. You know the drill: *Your mother doesn't live here, so please pick up after yourself!* You have to sweep the floors, put away the laundry, stack the dishes, and vacuum the floor. You have to keep things from getting too cluttered by taking out the trash regularly. You also need to clean out your closets once or twice a year and throw away things you no longer need. These are chores you do to make your home livable, and if you don't do them, your house won't function as well as you'd like.

Just as you take out the trash when you clean your house, you occasionally have to clean up the trash you've accumulated on your computer. *Therefore, getting rid of unnecessary files is the first step in degunking your computer.* If you're a pack rat, this could be painful, but I'll help you get through it! We'll take a look at what you've accumulated on your computer in the last few months (or years) and get rid of all the gunk you've added and don't need—music files, digital pictures that didn't make the cut, temporary files, documents you've created and mailed (or e-mailed), and anything else you don't need. You'll be surprised to find that you also have files from hardware you no longer own, and these files can include software programs, installation files, Help files, and other data. You may also have user accounts for people who no longer access your computer, as well as their related data files. It's amazing just how much gunk you'll uncover here, and how much free space and resources you'll have access to once you're finished.

CAUTION You should perform a comprehensive backup and create a System Restore point before you start the degunking tasks in this chapter. See Chapter 14 if you don't have a backup system in place already.

Clean Up the Default Folders and Libraries

Deleting superfluous files might not seem necessary if you have a 500GB hard drive, but it is. When Windows 7 looks for a file, it has to search the full hard disk for it. The more stuff on your hard disk, the more stuff it has to look through. Additionally, deleting unnecessary files is certainly essential if you've received the dreaded "low on disk space" error, although these errors are becoming less and less prevalent with the access most of us have to large hard disks. Beyond all of that, though, you don't want to wade through a thousand unwanted picture files to find the one picture you want to share and print. Why keep unwanted data? It's just gunk!

A Note About Saving Files

It's important to note that when you first got your new Windows 7 computer, the operating system prompted you to save your data in the proper places. It encouraged you to save pictures to the My Pictures folder, documents to the My Documents folder, music to the My Music folder, and videos to the My Videos folder. If you accepted the default saving options at any point, you'll have files in these default folders and you'll have a good foundation for degunking.

Unfortunately, you probably have not been quite so self-disciplined. You may have not known that it is important to save files in their related folders, or for that matter, even how to save files effectively. Perhaps you transferred all of your unorganized documents from your old PC to this one and placed them in your C: drive, bypassing the folder hierarchy entirely, in which case you really have a mess on your hands.

Whatever situation you're in, getting degunked starts with cleaning up this data.

You've likely seen some of the default folders as you've been using Windows 7:

- My Documents
- My Music
- My Pictures
- My Videos
- Downloads
- Contacts
- Saved Games
- Desktop
- Favorites

You certainly have noticed the libraries:

- Documents
- Pictures
- Music
- Videos

This is where you'll start, by organizing these folders and libraries. Once you've cleaned the gunk out of those, you'll need to locate files that should be there but aren't, and move them.

Precautions

Cleaning out files usually means that you'll have to open some of them to see what they are. Be careful! If you see a file with an .exe extension and double-click it, the file will run. While this will likely only start the installation of a harmless program and waste a few minutes of your time, if the filename is unfamiliar to you, it could potentially execute a virus on your PC. Other files with other extensions (including .scr, .bat, .vbs, .pif, and quite a few others) can carry hidden malware. It's always safe to open TXT files, and almost always safe to open image files like GIF and JPEG, but to be safe, keep your antivirus utility updated on a *daily* basis, and run a virus check immediately before spending any serious time "going hunting" for files to delete. If you have any doubts about a particular file, you can often right-click the file and select an option to check the file for viruses, depending on your antivirus software. See Figure 3-1.

And there's one other precaution before we continue: if your computer has multiple partitions, you'll have to repeat these steps on each partition you have. You can see if you have multiple partitions by clicking Start | Computer. You should have C:, the root drive, D:, the CD/DVD drive, and perhaps E: for a media card reader, F: for an attached external hard drive, and possibly further lettered partitions for other hardware options, but your hard drive, where you store data, hopefully only consists of one partition, C:.

For most people, and under ordinary circumstances, one partition is optimal. As with everything, though, there are exceptions. If you find that you have more than one partition and you aren't sure why, consider consolidating them. This is a risky and time-consuming process, though, and will involve either purchasing

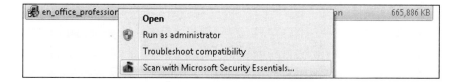

FIGURE 3-1   Right-click suspicious files and run a virus or security check before opening them if you are unsure of their contents.

third-party software to help you combine the partitions, or backing up all of your data and reinstalling the operating system. Either way, I think a single partition is best, because it's easier to keep files organized, you have less risk of running out of disk space, and backup software won't miss any data that's stored where it's not expecting it to be stored.

Delete Documents

Windows 7 provides a My Documents folder, which is where many users store all of the documents they create. This folder serves as the default location until it is changed. Windows 7 also offers a Documents library. The Documents library offers access to everything in your My Documents folder as well as what's in the Public Documents folder. To access the My Documents folder, click Start, click your username, and click My Documents. To access the Documents library, click Start | Documents, as shown in Figure 3-2.

FIGURE 3-2 Open the Documents library by clicking Documents in the Start menu.

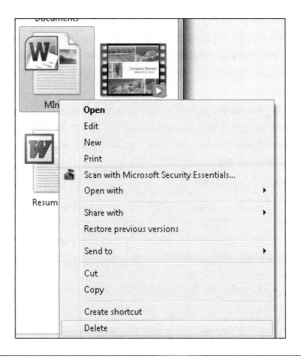

FIGURE 3-3   Right-click any file to delete it.

Stop reading for a minute and explore the Documents library to see what you can find. If you see something you don't like or you don't need, delete it. Here's how:

1. Click Start | Documents.
2. Right-click any file and choose Delete from the shortcut menu. See Figure 3-3.
3. In the Confirm File Delete dialog box, click Yes to delete the file.

TIP   If you prefer using the keyboard over the mouse, select the file and then press the DELETE key on the keyboard. When prompted to confirm the deletion, press the ENTER key. Alternatively, you can drag the item to the Recycle Bin.

Spend some time here and delete to your heart's content, but don't delete files if you don't know who they belong to or what they are used for. For now, let's just concentrate on taking out a bit of the garbage that *you've* created.

Delete Media Files

Let's now take a look at some other folders. Windows 7 also provides default folders called My Pictures, My Videos, and My Music for storing other types of files and related libraries. If you have a digital camera, for example, you might find that you have a lot of files in the My Pictures folder. If you take a lot of videos and make your own movies, I'll bet you've got some files in the My Videos folder you can delete as well. If you are a music hound, your My Music folder probably is really scary!

Pictures

Look at Figure 3-4 and you'll see an example of a Pictures library. It's pretty gunked up, although you can see that some prior attempt at organizing the images has been made. There are folders for the various image subjects, but there are lots of images haphazardly placed wherever. These need to be moved to the appropriate subfolders. Deleting pictures here is just the same as deleting from the Documents library. You simply right-click, choose Delete, and be done with it!

There's a lot wrong here and perhaps you have some of the same gunk:

- There are folders named for the phones the pictures were uploaded from. Those pictures should be distributed to appropriate subfolders that match their subjects, and renamed.
- There are folders names with dates (July 4th, for instance), but the images in them aren't only from the 4th of July; the pictures were simply uploaded that day and contain many pictures from months of picture taking.
- There are duplicate pictures in the folders and subfolders.
- There are pictures that are not in any folder.
- There's an odd shortcut to a personal folder.
- There are videos, spreadsheets, and documents in the subfolders, whereas everything should ultimately only be pictures.
- The pictures are not named properly.

FIGURE 3-4 Pictures are often the source of a lot of gunk.

Videos and TV

Deleting video files can be a little trickier than deleting images and documents because there are so many types of files to contend with. You may have video files you've downloaded from the Internet, videos you've taken with a video camera, files you've edited in video-editing programs, or even full-length movies you've purchased. You may even have recorded TV shows, depending on how you've set up your PC.

Although the sheer amount of possible data can be daunting and cause gunk, much of the problem in the Videos library stems from the process required to turn raw footage you collect and upload into a movie you can burn to a DVD. With some movie-making programs (like Movie Maker), you capture the video files (raw footage), upload them to your computer, and then you create a movie "project" using those files. The extension for these project files is different from the extension your raw footage has. You tweak the project (or working) file and then you create a movie, and the movie files are given a different extension still. The movie is the final product, so if you've turned a particular project file into a movie, you can delete that project file along with the raw footage. However, if you think you'll need any of those files later, if you want to save the raw footage for posterity, or if you are planning to use those files in another movie, you shouldn't delete them.

If you obtain video (think movies) from someplace like iTunes, they may not be in the My Videos folder or the Videos library, complicating things. Just look at the path for *Avatar* in Figure 3-5! It's actually in the Music library. (Recorded TV, podcasts, and other media may not be where you'd expect them to be either.)

TIP   When viewing files in any folder, note that you can change the view from the Change Your View button in the top-right corner. Try Large Icons for a simple, easy-to-see view, and try Details to see the name, date, size, type, and more for each file in the folder.

FIGURE 3-5   You'll find files in obscure folders on your PC, through no fault of your own.

Music

Ah, your music. I bet that you have quite a few files stored in your Music library if you're a music enthusiast. You literally can have thousands of music files, and if you've subscribed and unsubscribed to various online music sources, you may even have a lot that you can't even play because you don't have the proper licenses and are blocked by rights protection. Deleting music files is just as simple as deleting anything else described so far: simply right-click and delete. Lucky for you, iTunes and many other media programs store music in a subfolder of the Music library, so they are easy to find.

CAUTION   There may be a way to convert files that won't play to a type that will play, so don't delete a file just because it won't play, at least not yet.

As with Documents, Pictures, and Videos, there is a related Music library. You'll see these libraries in the right pane of the Windows Explorer window. Figure 3-6 shows the Music library on one of my computers, and it's pretty well-organized.

Use Public and Shared Folders

If you share a computer with another person (or with several people) and you don't belong to a large corporate network, you might have used the Public folders and/or created your own folders to share data. You may have even shared your own personal folders, a CD/DVD drive, or your root drive (although I suggest you don't do any of that—you have to have some private space and maintain computer and personal security).

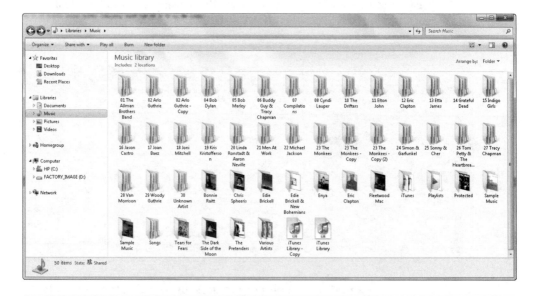

FIGURE 3-6   The Music library should have all of your music in it, even if you manage your music with iTunes or another program.

GunkBuster's Notebook: Saving Space by Spotting Duplicate Music Files

If you're like most people who collect music files, you gather them from wherever you can and then toss them into the Music folder on your (huge) hard drive. Chances are good that you have duplicate files in that directory—and since most music files are several megabytes in size, you can waste a *lot* of disk space that way. This problem often stems from inconsistent file-naming conventions. If you get music files from CDs you own, various media services, file sharing services, or your friends, the files' names may be arranged very differently, even though the songs are the same.

You can also have a problem with duplicates when you share music files over a home network. Your daughter may have the latest Lady Gaga CD in the Public folder on her PC, and you may have also burned the same CD to a media computer in the family room. If you've set up media sharing, you may see both in the Music library of each PC. These problems are difficult to resolve and require some effort to fix (usually by moving all music to one Public folder on a single PC, enabling Media Sharing, and working from there).

If you think you have duplicates but can't locate them by their names, first, look to your music management program. iTunes, for instance, has a feature called Display Duplicates that makes it easy to see what music you have duplicated, and other programs often include similar features. If you find duplicates, delete them.

If you don't use any music management program, you can download and install a third-party program that finds duplicate files. (Make sure to read the reviews and get one that's adware and spyware free.) If you'd rather not go this route, view the music files in Details view, and click the Size header in a Windows Explorer display to sort the files by *size*. That will bring all files of identical size together in the display. As you scroll down through your files in the Windows Explorer pane, look for multiple adjacent lines with the same file size and you'll discover that many of those are duplicates with slightly different filenames.

Using Public folders and creating your own sharing folders is an excellent way to keep your computer degunked in the long term, so don't worry that I'm going to advise you to move files that are already there. It's also a good way to avoid problems with duplicate files and avoid the gunk that's created when you e-mail a file from one computer in the house to another. Finally, it provides one receptacle for storing data and then backing it up. (Can you imagine? Having all of your media in one place, and backing it up to an external hard drive in a single step? Wow!) In the short term, moving all media to one, shared Public folder can practically eliminate (in a single step) problems with duplicate media files on your network.

CAUTION   Public folders are accessible by anyone with network access, even guests.

Now, I must point out that the Public folders can get gunked up quickly. The Public folders, at least for me, are kind of like the garage of a house. It's big, everyone has access, and stuff just collects there. Junk, gunk, things that don't work, things we don't want, and things, for whatever reason, we can't throw away. So while it's great to move data to the Public folders, it's also important to monitor those folders regularly.

The Public folders can be accessed from your personal folder, by expanding its related library. Just position the mouse over the library and click the down arrow appears. This will offer your personal and Public folders independently. If you want to manage your Public folders independently though, you may want to create a shortcut to them on your Desktop.

TIP   Create a shortcut to the Public folders on your Desktop. It'll be easier to manage, and seeing the icon each day will remind you to check in on it occasionally and remove, combine, delete, or organize the files in it.

Here's a novel way to locate the Public folders:

1. Click Start | Computer.
2. Double-click C:.
3. Double-click Users.
4. Right-click Public and click Send To | Desktop (Create Shortcut), as shown in Figure 3-7.

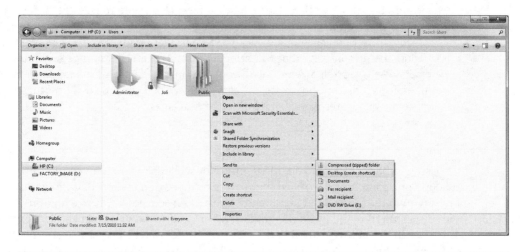

FIGURE 3-7   It's best to create a shortcut to the Public folders and place that shortcut on your Desktop.

5. Close the window and double-click the new shortcut on the Desktop. Note the folders inside.

If you take the time to clean out these default folders, you'll be well on your way to getting your machine running smoothly again. This is a good first step. Now, let's take a look at some of the other places you could have saved files that need to be deleted!

CAUTION   Don't empty the Recycle Bin just yet. Leave the files in there for a week or so, just to make sure you aren't going to miss anything you've deleted.

GunkBuster's Notebook: Use the Public Folders to Your Advantage

You can create subfolders inside the Public folder, and alongside Public Documents, Public Pictures, Public Music, and the like. Consider the following for subfolders to further personalize your Public folder:

- A Homework subfolder where junior can save his homework and you can check it.
- A Team Project subfolder where every employee on a project team can access and edit data stored there.
- A Family First folder where everyone has access to a shared calendar, address book, events schedule, wills, important documents, and other pertinent information.

(Continued)

- An Internet Downloads folder where downloads can be stored and accessed by everyone.
- A Compressed folder where compressed or zipped files can be stored and universally managed.
- An Attachments folder where users can save e-mail attachments so they aren't e-mailed to other users, gunking up each user's e-mail program.
- A Recipes folder with subfolders for each member of the family; Junior can find out here how long to put a hot dog in the microwave or a pizza in the pizza oven, while the hubby can learn how to boil water.
- A Teams folder that holds schedules, team rosters, rankings, and phone numbers.

Clean Up and Organize Your Hard Drive

Go ahead, admit it. Sometimes you just save files randomly to whatever folder you're prompted to. Sometimes you simply click Local Disk (C:), the Desktop, or some other partition in the Save As dialog box. (I won't make you admit that you sometimes can't find that stuff later.)

Saving randomly or leaving the files in a jumbled, disorganized mess is just going to get uglier as time passes. It's best to clean out the garage and do a little organizing now, before it gets completely out of control. In this section, I'll show you how to both clean and better organize your computer's hard drive and remove unwanted files that have been randomly saved on it.

Delete Files from the Root Directory (C:)

Your root directory may be a place where you are storing files inappropriately or storing files that you don't need. It may not be. It's harder to save to the C: drive than it used to be; Windows steers you in the right direction most of the time. However, take a look in there and see if there are any unwanted or misplaced files, and move files (if applicable) to better organize this directory. Open wide; let's take a look:

1. Click Start | Computer.
2. Double-click the C: drive.
3. If you see any files you created that you no longer need, right-click and choose Delete. These should be personal files you've created, not folders. You do not want to delete the Windows folder, the Program Files folder, or any system folder! Keep an eye out for compressed files, movie project files, picture files (.jpg, .bmp., .gif,. and .tif), documents, music, PDF files, PowerPoint and Excel files, or similar gunk you've created.

GunkBuster's Notebook: Be Careful What You Delete

As you begin exploring your hard drive and removing files, you'll notice lots of folders. Windows 7 has specific files it needs to function properly, to boot up, and to run effectively, and they are stored on your root drive. Windows files are stored in the Windows folder (makes sense), which contains many other folders, including Logs, Fonts, Setup, System32, and others. You certainly don't want to delete anything from that folder!

Another folder you'll notice on the root drive (often C:) is the Program Files folder. In this folder, you'll find subfolders that contain the files for the programs you've installed. I have folders entitled Adobe, Bonjour, Google, iPod, Microsoft Office, Microsoft Games, and many others. You certainly don't want to delete any of these folders or their files either. These are "program files," files the programs need to run.

TIP   If you want to delete a program, you don't do that by right-clicking and deleting the folder. Deleting programs is done from Control Panel. You'll learn about that later in this chapter.

So, what can you delete, and what should you look for? For the most part, you can delete anything *you've created* and no longer need: pictures you've saved to the hard drive; movies you've made; music you've downloaded; PDF files you've opened and saved; compressed files; Excel, PowerPoint, and Access files; and documents you've written. You can also delete temporary files that Windows has saved on its own.

Once you've finished deleting what you no longer need from the root directory in the C: drive, you might still have some stuff there that you want to keep. Take a look at Figure 3-8. Even though I've deleted most of the stuff I don't want in the C: directory, there are still two folders I want to keep. The next task is to move them to a better location.

Move Files Out of the Root Directory

You don't want to leave any personal remnants hanging around in your root directory. You want to move them to a more suitable holding area. Leave the system folders that belong there where they are, but move data you've created somewhere else.

CAUTION   If you don't know what it is—don't move it!

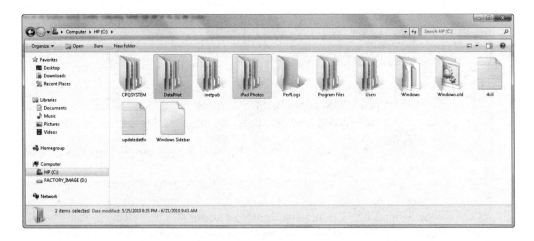

FIGURE 3-8   First, get rid of what you don't need, and then follow that up with organizing what you want to keep.

To move files to a better location, follow these steps:

1. Right-click any single file you'd like to move:
   a. Click Cut.
   b. Browse to the location to move the file.
   c. Right-click inside the desired folder and click Paste.
2. To move multiple files at once:
   a. Hold down the CTRL key on the keyboard and select the files to move.
   b. Right-click any of these and click Cut.
   c. Browse to the location to move the files.
   d. Right-click and click Paste.
3. To create a subfolder in any folder to hold the data, prior to pasting:
   a. Click New Folder.
   b. Name the folder. See Figure 3-9.
   c. Double-click the folder to open it.
   d. Right-click the open folder and click Paste.

NOTE   If you upgraded an older PC to Windows 7, you may have a folder named Online Services in the Program Files folder, or something similar. Look inside that folder, and if it contains files to help you get set up with an online service, delete it. Chances are, you're already online and you don't need to keep these files.

4. Repeat these processes as needed. When you're finished, the C: root directory should contain only folders that are necessary for the operating system and its programs to function. Don't move any folders created by other programs (like your instant messaging program), and don't move applications or system or hidden files.

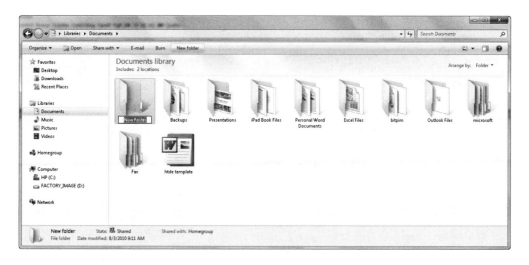

FIGURE 3-9   Create a subfolder to organize the data before you paste it.

There are other ways to move files besides cutting and pasting. You can drag a file from one folder to another, or you can open Computer along with Windows Explorer, resize the windows so you can see both, and then drag the files between them. When dragging, right-click the destination first and choose Move Here when you drop. If you just drag and drop, you'll most likely create a copy of the file instead of moving it.

TIP   When you move a file like a picture or a song and some application needs it later, it might not be able to find it. You may have to tell that program where the file has been moved. This might take a few minutes out of your day for the next few weeks or so, but take my word for it, you'll be glad you did!

Delete Unused Files in Other Locations

You've deleted unwanted files from your personal folders, and you've scoured your root directory for additional unwanted files. Make sure to check your Desktop too; you may have accumulated unwanted files there as well. But what about the rest of your hard drive? It is likely that you have unwanted files hanging out on your entire drive, hiding in places you haven't even thought to look.

Fortunately, you can use the Search option to locate files that are tucked away. For instance, if you have created art files in Photoshop, Corel, or a similar art program, you can locate those files by searching for their file extensions. Some of these files aren't stored where you'd think they should be. As an example, Arts & Letters is a program I use to create artwork. These program files all use the proprietary .ged filename extension. Those files aren't stored in the usual My Pictures folder either, making them hard to find. A quick search for *.ged will offer the folder they're stored in, and it's easy to delete what's unwanted there. You can also manually locate and delete misplaced music or video files by searching for their file extensions.

There are lots of ways to search. The easiest is to use Windows 7's Start Search window:

1. In the Start Search box on the Start menu, type ***.pdf**. Note the PDF files you find. You may not need any of these files and can delete them.

TIP   You can right-click any file in the Start Search results list and click Delete.

2. If you'd like to access the folder that contains the file, right-click any file and click Open File Location. This is not mandatory for deletion.
3. Delete the files as desired.
4. Repeat the search.
5. To see all results for PDF files, click See More Results in the search results pane.
6. Delete the files as desired.
7. Continue in this manner as time permits, searching for
   a. *.jpg and *.jpeg to locate missing digital camera files and pictures
   b. *.psd to locate missing Photoshop files
   c. *.gif, *.tif, *.bmp, and *.tiff to locate art files
   d. *.midi, *.mp3, *.mp4, *.wav, *.avi, and *.wma to locate music files
   e. *.doc for Word documents

Note that there are hundreds of other file types to search for; this is only the beginning, but it will probably keep you busy for a while.

TIP   Google **"common file extensions"** to see other file types you can search for.

To be really successful degunking via searches, you need to click the See More Results option in the search results pane after searching for any file type. The results Windows finds will appear in their own window. You can sort the results in just about any way imaginable, and this will help you root out even the most obscure files in the most remote locations. Clicking once on the Name title sorts the files alphabetically, for instance, allowing you to locate specific files; clicking once on the Size title sorts the files by their size, allowing you to locate and delete the largest files. Clicking Type sorts the results by the type of file they are, allowing you to group all files of a specific type together.

Finally, if you really want to get specific about searching, open the Computer window, open your root drive, and use the Windows 7 Search features to locate unwanted files. The window has its own Search options, and you can really narrow down what you're looking for. In this example, you'll employ the technique required to locate the largest files on your computer:

1. Click Start | Computer.
2. Double-click the C: drive.
3. Click inside the Search box on the far right side, and click Size. See Figure 3-10.
4. Click Gigantic >128 Mb.
5. Note the results. Mine are shown in Figure 3-11.
6. Right-click to delete any file, or select multiple files before right-clicking (by holding down the CTRL key or the SHIFT key when selecting).

TIP   You can also use Windows 7 utilities to search for temporary files. I like a utility called Disk Cleanup. I'll talk about that shortly, and I'll also give you more insight into temporary files. However, if you are so inclined and want to remove your temporary files manually, search for *.tmp. You can safely delete files that are more than a week old.

FIGURE 3-10   Every Windows 7 Explorer window has a Search option.

Name	Date modified	Type	Size
Avatar (2009)	5/3/2010 1:37 PM	MP4 Video	2,458,744 KB
Data1	6/12/2008 6:12 AM	Cabinet File	1,275,791 KB
Outlook	8/3/2010 9:51 AM	Outlook Data File	1,220,177 KB
en_office_professional_plus_2010_x86_515486	5/7/2010 7:38 AM	Application	665,886 KB
Outlook May 25 2010	5/25/2010 12:43 PM	Outlook Data File	586,785 KB
01 Midnight - 1_00 A.M.	5/11/2010 2:38 PM	MP4 Video	500,028 KB
Leo Laporte - The Tech Guy 658	5/11/2010 12:31 PM	MP4 Video	483,164 KB
Leo Laporte - The Tech Guy 660	5/11/2010 12:06 PM	MP4 Video	478,028 KB
Leo Laporte - The Tech Guy 661	5/11/2010 12:07 PM	MP4 Video	442,818 KB
Outlook PST September 2009	4/27/2010 6:06 PM	Outlook Data File	361,601 KB
Outlook May 25 2010	5/25/2010 12:44 PM	Compressed (zipp...	312,415 KB
01 The Shack_ Special Edition (Unabr	6/1/2010 9:21 AM	MPEG-4 Audio Fil...	247,987 KB

FIGURE 3-11   The largest files on your computer are probably full-length movies, installation files, and backups.

Get Rid of Unwanted Programs

You have programs you don't use. Most are likely associated with hardware you no longer own. Some will be stand-alone applications. Some will be trialware that came with your new PC. Some will be unknown to you! Because most unwanted software these days is likely the result of hardware, gadgets, cell phones, and the like, let's start there.

Take a look around the room and make a list of all the hardware you currently have connected to your computer, hardware you can connect, and hardware you used to connect but no longer use. Include printers and networked printers, business card readers, external hard drives, scanners, speakers, CD and DVD burners, TV tuners, and web cams, and don't forget items like MP3 players, iPods, iPads, iPhones, your BlackBerry, Android, PDAs, and digital cameras.

Next, take a look at the boxes, drawers, or closets that hold your dead hardware, like that pen/camera/web cam/coffeemaker combination your mom got you for your birthday last year. It's highly likely that all of these things have related software that's installed on your PC. Now, make a mental list of all the things that you no longer use, that are broken, or that were lost or stolen. If your memory isn't that great or if it's a long list, write them down on a piece of paper.

NOTE   Printer and scanners are the worst hardware culprits because these generally come with programs for enhancing photos, cropping them, publishing or e-mailing them, and performing similar tasks. If you use a different program (such as Photoshop or Photoshop Elements) or any of the available Microsoft tools (like Windows Live Photo Gallery or Paint), you probably don't need this additional software at all.

Now, take a look at your All Programs list to see some of the programs you have installed on your computer. You can do this by clicking the Start menu and pointing to the All Programs option. If anything strikes you as odd or if you don't know what a program is, open it and take a gander. If it's a program you don't need or one that doesn't open, make a note of it. You'll uninstall it next. You should also make a list that includes programs you are not sure you use. You might encounter some programs that have names that are so cryptic or shortened that you can't easily determine if the program is needed. Later, I'll show you how to play detective and uncover the mysteries of your installed programs.

Keep going! My test machines are running faster than ever, and I've only just begun!

Use Control Panel to Remove Programs

Control Panel offers the Uninstall or Change a Program window for uninstalling any program on your computer. This is the best way to uninstall a program. The steps are as follows:

1. Click Start | Control Panel.
2. Under Programs, click Uninstall a Program.
3. Scroll through the list of installed programs. When you see a program you no longer need, click it once.
4. Click Uninstall. See Figure 3-12.

Uninstall or change a program

To uninstall a program, select it from the list and then click Uninstall, Change, or Repair.

Organize ▾   Uninstall

Name	Publisher	Installed On	Size	Version
AAdvantage eShoppingSM Toolbar		7/16/2010		1.514
Adobe Flash Player 10 ActiveX	Adobe Systems Incorporated	4/28/2010		10.0.45.2
Adobe Reader 9.3.3	Adobe Systems Incorporated	7/27/2010	210 MB	9.3.3
Apple Application Support	Apple Inc.	6/21/2010	42.8 MB	1.3.0
Apple Mobile Device Support	Apple Inc.	6/21/2010	19.9 MB	3.1.0.62
Apple Software Update	Apple Inc.	4/30/2010	2.25 MB	2.1.2.120
BitPim 1.0.7	Joe Pham <djpham@bitpim.org>	6/21/2010		1.0.7
Bonjour	Apple Inc.	6/21/2010	1.05 MB	2.0.2.0
Canon SELPHY CP770		5/10/2010		
DataPilot	Susteen	6/21/2010	201 MB	6.01.0000
GoToMeeting 4.5.0.457		7/13/2010		
iTunes	Apple Inc.	7/22/2010	161 MB	9.2.1.4
LG Android Driver	LG Electronics	6/21/2010		1.0
LG USB Modem Driver	LG Electronics	6/21/2010		4.9.7
LG USB WML Modem Driver	LG Electronics	6/21/2010		1.0

FIGURE 3-12   Look for programs that were installed with hardware you no longer own and uninstall it.

5. Work through the installation process, which differs depending on the program being uninstalled.

6. Do not uninstall Silverlight, SQL Server, or other Microsoft programs. Yet.

TIP   Although toolbars, like the AAdvantage eShopping SM Toolbar listed in Figure 3-12, are often undesirable additions to a PC, if you use a toolbar to earn miles, check e-mail, or perform other tasks in Internet Explorer, it's okay to keep it. Delete toolbars you don't use, though.

Use a Program's Uninstall Command

Some computer experts believe that you should always use the program's Uninstall command instead of Control Panel, because doing so will take care of a number of important cleanup and "bookkeeping" tasks, such as updating the Windows Registry. While this used to be the case, I haven't had any problems using Control Panel in recent years, and this issue may be moot now. However, if you'd rather use a program's Uninstall option (or if, for whatever reason, Control Panel won't work for you), check the All Programs list. You may find an Uninstall option there.

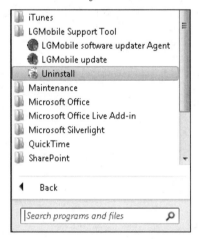

CAUTION   If you receive a message that you are going to uninstall some shared files when uninstalling, be sure to choose the option to not delete them. These files don't take up much room, but uninstalling one that is needed by another program can cause problems.

Be Persistent and Use Precaution

If you purchased a computer that had Windows preinstalled, you probably have programs that were installed by the manufacturer. Some of these you may actually use, but most, probably not. When uninstalling programs, look for programs whose names are created from a variation of the manufacturer's name. My HP computer came with several, including HP Games, HP Share-to-Web, and others. Also look for programs that offer online services, help and support, and antivirus software trials.

TIP   If you're unsure what a program does or is used for, Google the name. You can find out easily if the program was installed with a printer, with the PC by the manufacturer, of if it's simply a cryptic name for a program you installed but don't remember.

Be careful, though. When choosing what to uninstall, don't uninstall any program if you aren't sure what it is used for. In addition, shy away from uninstalling Microsoft Updates and any programs that were upgraded from one version to another. If your computer came with Windows 7 preinstalled and included several programs with it, and all you got was a recovery disc, you shouldn't uninstall any of these programs unless you are positive you don't want them anymore. Many times, the only way to get these programs back (without the application's discs) is to format the drive and use the computer manufacturer's recovery discs.

NOTE   If all you got was a recovery disc, and not an actual Windows 7 DVD and application CDs, call the computer store where you bought your computer and complain. There is a slim chance you can get "real" discs if you bark loud and long enough.

Turn Off Extraneous Windows Components

If you're really obsessed with degunking, you can also clean up your hard disk by turning off Windows components you don't use. You can turn off items such as Indexing, Games, Tablet PC Components, Windows DVD Maker, and others. Turning off these services may or may not provide relief to your overworked computer, depending on what you currently have turned on and what you decide to disable, but if you find that you have all of the features and services running, you can certainly make headway by working a little here.

To see what Windows components you have installed on your system and to turn off the ones you don't need, follow these steps:

1. Click Start | Control Panel.
2. Under Programs, click Uninstall a Program.
3. Click Turn Windows Features On or Off.
4. Look through the list. If you are unsure what any item is, hover your mouse over it, as shown in Figure 3-13.
5. Deselect any item to turn it off. Do not turn off any feature if you do not understand its purpose.

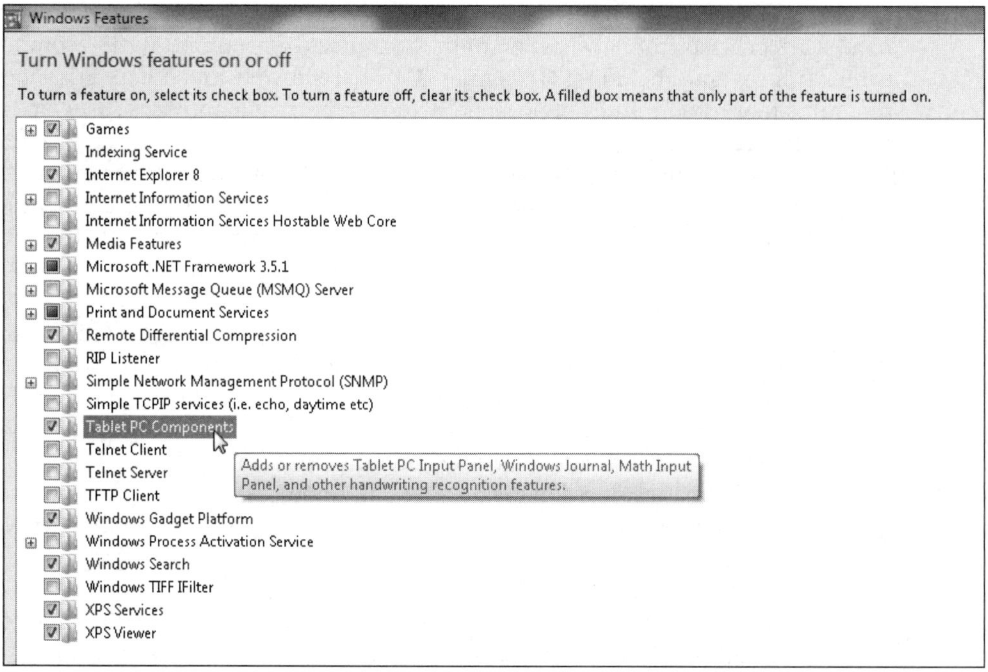

FIGURE 3-13 Turn off unwanted Windows features.

GunkBuster's Notebook: Centralizing Storage of Install Suites

Windows provides ready-made folders for storing documents, music files, video files, and digital photo files. It also provides a folder for installation files you download from the Internet. You use these files to perform the actual installation of the program you purchase or obtain. Because most programs that you download from the Internet prompt you to copy (save) the installation files to your computer, that folder is called *Downloads*. When you download a utility from the Web (whether free or something you paid for), you're downloading a file and should save it to the Downloads folder when prompted.

However, and this is a big however: once you've installed a program, you don't need its install suite. That is, you don't need it until you buy a new machine and need to install it on there, or until your old machine crashes hard and must be reformatted and everything must be reinstalled. If you try a piece of software and don't like it (and then uninstall it), deleting its install suite

is just good housekeeping. If you *do* like it, keeping the install suite file is essential, but it can be burned to a CD if you want if off your PC.

One final note on install suites: programs that you purchase by downloading from a web site generally require an "unlock code" to make them fully functional. It's a good idea to create a document file that details all your unlock codes and the programs to which they apply. Create an Install Suites folder and store the document there, and also print it out and keep a hard copy in your desk drawer in case your computer crashes. An install suite without its unlock code is useless!

Clean the Nooks and Crannies

It may just about blow your mind to think that there are still places on your hard drive that contain gunk! Trust me, there are. If your computer is like mine, you likely have temporary (*.tmp) files hiding in every nook and cranny. You learned a little about finding temporary files using Search earlier in this chapter. If you've never taken the time to clean up your temporary files, though, or if you did a search for them earlier, you no doubt will get (or got) a big surprise! You can free up lots of hard drive space quickly and easily simply by deleting these unnecessary files.

There are lots of reasons temp files are created. If Windows locks up or crashes, or if you have to use CTRL-ALT-DEL to restart, some temporary files get left on your hard disk. Some installation routines also leave temporary files. Temp files can be files that the computer creates to use as backup files for office programs like Microsoft Word so that, if something happens and the program shuts down unexpectedly, a saved copy will be available. Programs create temporary files, too, to store frequently needed information in an easily retrievable folder. Temporary files are also created when you surf the Internet, and these files store information about the web sites you visit. Most of the time, these files are created to save you time, but after a while, their buildup can cause a hard disk to bog down.

It's best to clean up your temporary file folders occasionally, just to make sure you aren't causing the hard drive any unnecessary strain. There are several ways to do this, and using Disk Cleanup is the easiest.

Use Disk Cleanup

Disk Cleanup is a utility that ships with Windows 7 and can be used to delete temporary Internet files, temporary (computer) files, offline web pages, the files in the Recycle Bin, and more. Temporary files aren't needed, and if you've used offline web pages, they're just taking up space too. Disk Cleanup is easy to use, but this first time you might want to lay off emptying the Recycle Bin, just to be safe.

Here's how to use Disk Cleanup:

1. Click Start and in the Start Search window, type **Disk Cleanup**.
2. Right-click Disk Cleanup in the results, and click Run As Administrator.
3. Choose your root drive if prompted, which is likely C:, and click OK.
4. Click Clean Up System Files, if it's available. Note you can opt to view the files prior to deleting them.
5. After that process completes, perform any required steps to return to the list of options, and then select everything except the Recycle Bin. (You don't have to select everything; click each option in the list to view it if you aren't sure you're ready to commit to, say, deleting old setup files or previous Windows installations.)

TIP   If you're cleaning up a netbook, be extremely observant. You want to clean up as much as possible because of the limited resources available.

6. Note the other tab, More Options, noting you can return here to clean up System Restore files and Shadow Copies.
7. Click OK.

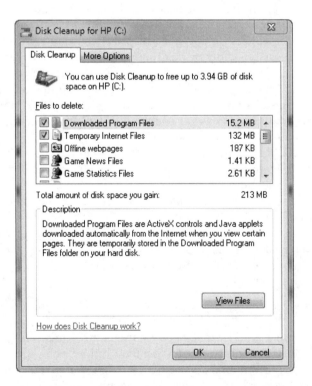

NOTE   As you can see in this illustration, the hard drive space that can be freed up is 3.94GB. That's quite a bit. However, the real advantage is cleaning out unwanted files; 3.94GB by today's standards is negligible.

Empty the Recycle Bin

After a week or so, if you're sure you don't need any of the files or programs you've deleted, you can empty the Recycle Bin. Before you do, though, you may want to see just how much progress you've made. In the example shown in the following illustration, emptying the Recycle Bin will recoup 7.4GB of space. (I ran Disk Cleanup again to see how much data the Recycle Bin is holding.) That's a lot of space! Remember, though, that with today's larger hard drives, space isn't the biggest benefit; the biggest benefits come from

- Removing unwanted data so it's not in your way
- Removing unwanted programs so they aren't running in the background and using system resources
- Removing temporary files so they aren't bogging down your web browser or computer
- Moving data to their correct places so Windows can find them faster when you need them

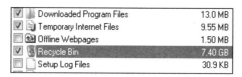

To empty the Recycle Bin, right-click it and choose Empty Recycle Bin. (If you are viewing this in Disk Cleanup, simply click OK.)

Remove Unwanted User Accounts

If you've ever created a user account for someone else so that they could access your computer, you'll have user account files for that person stored on the hard disk. If that person no longer accesses the computer and doesn't need the files they created, you can safely delete both the account and the files.

Here's how to do both:

1. Click Start | Control Panel.
2. Under User Accounts and Family Safety, click Add or Remove User Accounts.
3. Click the account to remove.
4. Click Delete the Account.
5. Click Delete Files.
6. Click Delete Account.

TIP   If the account had a lot of user data, you may want to empty the Recycle Bin again.

Summing Up

If you've deleted all of the unnecessary documents, temporary files, pictures, movies, and music from your PC, you've taken a gigantic step forward in reducing the amount of clutter on it. As you've learned, when you reduce clutter, you improve the performance of your system because your PC's hard drive doesn't have to sift through unnecessary data to find what it needs and the information you want.

If you followed that up and removed the programs you don't use and their related files, you've made great progress. As with removing data files, removing program files frees up hard drive space; however, by removing program files, you sometimes get even more bang for your buck. Some programs start automatically each time you boot up, and run in the background without your knowledge.

In addition to removing programs you don't use (or don't want), though, hopefully you also removed programs that you *can't* use, like programs that you installed with a digital camera you've lost, applications for a printer you no longer own, or programs for a phone you no longer have.

4

Organize Your File System

Degunking Checklist:

☑ Organize the default folders by creating additional, embedded, subfolders

☑ Rename, copy, move, or delete folders

☑ Create folders on external drives, network drives, or partitions

☑ Use libraries effectively by adding folders to a library, creating new libraries, sharing a library, and adding shortcuts to libraries

☑ Use the Public folders effectively

☑ Configure Public Sharing

☑ Share a personal folder, new folder, drive, or other item

☑ Run Disk Cleanup, Disk Defragmenter, and finalize this part of the degunking process

Now that you've deleted unnecessary files, programs, and software and hardware gunk, it's time to organize what you have remaining on your hard drive. Compare this to our housecleaning analogy, and this part of degunking is like cleaning out the garage: You need easy access to all of the stuff you have stored there, even the stuff you don't use very often (like holiday decorations and the fertilizer spreader). And, while you want quick access to items when you do need them, you don't want to trip over them when you don't. Those items should not impede your ability to regularly get to the mower or to your car, for instance. Organizing your possessions for both long-term storage and quick access can be a difficult task.

In this chapter, you'll learn how to organize your stuff, except in this case, your "stuff" will be the data on your hard drive. You're on your own in the garage! I'll walk you through how to create folders and subfolders and organize data in them. You'll also learn some techniques for getting organized (and staying that way), including naming your folders effectively. After that, you'll learn how to manage data you share by employing the features of Windows 7 libraries, creating your own libraries, and sharing libraries. You'll be encouraged to use the Public folder for storing anything you want to share, including the media you share over your network. Once this final bit of organizing is out of the way, it would benefit you to run Disk Cleanup one more time and empty the Recycle Bin, and run Disk Defragmenter (or at least see when it'll run on its own). Once all this is done, your PC should be zipping along at breakneck speed.

Manage Data in Folders

The simplest way to organize your files is to create personal folders inside the default folders. As we've discussed, the default folders are My Documents, My Pictures, My Music, and My Videos, along with others such as Downloads and Contacts. You can create subfolders inside of those and move data into them to further organize what you want to keep. These default folders make great storage areas and can be used to organize everything from your accounting files to your zoo pictures. Hopefully, you've moved some of your files there already.

Because I'll encourage you to put just about everything in these default folders, you might encounter a common problem when using them—they are very likely to get really disorganized, really quickly. That's because in this age of large hard drives, we tend to save everything, even things we don't need. You'll have to be disciplined, and continue to degunk regularly, and I'll give you some tips for doing this at the end of the chapter.

GunkBuster's Notebook: Regarding Partitions

Older computers were notorious for being partitioned, and you may have such a system. While you don't hear much these days about partitions on new PCs, an overzealous computer geek still might build a computer that way, and you may have ended up with one. When a computer is partitioned, its hard drive is split up into "sections," and one section is used for the operating system while the other is used for data. (Some computers even have two hard drives.) This sounds good in theory, but unfortunately many people store personal stuff in the default folders on drive C: and completely ignore drive D:. One day these people wake up and realize that their 80GB C: drive is full, and their 500GB D: drive is empty! What a mess.

If you have multiple partitions, which you can easily determine by viewing the Computer window, you have some choices: deal with it and work around it, combine the partitions with software made specifically for that task, or format and reinstall the OS on a single partition. If you decide to deal with it, keep in mind throughout this chapter that you have multiple partitions to deal with and degunk accordingly.

To resolve any questions before they arise, regarding the very small partition you *may* see on your computer, note that lots of computers do come with a "recovery" partition. This is different from the partitions I spoke about previously. You would never store data on a recovery partition, and you'd only ever access it for the purpose of reinstalling the computer with its original operating system and applications. Basically, a recovery partition holds the reinstallation files you used to get with "recovery CDs."

Create Personalized Subfolders

You've taken the first step; you've moved your files to their proper folders (documents to My Documents, pictures to My Pictures, and so forth), and your next step is to organize what's left. You'll continue the degunking process by dealing with what's now in your default folders and libraries.

NOTE   Because a library offers access to both the personal and Public folders they represent, any subfolder you create in a personal or Public folder will be accessible here after you've created it. Any folder you create in a library will be included with your personal folder (not the Public one).

Click Start | Documents. This will take you to the Documents library. In the left pane, click the arrow by Documents so you can access both the My Documents folder and the Public Documents folder, as shown in Figure 4-1. Note that you won't see the down arrow until you position your mouse over that area.

Take a moment now to mentally categorize the documents in both the My Documents folder and the Public Documents folder. Think about what you could put in the Public Documents folder. Perhaps you have items that all family members need access to, such as contact lists, wills, inventory lists, and similar items. You could create a repository for school lunch menus, sports schedules, and homework. Before continuing, move what you can to the Public folders and consider how your whole family (or small business) can benefit from having access to the data they need in a single place on the computer or network. (Later you'll learn how to make sure those folders are available to everyone.)

FIGURE 4-1   Each library offers access to its related Public and personal folders.

Now, consider what subfolders you can create. In your personal My Documents folder, you can create a subfolder for each project you're working on, one to hold tax information, one to hold resumes, one to hold presentations, and so forth. In the Public Documents folder, consider creating subfolders for each member of your family, or subfolders for family-specific documents, such as Contact Lists, Emergency Numbers, Wills and Power of Attorney, Grocery Lists, To Do Lists, and so on.

To create a subfolder:

1. In any folder, click New Folder.

2. Name the folder appropriately.
3. Press ENTER on the keyboard or click outside the naming box to apply it.

Pictures, Videos, Music, and More

While it would be easy enough to tell you to "repeat this practice for each of the remaining default folders," meaning you should continue to create subfolders and move data into them while also incorporating the Public folders, I'd be doing you a disservice. That's because media differs from documents, and while you may have less than 50 documents, you probably have 1,000 + pictures or 500 + songs. It's much, much more to deal with.

It's not just quantity, though; while your documents are probably named appropriately (or most of them anyway), your pictures probably have names like IMG0001_JPG and 100535_PNG. Raw footage you've uploaded from your video camera probably also has obscure filenames (like something out of a sci-fi movie). And if your music is managed by iTunes or another music service, it's best not to go mucking about in the Music library at all! You don't want to cause problems by messing up the system the program has put in place. There's quite a bit to do, but also a lot to consider!

Pictures

Let's start with your Pictures library. Click Start | Pictures and, as with the Documents library, click the arrow under it to have easy access to both the My Pictures and the Public Pictures folders. See Figure 4-2. Again, take inventory. Consider what subfolders you could create: Weddings, Travel, Friends, Family, Pets, House, and so on. Now think a little more deeply. Do you have three cats? Consider creating three subfolders inside the Cats folder you create. Have you traveled a lot? Consider creating subfolders inside Travel for each place you've visited.

With all of your pictures in their proper subfolders, you can start the renaming process. (Right-click any picture and click Rename. Type the new name.) Yes, I know, this could take weeks, if not months, of degunking to complete. To shorten the process, as you're renaming, delete pictures you don't need or want.

FIGURE 4-2   Create subfolders, and then create more subfolders to truly organize your pictures.

Videos

You probably either have a ton of data in your Videos library or virtually none at all. At least that's my experience. For the most part, movies are stored elsewhere (like in an iTunes folder or someplace similar). To find out what's in your Videos library, click Start, click your name to open the Windows Explorer window, and expand the Videos library in the left pane. I'm embarrassed to say that Figure 4-3 shows what my My Videos folder looks like. It's really gunked up, but at least there isn't a lot of data to deal with. (How did those copies get there?)

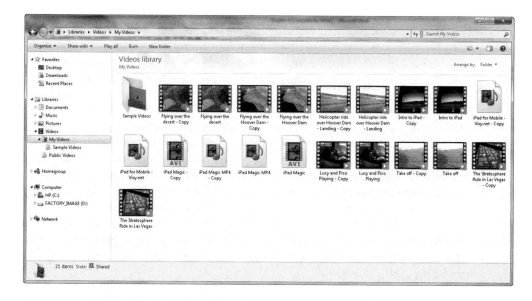

FIGURE 4-3   Videos have a way of being forgotten, and are often a source of gunk.

Degunk as warranted, renaming files, deleting copies and unwanted video, and creating subfolders to manage what you want to keep. Consider folders named for your pets, trips you've taken, or pictures you sync with other devices, to name a few.

Music

Unless you manage your own media and know what you're doing, the only thing you should consider undertaking in your Music library is to move all the data in the My Music folder to the Public Music folder and delete duplicate files. When you do this, you achieve a few things:

- You make your music available to everyone on the network.
- You make your music available from any compliant device on the network.
- You make your music available to anyone who uses your computer.
- You avoid problems with duplicate files or file listings when you access your music over a network (provided that you meet certain other criteria, outlined in Chapter 11).

You may create a problem when you move your music from your personal folder to the Public one, though. Some music programs will only look to the My Music folder for music files. They may not look to the Public Music folder. If you find that to be the case, you'll need to either have the program rescan for music files (noting that it must scan networked drives if the music is stored on the Public Music folder of another computer), or tell your music program specifically where to look. For instance, you can verify that Media Player looks to the Public Music folder for music (see Figure 4-4), or make sure that iTunes does (see Figure 4-5). To access the screen in Figure 4-4, in Media Player, click Organize | Manage Libraries | Music.

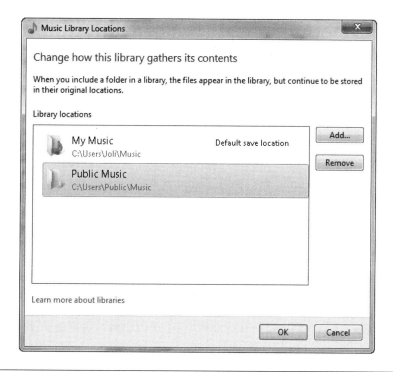

FIGURE 4-4   Media Player can access the Public Music folder.

TIP   Leave the Contacts folder as is, but do consider organizing the Downloads folder (deleting what you don't need), along with Saved Games, if applicable.

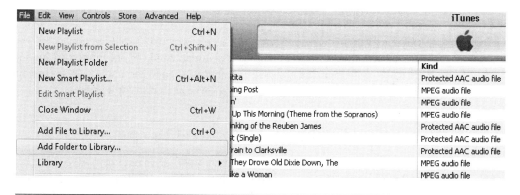

FIGURE 4-5   iTunes has the option to add a folder to its library.

Rename, Cut, Copy, Paste, and Delete Folders

You can rename, cut, copy, paste, and delete folders by right-clicking them. You can also *send* a folder to various places, including My Documents (a copy is made). There are other options too, including opening the folder in a new window (which is great when you want to drag and drop files between two folders), creating a shortcut, and additional options unique to programs you have installed on your computer, such as scanning the folder for viruses with your antivirus program. For now we'll focus on the organizational features: Rename, Cut, Copy, Paste, and Delete.

Renaming is an extremely important part of degunking. If you have a folder named January 2009, but it contains pictures of your vacation to Italy, then you should rename it. You'll use the Rename command often.

To rename a folder (and you'll use the same right-click technique for other commands):

1. Right-click any folder to rename.
2. Click Rename.
3. Type the new name and press ENTER.

The Cut, Copy, and Paste commands work the same with folders as they do with single files. Use Cut to move a file, use Copy to copy a file, and use Paste to place the file. Use the Copy command sparingly, though. You should copy a file to back it up to an external or network drive. You should also create a copy of the file if you want to edit it while hanging on to the original. This is often the case with pictures. You can also delete the original later—if you remember to! Other than these two situations, though, there's rarely any point in having multiple copies of the same file on a single computer.

Of course, the Delete command can be your best friend or your worst enemy! I'm a big fan of deleting data you no longer need, especially pictures and to-do lists, and as long as you don't empty the Recycle Bin, you have a window of reprieve. If you change your mind about any deleted file, you can get it back. (Once you've emptied the Recycle Bin, you're out of luck—unless you have an old backup or you can hire the FBI to recover it for you if you don't!)

NOTE   There are file recovery utilities you can buy and use, should you ever empty the Recycle Bin and then decide you really do need to recover something in it. However, time is of the essence here, because once the hard drive space containing the deleted Recycle Bin data is written over, it's gone for good.

Organize Additional Drives or Partitions

If your computer is partitioned or you have an external or network drive to back up your data, you'll want to create folders and subfolders on those drives to keep them organized. For instance, on a backup drive, you may want to create folders for the months of the year, and place any backups created during those months in them. You may also have folders for dragging and dropping files, such as Pictures, Documents, Videos, and so on, just as you have on your root drive. It would also be good to have a folder just for e-mail backups.

Figure 4-6 shows an example of a computer that contains various drives and hardware. HP (C:) is the root drive, the hard drive used for the operating system, data, and installed programs. FACTORY_IMAGE (D:) is a small partition created by the manufacturer that can be used for recovery should the PC ever need to be reformatted and reinstalled. Backup Drive (K:) is an external drive used exclusively for backing up data. DVD RW Drive (E:) is a rewritable DVD drive. Removable Disk (H:) is a media card reader with a card in the slot. CD Drive (J:) WD SmartWare is the software installed on the backup drive (even though it appears here as a separate drive). Finally, Removable Disk (L:) is a USB flash drive; it's currently empty.

For the drives shown in Figure 4-6, the only drive you really want to degunk is the Backup Drive, K: (well, after degunking C:, of course). You could create folders and subfolders on the USB drive, but it's pretty small and should really be used only to store small bits of data. You don't want to muck about in the recovery partition because, first, there's not enough extra space worth reclaiming and, second, the recovery partition (D:) is there for the purpose of recovery only and should not be tampered with. You can't create folders on CD and DVD drives, only on the data prior to burning it, so that's out. And unless you're using your media card for the purpose of backing up data, there's no point in adding folders to that.

Think about how you'd like to configure the drives you have access to. There is probably an external drive of some sort. Write down what folders and subfolders you'd like to create, and create them:

1. Open My Computer and open the drive where you want to place your data.
2. Right-click an empty area of the folder window, point to New, and click Folder.
3. Repeat step 2 and create other folders as desired.
4. Continue by adding subfolders, moving or copying data, and degunking!

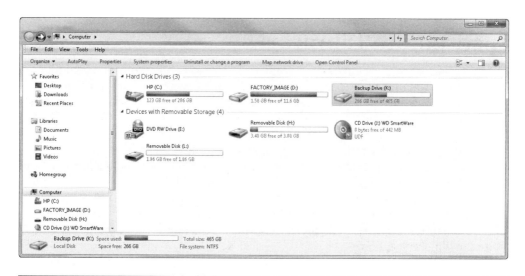

FIGURE 4-6   Your computer may have all kinds of hardware, card readers, and CD/DVD drives available.

GunkBuster's Notebook: Create Multiple Backups

Just how valuable is your data? Do you feel comfortable with your family photos being backed up to an external drive and nowhere else? What about your resume, wills, and other personal data? If a fire destroyed your home, would it destroy your backup too? The real question is: Is moving data the right move for you?

It is okay to move data off of your computer to your external drive, provided you trust your external drive and provided your data isn't that valuable. However, I suggest you leave valuable data on a PC and on a backup drive. If one fails, you still have the other. On that same note, extremely valuable data should be stored on a PC, a backup drive, and somewhere else, like the free Windows Live Workspace, your parent's house, or a child's house. If you consider the possibility of a disaster like a fire or flood, you can easily see that any data stored on your PC and on the backup drive would both be destroyed. Windows Live workspace, with 25GB of free storage, is shown in the illustration, and will be briefly discussed in Chapter 14.

Incorporate Libraries

Libraries are new to Windows 7 and offer access to both your personal files and Public ones. You know that. But you can also tell Windows to look at other folders when amassing data for a library. This means that if you have a folder on your Desktop named My Personal Files, you can tell the Documents library that you want to include that folder in it. Then, when you open your Documents library again, you'll have access to My Documents, Public Documents, and My Personal Files.

You can also create your own library. This means that you can stray from the Documents, Pictures, Videos, and Music libraries you've grown to love, and add others of your own, like My New Invention, Travel, Kids, or Pets. (In a Pets library you could include folders from the Pictures library, veterinary documents from the Documents library, and videos from the Videos library. All pet-related things would be in one location.)

Finally, you can share libraries. You can share a library with everyone, with people in your HomeGroup, or with specific people you name. You can even decide whether they can only access the data or change it and add their own.

TIP   Libraries work in conjunction with homegroups, and you can easily share libraries with other people on your home network. Homegroups are discussed in Chapter 10.

Add a Folder to a Default Library

Since you already know about the default libraries and how to use them, let's jump right in and add a folder to a library. As mentioned, only your personal folder and related Public folder are included in a library by default. If there's a folder you'd like to include, you have to tell Windows to watch for it. This allows you to degunk your computer by making it easier to access the data you want, while at the same time keeping that data organized in folders where you want them (like on the Desktop, on a network drive, on an external drive, and in other places).

CAUTION   If you add a folder to a library that is stored on another drive, that drive must be connected for you to have access.

To add a folder to a default library:

1. Click Start and click your username.
2. In the left pane, select the library to configure.
3. Click Organize | Properties.
4. In the Documents Properties dialog box, click Include a Folder.

5. Browse to the folder to add, and click Include Folder.
6. Click OK.

Create a New Library

You should create a new library to organize a group of related data that is not *all* documents, *all* pictures, *all* videos, or *all* music, but instead, a combination of these. For instance, you may have a project that includes documents, blueprints, training videos, pictures, expense reports, tax receipts, presentations, flyers, and brochures, and organizing these separately in their related default folders would prove futile. You need the data in a single place. You should also create a new library if you still, after all of this degunking, have stray folders on your hard drive that just can't be placed in any of the default folders, or included with them. You should create a new library for data that doesn't fit in any of the default folders, such as data you sync from a PDA or cell phone. You could create a library that offers access to everything you sync, even if the data is managed by third-party software.

To create a new library:

1. Click Start and click your username.
2. Right-click Libraries and choose New | Library, as shown in Figure 4-7.
3. Name the library.
4. Select the new library, and in the right pane, click Include a Folder.
5. Add folders as desired.
6. To add more folders, select the library, click Organize | Properties, and then click Include a Folder, as outlined in the previous section.

To view and/or remove a folder from a library, select the library, click the number of locations (in Figure 4-8, that's 2 Locations, in the Pets library), select the folder to remove if applicable, click Remove, and click OK.

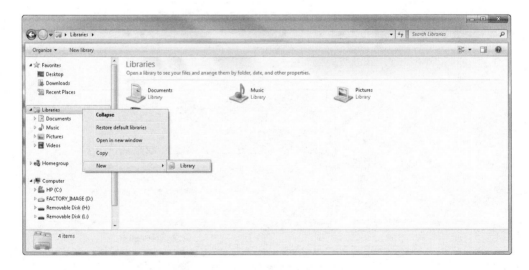

FIGURE 4-7   Create a new library with a right-click on Libraries.

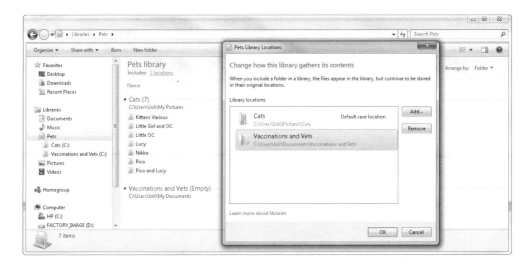

FIGURE 4-8 You can see what folders are included in a library by clicking the location number.

Share a Library

Sharing a library is ultimately better than copying the data to a second or third computer. You don't need duplicate data on your network. Sharing a library is also the best choice if making the data public (by moving it to the Public folders) is not a good idea because you don't want everyone to have access to it. Putting data into libraries and sharing it with only those who you want to have access is a great way to share and secure your data at the same time. When you opt to share a library, you have four options: Nobody, Homegroup (Read), Homegroup (Read/Write), and Specific People.

NOTE Depending on how the wind is blowing, Microsoft may refer to a homegroup as HomeGroup or Homegroup.

If you have yet to hear the term *homegroup*, a homegroup is a group you can create if you have other Windows 7 computers on your network. Often, this gets set up during the installation process or when you create or manage your network. Windows 7 knows when other Windows 7 machines are on the network. A homegroup makes it easier to share data with others on your network. If you have a homegroup, you can choose this option; otherwise, you'll want to select Specific People, as shown in Figure 4-9.

To share a library with specific people:

1. Right-click the library to share, and click Share With.
2. Click Specific People.

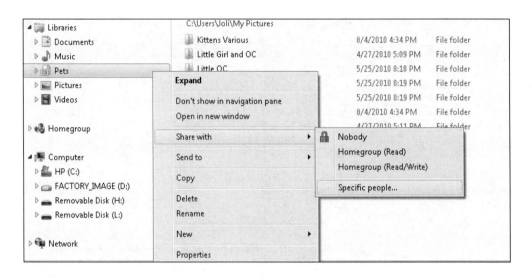

FIGURE 4-9   When sharing a library, you have several options, including specifying which users have access and what they can do once connected.

3. Click the arrow to see which people you can add.
4. Select a person and click Add. Repeat if desired.
5. Under Permission Level, click Read or click Read/Write.
6. Click Share.

TIP   To add a shortcut on the Desktop to any library, right-click the shortcut and choose Send To | Desktop (Add Shortcut).

Use Public Folders to Your Advantage

If you start, right now, to move data to the Public folders that you want to share across your network (with everyone), you'll reduce the number of headaches you have later on. You can move music, videos, pictures, and even documents. You can create subfolders in the Public folders to hold e-mail attachments. You can save travel plans, calendars, contact lists, and myriad other data that your family or small business needs access to. There are lots of advantages to doing this:

- You make the desired data available to everyone on the network.
- You avoid having copies of the same data on various computers across the network (which in turn can cause version-control issues).

- You make your media available from any compliant device on the network.
- You make the desired data available to anyone who uses your computer.
- You avoid problems with duplicate files or file listings when you access media over a network (providing you meet certain other criteria, outlined in Chapter 11).

There are a few caveats to using the Public folders, though. You have to verify that Public folder sharing is enabled, you have to configure how you want that sharing to work, you have to point media programs that are used to finding the data in personal folders to the Public ones, and you have to be sure that you're ready to share the data with everyone with network access.

Configure Public Folder Sharing

Let's assume you've moved data over to the Public folders. You should. Move everything you want to share with others. Move all media you access from networked devices. Move all music, movies, pictures, and videos you play on a compliant device like an Xbox or other media extender. Now, whew, configure Public folder sharing:

1. Click Start, and in the Start Search window, type **Network**.
2. In the results, click Network.

TIP If you use Network often, you can add it to the Start menu. See Chapter 5.

3. Click Network and Sharing Center.
4. Click Change Advanced Sharing Settings in the left pane of the Network and Sharing Center.
5. Verify that the following settings are enabled (or enable them), as shown in Figure 4-10:
   - Network discovery—Turn on network discovery
   - File and printer sharing—Turn on file and printer sharing
   - Public folder sharing—Turn on sharing so anyone with network access can read and write files in the Public folders
   - Media streaming—Choose media streaming options; turn on media streaming and accept default settings.
   - File sharing connections—Use 128-bit encryption to help protect file sharing connections (recommended)
6. Click Save Changes.

Point Programs to the Public Folders

Your media programs and devices need to be able to find the media you collect. When you set them up, they likely scanned your hard drive and configured themselves automatically. In Media Center, for instance, a program included with Windows 7,

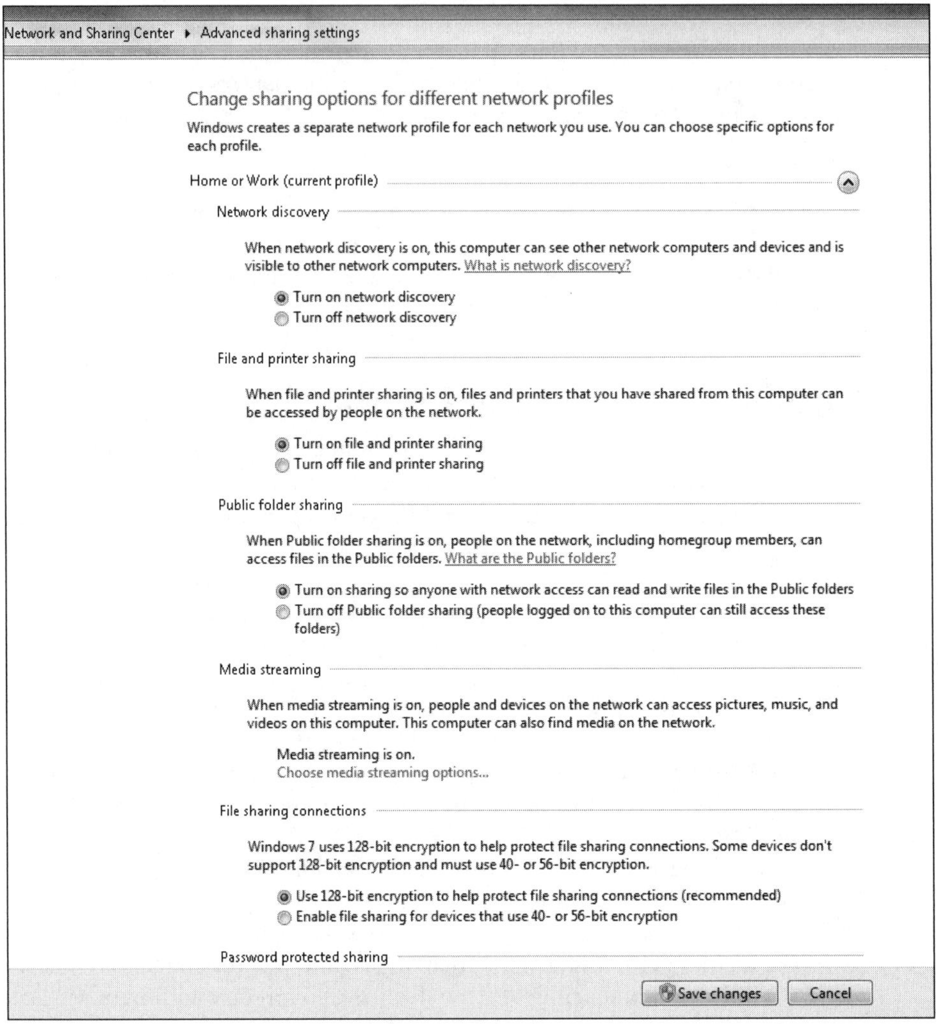

Network and Sharing Center ▸ Advanced sharing settings

Change sharing options for different network profiles

Windows creates a separate network profile for each network you use. You can choose specific options for each profile.

Home or Work (current profile)

Network discovery

When network discovery is on, this computer can see other network computers and devices and is visible to other network computers. What is network discovery?

◉ Turn on network discovery
◯ Turn off network discovery

File and printer sharing

When file and printer sharing is on, files and printers that you have shared from this computer can be accessed by people on the network.

◉ Turn on file and printer sharing
◯ Turn off file and printer sharing

Public folder sharing

When Public folder sharing is on, people on the network, including homegroup members, can access files in the Public folders. What are the Public folders?

◉ Turn on sharing so anyone with network access can read and write files in the Public folders
◯ Turn off Public folder sharing (people logged on to this computer can still access these folders)

Media streaming

When media streaming is on, people and devices on the network can access pictures, music, and videos on this computer. This computer can also find media on the network.

Media streaming is on.
Choose media streaming options...

File sharing connections

Windows 7 uses 128-bit encryption to help protect file sharing connections. Some devices don't support 128-bit encryption and must use 40- or 56-bit encryption.

◉ Use 128-bit encryption to help protect file sharing connections (recommended)
◯ Enable file sharing for devices that use 40- or 56-bit encryption

Password protected sharing

[Save changes]   [Cancel]

FIGURE 4-10   For Public folder sharing to work, you must configure specific settings in Advanced Sharing Settings.

music and other media are added automatically from your default folders, even Public ones. You have the option to choose additional folders, though, as shown in Figure 4-11.

Most, if not all, Windows 7–compliant programs will scan the media libraries for data automatically, and this includes the Public folders. This means that if you move the data from your personal folder to the Public one, you probably won't have to do anything. However, other computers and older devices may not be so smart. You may have to tell the programs on those devices where data is stored. It's different for every program.

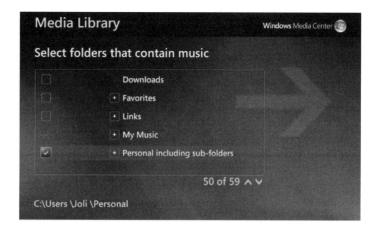

FIGURE 4-11   Media programs always offer the option (somewhere) to scan for media or choose a folder that contains it.

This illustration shows the Music library, and you can see it contains both the personal Music folder and the Public one.

Share a Personal Folder You Create

At this point, you should have all of your data organized in default folders, libraries, or Public folders. However—and I heave a large sigh here—if you still have personal folders that contain data, and you want to share that data, you can. Sigh again.

CAUTION   You should never share your C: drive. It would be best never to share your My Documents, My Pictures, and other personal folders. It's always good to keep some things private, and you'll need a place to put sensitive data.

You share a personal folder the same way you share a library:

1. Right-click the folder to share, and choose Share With | Specific People, as shown earlier in Figure 4-9.
2. Click the arrow to see what people you can add.
3. Select a person and click Add. Repeat if desired.
4. Under Permission Level, click Read or click Read/Write.
5. Click Share.

NOTE   You can share a physical drive the same way. You may want to share a CD/DVD drive over a network to install software on a netbook or other device that does not have a CD/DVD of its own. You may also want to share an external backup drive.

Finalize the Organizational Process

You've deleted, moved, and copied data and have really changed how your computer is organized. That part of degunking is about complete. From here we'll focus more on the *computer* and less on the data, and tackle topics such as optimizing the hard drive, cleaning up Internet Explorer and your e-mail program, securing your computer and network, and resolving the problems associated with media, syncing, and error messages. That means we need to do a couple of things to finalize this part of the degunking process. We need to run Disk Cleanup once more, run Disk Defragmenter, and then verify that Disk Defragmenter will run on a schedule in the future. We also need to discuss how to stay degunked—at least as far as managing your own data goes.

TIP   Run Disk Cleanup now (see Chapter 3). If you feel inclined, empty the Recycle Bin during the process. Remember, once you've emptied the Recycle Bin, you can't restore anything in it.

Disk Defragmenter

You can count on one thing: if you've deleted a lot of files, moved files from one area of the computer to another, deleted programs and applications, and emptied the Recycle Bin, your hard drive will be a mess. When I say "a mess," I don't mean it's disorganized by my standards. I mean that the files on the actual hard drive are *fragmented*, or disorganized by Windows standards. There are files and parts of files stored everywhere, and they aren't stored contiguously. That causes problems and degrades the performance of your hard drive.

Here's basically how a hard drive works, and this is assuming you actually have a hard drive and not a newer, more expense solid-state drive (SSD), which you often find on netbooks and tablet PCs. A hard drive is a circular disk, kind of like an old LP record. As data is written to the hard disk, it is written sequentially using the first open space it finds. If you installed a program on that hard disk the day you purchased the computer, it would be located near the beginning. As time passes, files are saved after it and the disk begins to fill up. If you uninstall data or programs later, you'll have a big gap on the hard disk where that program once was. The next time you install a program or save a file, Windows will begin writing that data to the first open space it sees, most likely this gap where you uninstalled the program and freed up some space. This means you could have part of a file stored at the very beginning of the hard drive, another part stored in the middle, and the rest of the file saved at the end. When you open that file, Windows has to search the entire hard drive to put the pieces together.

When Windows has to piece together a file in this manner, the computer slows down because it simply takes longer to find the data. The disk might have to spin several thousand more times than it should have to, which not only causes a slow response but also causes unnecessary wear and tear on your computer. After a computer is *defragmented*, the files are stored (more) contiguously and the computer's hard disk has to spend less time spinning around and looking for files. This makes for better performance and less stress on the computer. The problem is worse if *program files* are stored in a noncontiguous manner.

Fortunately, Windows provides a utility called Disk Defragmenter that is designed to clean up the fragments in your hard drive. When you run this utility, Windows rearranges the files it knows should be placed together so that the disk will operate more efficiently. You'll see a huge difference after defragging your drive.

By default, Disk Defragmenter runs on a schedule, once a week. If it's set to run on Wednesday at 1:00 A.M., though, and it's Friday morning, you may want to run that program now to see just how far you've come in the way of increasing the performance of your computer. You'll also want to leave your computer on so Disk Defragmenter can run while you aren't using the computer! You can run Disk Defragmenter manually anytime you want, and you can schedule it to run anytime you want.

TIP Removable storage devices such as USB flash drives can also become fragmented.

To run Disk Defragmenter now:

1. Close all programs and disable screen savers. Windows can ignore these, but it's best to take the extra precaution.
2. Click Start, and in the Start Search window, type **Defrag**.
3. In the results, click Disk Defragmenter.
4. Click Configure Schedule and verify that Disk Defragmenter runs at least weekly. If not, configure it to do so.
5. Click the root drive of your computer, generally C:, and click Analyze.

6. Wait while the process completes, as shown in Figure 4-12.
7. If the drive is fragmented, click Defragment Disk. Note that you should do this when the computer is not being used.

NOTE   The length of time it takes for Disk Defragmenter to complete depends on the size of your hard disk and how fragmented it is. It also depends to some extent on how fast your PC is. It's best just to let it run while you're asleep because it can take several hours on slow or extremely gunked-up machines.

Stay Degunked

Keeping your PC degunked is hard, I'll give you that. In fact, it's just as hard as keeping a sparkling-windowed, newly mopped, freshly dusted, vacuumed, trash-free home unsoiled. You can't. However, you can put your dishes in the dishwasher after you're finished eating, take out the trash every other day, and stay on top of the dusting and vacuuming by cleaning one item a day and rotating rooms. The same is true of keeping your computer pristine.

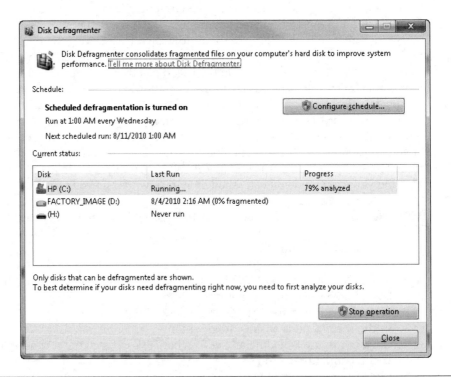

FIGURE 4-12   Analyze your hard disk to see if it's fragmented.

TABLE 4-1   Schedule for Staying Degunked and Organized

Task	How Often to Perform	Tips for Remaining Degunked
Clean up the default folders, like My Documents and My Pictures	Once a week	Put data in the correct subfolders each time you save a file and always delete items you know you do not need.
Use Disk Cleanup and Disk Defragmenter	Once a week	Remember to run Disk Cleanup regularly and verify that Disk Defragmenter is set to run on a schedule.
Uninstall unwanted applications	Once a month	Do not install freeware or shareware unless you're sure it's from a trusted source, and only install third-party software you know you'll use.
Keep unwanted data off your computer	Every day	Purchase, configure, and automatically run third-party antivirus and antispyware software. Do not save data you know you don't need. Get updates each night.
Create subfolders	Whenever necessary	Create a new subfolder every time you upload pictures from your digital camera to your My Pictures folder, create a new movie, or obtain a new hobby, client, or work project. Keep files in their proper folders.
Empty the Recycle Bin	Monthly	Restart your computer before emptying the Recycle Bin, especially if you've recently uninstalled an application.

You may be wondering just how often to perform the tasks introduced so far and what plan of action is required to remain degunked. Now that you've rid your PC of unnecessary files and applications and organized what you want to keep, you'll want to keep it that way. Table 4-1 outlines the tasks introduced in Chapters 3 and 4. Use this table to guide you through the process of staying degunking and organized.

Summing Up

In this chapter, you completed the optimization of the hard drive by organizing the files you decided to keep, moving them to their proper places on the hard drive, emptying the Recycle Bin, and running Disk Defragmenter. All of these things, especially running Disk Defragmenter, are "must do" items if you want your computer to run at its best possible and peak performance. Since the hard drive is an extremely important part of any computer system, it's important to regularly perform the tasks detailed here.

5

Clean Up Your Desktop, Start Menu, and Taskbar

Degunking Checklist:

☑ Get rid of unwanted Desktop icons

☑ Create Desktop icons you'll use

☑ Change the wallpaper and screen saver

☑ Clean up the Start menu

☑ Pin items to the Start menu

☑ Personalize the Taskbar

☑ Pin items to the Taskbar

☑ Change Taskbar settings

☑ Clean up the Notification area

☑ Personalize the Notification area

In the previous chapters you learned how to remove and organize a lot of data and programs that reside in your folders. You might not realize it, but there are also a number of personalization and organizational tasks that you can perform on your Desktop to make Windows run better. Personalizing Windows 7 might not seem like a big deal, but it is. You can tell Windows 7 how you want the Taskbar and Start menu to look, and what should or shouldn't appear on the Desktop. By personalizing Windows 7, you can work faster and smarter and perform tasks more efficiently than if you didn't personalize at all. You can put what you need where you need it, making it a snap to open a program, locate a file, or perform a task. This is the fun part of degunking.

You can also configure what appears in the Notification area of the Taskbar. The items there are running in the background and using system resources. You might find things there like calendar syncing tools, upload tools, music players, or applications you downloaded from the Internet. You can disable the programs you don't need all the time, to improve performance. Disabling these programs in the

Notification area doesn't remove them; it only prevents them from starting when you boot your computer. Fewer programs to start means a faster boot time; fewer programs running in the background means more available RAM for other programs.

The Desktop

There's really only one more item we're going to clean up and then personalize with our own touches, and that's the Desktop (then we'll move on to more system-related things like optimizing your hard drive and securing your web browser). You can make the Desktop look however you want it to. It can have lots of icons or none at all; it can show Computer, Recycle Bin, User's Files (that's your personal folder), Control Panel, and Network; it can have shortcuts to programs you use a lot, folders you access daily, networks you connect to, and more. You can also choose screen savers, although for the purpose of degunking, we'll talk about non-system-intensive ones as well as non-system-intensive themes. The place to start, though, is to get rid of unwanted Desktop icons—so that we can see the Desktop!

NOTE You can add anything you want to a Windows 7 Desktop. This makes it quite easy to gunk up. You'll have to keep an eye on your Desktop to make sure you're keeping it degunked.

Get Rid of Unwanted Desktop Icons

Let's face it: the Desktop gets really messy, really fast. Once a Desktop is gunked up, it's difficult to find the program, file, or icon you need, especially if you need to find it quickly. Beyond the simple inconvenience, though, you may have links on your Desktop to data that doesn't exist anymore, or data you have no use for. You need some breathing room!

My recommendation is that you develop a strategy for what you will allow to be displayed on your Desktop and what you will not allow. You should be very picky. If you're right-brained, think of your Desktop as really valuable real estate, like beachfront property—you don't want to junk it up with a bunch of broken beach chairs and fishing poles. If you're left-brained, imagine it's a filing cabinet, and the icons on your Desktop are the tabs on your file folders. Either way, the idea is to clean it up, make it nice, and configure it so that you can find what you want, when you want it.

TIP Before continuing, right-click any unwanted shortcut to any program or file you don't need on your Desktop and click Delete. Make sure it's a shortcut, though; shortcuts have an arrow on them.

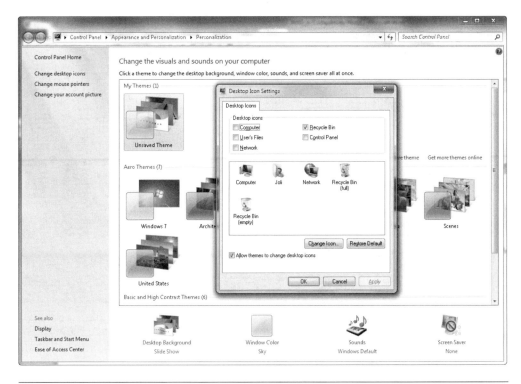

FIGURE 5-1   Add the Desktop icons you use, and delete what you don't.

Your first step should be to remove any of the default icons you don't need (or add them if you do). To add or remove default icons, follow these steps:

1. Right-click an empty area of the Desktop and click Personalize.
2. In the Personalization window, click Change Desktop Icons to open the Desktop Icons Settings dialog box. See Figure 5-1.
3. In the Desktop Icons Settings dialog box, select the icons to show or hide.
4. Click OK, and close the Personalization window.

Next, look for gadgets you've added but no longer use. You may have added gadgets from the Desktop Gadget Gallery, which is fine if you use them, but gunk if you don't. It's easy to remove a gadget from the Desktop; just hover the mouse over it and click the X, as shown here.

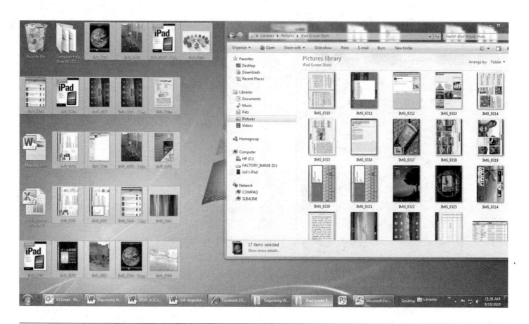

FIGURE 5-2   Select related files saved to the Desktop and move them to an
appropriate folder.

NOTE   Deleting a gadget from your Desktop does not delete it from the gallery.

Finally, while you're focused on the Desktop, look for files that should be moved into folders. You can see in Figure 5-2 that, ahem, *someone* has dumped quite a few iPad screen shots onto the Desktop. What would have been better is if, ahem again, *this person* had created a folder before copying these pictures, a subfolder preferably in the Pictures folder, and uploaded them there. Unfortunately, it looks like there are duplicates too. You may have also noticed that there's a document called Monthly Bills and a spreadsheet for the months of August to January. These could both be moved to a personal folder or a subfolder within it, unless those files are accessed daily.

Create Desktop Icons You'll Use

Having items on the Desktop that you use often can help you work faster and smarter. You can add folders to the Desktop by either creating shortcuts to existing folders or creating completely new folders. You can add program shortcuts just as easily, by browsing to them and right-clicking, although I prefer to pin them to either the Start menu or the Taskbar. If you go this route, the program icons are still easily accessible, but they aren't on the Desktop.

To create a shortcut to an existing folder that contains documents you access often, simply follow these steps:

1. Browse to the folder using the Start menu, Computer window, Network window, or other resource.

TIP   Consider creating a shortcut to the Public folder if you use it often. It's in C:\Users.

2. Right-click the folder and choose Send To | Desktop (Create Shortcut). A shortcut will be placed on the Desktop.

TIP   If you click Create Shortcut in step 2 (vs. Send To), a shortcut will be created in the window (folder) that you are in. You can then drag that shortcut anywhere you'd like to move it, but that requires a second step.

To create a new folder on the Desktop:

1. Right-click an empty area of the Desktop and choose New | Folder.
2. Name the folder, and then drag and drop files in there or add them there as they are created.

It's okay to add folders to your Desktop if you use them. My Desktop may look cluttered to a neatnik, but I need easy access to these folders and I don't want to spend the time necessary to drill into the Start menu, the Documents library, the folder I need, and then the chapter folder and file. If what is on your Desktop works for you, it's fine by me! Figure 5-3 shows my Desktop.

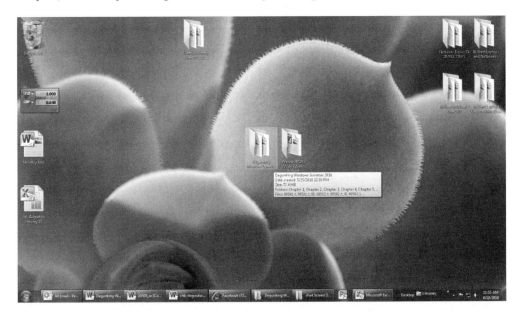

FIGURE 5-3   It's okay to have things on your Desktop, provided you use them.

To bring home the point that a busy Desktop is not necessarily a bad one, let me explain mine: I need my Excel spreadsheet on the Desktop because I use it to track the calories I eat at every meal, along with my blood sugar and the amount of exercise I get. I work a lot for a publisher in the U.K. and need access to the daily exchange rates between the dollar and the British pound (hence the gadget). I need easy access to every folder that contains the book files I'm working on. You can see the Degunking Windows folder selected here. And yes, I do need access to the Monthly Bills file. It helps me stay focused on my budget and keeps me from taking online shopping trips in my spare time.

Remove Folders

Removing shortcuts from the Desktop is as easy as right-clicking and choosing Delete. They just go away; no harm, no foul. You can tell an item is a shortcut if it has an arrow beside it (or technically, on it). You can also right-click and delete default folders like Recycle Bin, Network, Computer, Control Panel, and your User's Files folder. Even though they aren't technically shortcuts with arrows on them, they'll be safely removed and their contents won't be deleted and moved to the Recycle Bin. (I prefer to remove the User's Files folder via the Desktop Icons Settings dialog box detailed earlier, though, just to be safe.)

However, if you want to remove a folder that *you created* on the Desktop and the folder is not a shortcut to another folder, you have to be more careful. If you delete a folder you've created on the Desktop, its contents will be deleted as well. Figure 5-4 shows the warning box you'll see when you try to delete a folder that is not a shortcut to another folder.

Therefore, if you have created a folder on the Desktop and added data to it and you later decide that you don't want it on the Desktop anymore, your best bet is to *right-click* the folder, and then drag and drop the folder to another area. (You can drag it to another folder, to the Start menu, and to an open Windows Explorer window, among other places.) You can drag it to the Documents library, to somewhere in

FIGURE 5-4   Be careful not to delete folders you created on the Desktop or the folder and all of the data you saved to it will be deleted.

Windows Explorer, to a separate hard disk, or even to a network drive. Right-clicking during the process gives you the option to Copy Here or Move Here when you drop it, as shown next. (Left-clicking, dragging, and dropping will either copy or move the data depending on where you're dragging it off to, and there's no need to dedicate brain space to the rules behind this.)

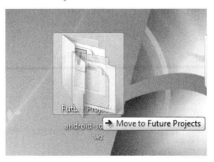

Change the Wallpaper and Screen Saver

If you've chosen a wacky screen saver, one that is complex, one that requires complex calculations, or one you've downloaded from a web site that can't be trusted to create efficient program code, you might be seeing the effects of running a system-intensive or poorly designed screen saver. (I loved my "aquarium" screen saver, complete with its 20 fish, but it was hanging up on me and I had to disable it.) When a screen saver is used, the computer must offer up system resources to run it. If you're having problems with system performance, including slow response coming out of a screen saver, a screen saver that hangs or freezes up, or one that locks up the computer, you should switch to a non-system-intensive or a default Windows 7 screen saver. Of course, the best option is to select None and configure your computer to sleep when you aren't using it. This way, no system resources are used, you extend the life of your computer and monitor, and you save a little on your electricity bill. However, if you must, a screen saver is fine and dandy, provided it's not using a lot of system resources or causing problems.

TIP   The savings add up even more if you're using a laptop. Screen savers use battery power when you aren't using the computer, and drain the battery. For a laptop, it's certainly best to let it sleep or hibernate.

If you're having screen saver problems, select a screen saver that's not so complex, like the Windows 7 screen saver Bubbles (or none at all):

1. Right-click an empty area of the Desktop and click Personalize.
2. Click Screen Saver.

3. In the Screen Saver Settings dialog box, shown in Figure 5-5, select a screen saver and apply any desired options, such as how long to wait until the screen saver is enabled. The screen saver you select may also offer "settings". Click Settings to find out.

4. Click OK.

NOTE   Screen burn-in is a thing of the past, unless, I suppose, you have an extremely old monitor. It's better to let your computer sleep or hibernate than to use a system-intensive screen saver.

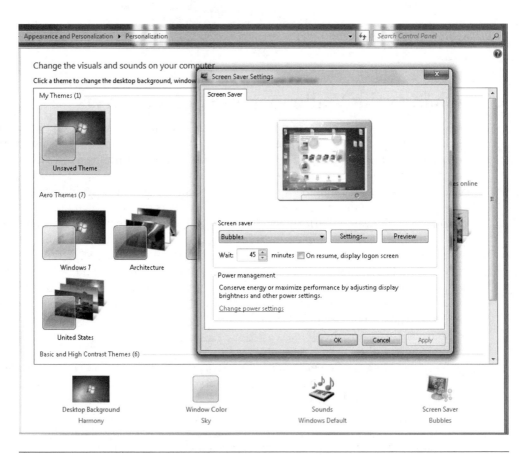

FIGURE 5-5   Choose a screen saver if you must, but it's best to let the computer sleep or hibernate, as discussed in Chapter 9.

Regarding backgrounds and wallpapers, choose one that does not impede your ability to discern the icons on the Desktop. Some backgrounds can do that, as shown in the illustration.

GunkBuster's Notebook: Using Themes

Themes are groupings of backgrounds, screen savers, mouse pointers, sounds, colors, and similar computer-related features. If you're concerned about performance or battery life, it's best to avoid themes, especially from third-party web sites. However, if you really enjoy themes, try one of the default Windows 7 themes, like Windows 7, Architecture, or Landscapes. Keep in mind, though, that it will take some system resources to change the backgrounds regularly and employ the Aero interface (a premium visual experience with translucent glass effects and subtle window animations, among other things), and the background or screen saver applied at any given moment might be distracting. Themes may also use more resources, with their fancy sounds and other amenities, such as how menus appear, animated controls, or shadows under windows. If you're in it for the simple pleasure of having a nice background, screen saver, mouse pointer, colors, and interface, and if you have plenty of resources, by all means, browse for and choose a theme! You can access themes from the Personalization window.

The Start Menu

In order to work faster and smarter, you need to personalize the Start menu so the things you need are readily available and the things you don't need or no longer have installed aren't taking up unnecessary space. There's nothing worse than having to wade through a disorganized Start menu looking for some program you think should be there but isn't! Beyond that, though, you also need to take advantage of the Start Search window; you can use it to find any program quickly, even if your Start menu is completely gunked! The illustration here shows a Start menu that has been slightly modified, with some items unpinned from the Start menu and some new ones pinned. (You'll learn about pinning shortly, but briefly, you're saving a program icon to the Start menu for easy access.)

Your Start menu can and will look much different, though. My most-used programs won't be the same as yours. My most-used programs often have arrows beside them. Pointing to this arrow or any other on the Start menu opens another menu with the item's contents, which generally include recent documents, pictures, and TV shows I've recorded in Media Center. For instance, SnagIt 8's arrow shows the screen shots I've taken so far today, for this chapter!

There are many ways to customize your Start menu, including how the icons, links, and menus appear on it, what the "Power button" command is (Switch User, Log Off, Lock, Restart, Sleep, Shut Down), and whether or not to display recently

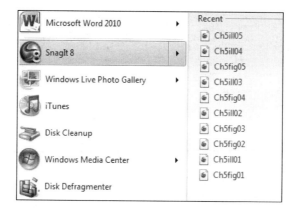

FIGURE 5-6   Your most-used programs will appear in the Start menu and may have an arrow beside them.

opened items. You can also pin items to the Start menu that you use often. In Figure 5-6 and the preceding illustration, Microsoft Word 2010 is pinned to the top of the Start menu, making it easy to access.

Explore Start Menu Options

To change how the Start menu looks and responds to your clicks, you need to access the Taskbar and Start Menu Properties dialog box:

1. Right-click the Start orb in the bottom-left corner of the screen and click Properties.

2. On the Start Menu tab, choose a setting for the Power Button Action field.
3. Under Privacy, choose the privacy options you prefer.
4. Click Customize to open the Customize Start Menu dialog box, shown in Figure 5-7.
5. Read each option and make changes as desired:
   - **Display as a link**   Shows only the option and no menu. When you click the link, the resulting window opens. By default, almost all options on the Start menu are a link only.
   - **Display as a menu**   Shows the option, and a menu appears when you click that option. By default, Recent Items shows a menu.
   - **Don't display this item**   The item is not shown. By default, many aren't, including Downloads, Recorded TV, System Administrative Tools, and Videos.

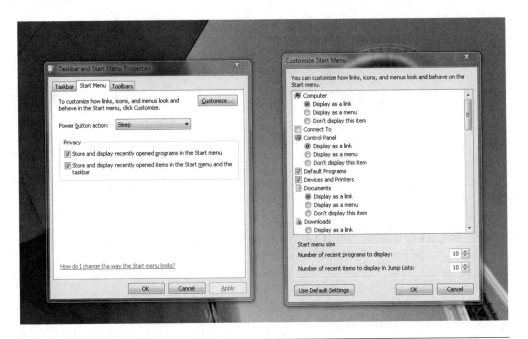

FIGURE 5-7   Click Customize to access options for how the Start menu looks and reacts to a mouse click.

6. Select the number of recent programs to display and the number of items in Jump Lists (the lists that jump out when you click an icon in the Start menu).
7. Click OK. Click OK again.

> TIP You can right-click any item in the Start menu to remove it. Just right-click and choose Remove from this list.

Pin Items to the Start Menu

Pinning an item to the Start menu enables you to access it all the time, no matter how the list of items on your Start menu changes. Pinned items appear at the top of the list, above a line that separates them from the list of most-used programs. You can pin an item to the Start menu easily if it's showing in the Start menu; just drag it from its place in the Start menu to the top, as shown in Figure 5-8.

You can also pin any program icon to the Start menu by right-clicking its icon and choosing Pin to Start Menu. This illustration shows a pretty clean Start menu, with four items pinned to it and three programs I use often.

FIGURE 5-8   If a program is showing on the Start menu, drag it to the top and drop it there to pin it.

Finally, you can pin folders and files too. You can try right-clicking the file or folder to access the Pin to Start Menu option, but if you can't find it, simply drag the file or folder to the Start orb, wait for the Start menu to appear, and drop it on the Start menu. It will be pinned automatically.

The Taskbar

The Taskbar is the translucent, possibly gray/blue, bar that runs across the bottom of your screen. Its color depends on the theme you've selected. You can use it to immediately find out what programs are running, what programs started automatically when you booted Windows, and what programs you have pinned to it. The Taskbar is full of information and, by its very nature, a busy place that tends to get more than a little cluttered.

The Taskbar contains four main components (see Figure 5-9): In the bottom-left corner, you'll find the trusty Start button, also called the Start orb. To the right of the

FIGURE 5-9   The Taskbar has many sections and features.

Start button are items pinned to the Taskbar, which enables you to quickly launch the programs they represent, along with icons for the programs currently running on your computer. Depending on how you've set up your Taskbar so far, you may also see libraries and toolbars listed. Finally, the section to the far right is the Notification area. The Notification area shows the programs that started when Windows did, and each runs automatically and in the background.

NOTE Your Taskbar and Notification area may look quite a bit different from Figure 5-9, as the look of the Taskbar depends on the settings configured.

Pin Items to the Taskbar

You pin items to the Taskbar in the same manner as you pinned them to the Start menu. You right-click the item and select Pin to Taskbar. You can't pin just anything, though; you can't pin printers and other hardware, for instance, but you probably wouldn't want to anyway. When you right-click a networked computer, there's no option to pin it to the Taskbar either. You can pin programs icons, though, and this alone can make using the Taskbar more effective.

TIP If you really want to pin "anything" to the Taskbar, google "How to pin anything to the Windows 7 Taskbar." You'll find tutorials on how to do this, but your Taskbar may get a little "gunky" if you pin too many things.

When an item is pinned to the Taskbar, its icon appears there. The icon appears "indented" when it's open, and appears to have other icons behind it if there are multiple documents, spreadsheets, web pages, or the like open in it. When you click an icon with multiple files or web pages opened, you see their thumbnails. You can then click a thumbnail to open the desired item. (If this gets annoying, change the Taskbar Buttons setting from Always Combine, Hide Labels on the Taskbar tab of the Taskbar and Start Menu Properties dialog box, detailed in the next section.) The way your Taskbar appears is dependent on your settings, though; Figure 5-10 shows what you'll see if the Taskbar settings are configured to combine and hide labels,

FIGURE 5-10 The Taskbar can be configured to compress everything, including multiple documents open in Word or multiple web pages in Internet Explorer.

among other things. Here, Photo Gallery, my personal folder, Excel, and PowerPoint are pinned but are not open. Outlook, Word, and Internet Explorer are open. There are other options, though, and they offer different looks.

If you want to pin a *folder* to the Taskbar, drag it there and choose Pin to Windows Explorer. This will place a link to the folder in your personal folder, which is available from the Taskbar. In Figure 5-11, I've pinned quite a few things to "Windows Explorer," available by clicking the personal folder icon.

However you decide to set up your Taskbar, it's important to note here that you can pin items to it. That's all you need to know, and you may want to pin a few items to it now to personalize the Taskbar before continuing. (You know not to gunk up the Taskbar with too many items, don't you?)

NOTE   You can also incorporate libraries and toolbars into your Taskbar. I won't go into this, but you can explore it by right-clicking an empty area of the Taskbar. Click Toolbars to get started.

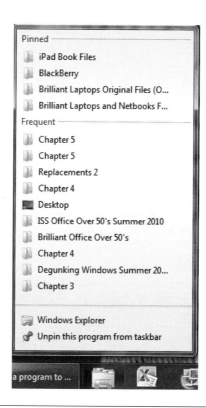

FIGURE 5-11   You can easily pin folders to Windows Explorer by dragging them to the Taskbar.

Configure Taskbar Settings

You can lock the Taskbar so that it cannot be moved or resized, or you can configure it to hide when inactive. You can also configure it to group files that are opened by the same program in the same area of the Taskbar. If you choose to group files, when the Taskbar becomes crowded, the buttons for the same program are collapsed into a single button. You can also opt to always have similar items grouped. You then click to see the options for opening any file or pinned item in it.

To apply AutoHide, to lock the Taskbar so it can't be moved, to reposition the Taskbar, or to group items, right-click the Taskbar, choose the Taskbar tab, and select the appropriate boxes.

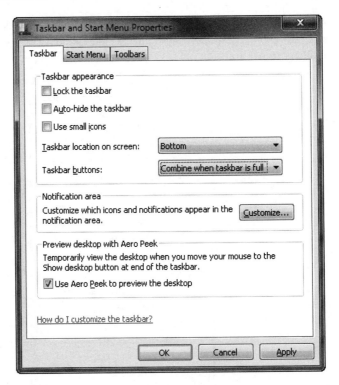

TIP   You can drag icons on the Taskbar to reposition them.

Manage the Taskbar's Notification Area

The Notification area is where we'll focus our energies now. Degunking the Notification area will free up system resources and help your computer run faster and is well worth the effort. If I lost you a little in the Start menu and Taskbar sections, because you didn't feel as if you were really "degunking," sit up and pay attention now. I'm talking about making your computer run faster and boot more quickly. This isn't just cosmetic.

NOTE Every item in the Notification area is slowing down the boot process and bogging down your computer. It's that simple. If an icon is in the Notification area, it's running in the background whether you like it or not, and it's starting with Windows, like it or not (thus increasing how long it takes your computer to boot).

Programs, especially those downloaded from the Internet, might place their icons in the Notification area without your permission. If you don't monitor your Notification area regularly, it could become really cluttered. When an icon is showing in the Notification area, the program it represents runs in the background all the time and uses valuable system resources. You don't want a lot of icons there for that reason; their programs hog valuable RAM. It's best to have as few items as possible in the Notification area.

Some of the items you should see running in the Notification area are programs you use every day (such as an antivirus program) and icons for applications or hardware that you use often (in my case, SnagIt for screen captures, the external hard drive and related backup software, and Outlook for e-mail). Some items that you probably don't want there are icons for programs you downloaded, tried out, and didn't like, such as music programs, calendar syncing programs, upload tools, and backup software you no longer use. There's no reason to leave running all the time a program that you don't use regularly. To see what's in your Notification area, click the up arrow, as shown in the illustration. Click Customize to change what icons and notifications you see here.

NOTE You should have already uninstalled all the programs you no longer want from Control Panel. If you see icons for programs you don't want in the Notification area (implying you missed these in the degunking processes outlined in Chapter 3), uninstall their programs from Control Panel now. If you want to keep the programs but do not want them to run when you aren't using them, continue here.

Although you can look for and disable a single program's ability to run all the time and in the background through its various menus and settings, the easiest way is to tell Windows what you do and do not approve of. Using the System Configuration utility, you can be in control of what programs start with Windows. You can configure all programs at once this way. Note that if you deselect an item in the System Configuration dialog box, it is not permanently disabled or uninstalled. It simply won't start when Windows boots. If you want to use these programs, you simply start them manually from the Start menu or program icon!

Here's how:

1. Click Start, and in the Start Search window, type **msconfig**.
2. Click msconfig in the results.
3. Click the Startup tab of System Configuration, shown in Figure 5-12.
4. Deselect items that you recognize and don't want to start automatically. Do not deselect anything you don't recognize or the Windows operating system.

TIP   If you are unsure about any item under the Startup tab of the System Configuration dialog box, jot down the path to the program and see if you can figure out what it is by browsing there and starting the program. If that doesn't work, you can look up the program in question on the Internet.

---

5. Click OK and restart your computer.
6. On reboot, read the information and click OK in the System Configuration dialog box.
7. Notice that the bootup processes completed more quickly, and that there are fewer icons in the Notification area.

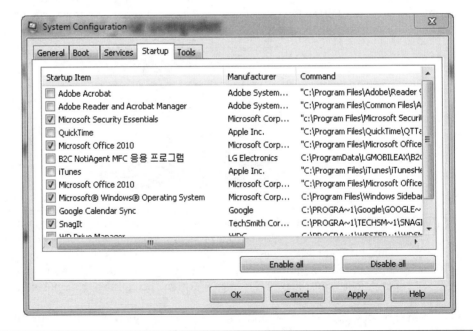

FIGURE 5-12   Deselect items like iTunes, QuickTime, Adobe Acrobat, calendar syncing programs (if you don't use them), and other items unnecessary at bootup.

TIP   In a general sense, if you get error messages on startup, find out what program those errors are related to and uncheck that item in the System Configuration utility. You might find that those error messages go away on the next bootup, and you can then decide if you want to uninstall the program, reinstall it, or replace it with something more compatible. Additionally, www.bleepingcomputer.com has a helpful Startup Programs Database at www.bleepingcomputer.com/startups/.

There are a few other things you can do if you want to clean up the Notification area, although the performance results won't be nearly as noticeable as disabling 20 programs from starting when you boot your PC! However, in the desire for full disclosure, here is one other thing you can do to "enhance" your Notification area:

1. Right-click the Taskbar and click Properties. Under Notification Area, click Customize. (Alternately, click the up arrow in the Notification area and click Customize.)
2. Change everything to Only Show Notifications, unless you feel strongly about another setting such as Hide Icon and Notifications. See Figure 5-13.
3. Click Turn System Icons On or Off.

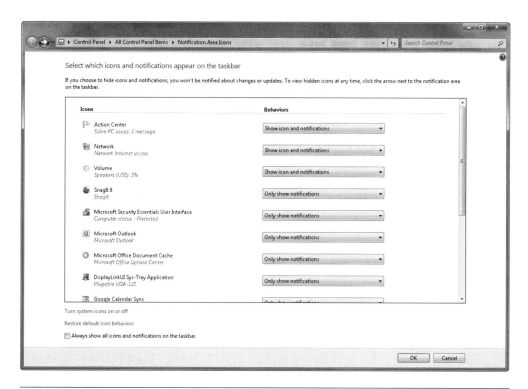

FIGURE 5-13   You can tweak the Notification area in Control Panel.

4. Opt to turn on or off system icons, including the clock, volume, network, power (for laptops only), and Action Center.
5. Click OK.
6. Click OK again.

Summing Up

Cleaning up and tweaking the Start menu, Desktop, and Taskbar might seem like simple cosmetic enhancements at first, but they aren't. Making programs readily accessible by having what you need on the Start menu and Taskbar will help you, and thus Windows, work faster. Cleaning up the Notification area, limiting what programs start automatically when Windows starts, and using non-system-intensive screen savers and themes dramatically increases performance as well. Of course, keeping a tidy house doesn't hurt, so keep an eye on your Desktop, Start menu, and Taskbar, and keep them clean!

6

Optimize Your Hard Drive

Degunking Checklist:

☑ Convert your file system to NTFS

☑ Get rid of unsigned drivers

☑ Run Check Disk

☑ Run performance tests

☑ Tweak features and use advanced tools to enhance system performance

☑ Schedule Disk Cleanup

☑ Clean up the Registry

The hard drive must be optimized for you to get the most out of your computer. The hard drive is the spinning, whirling, cylindrical disk that is housed inside almost all computers, and it holds the program files, operating system files, and data. The hard drive is very important to overall system performance, because when Windows needs something, it must find it on the hard drive before it can use it. The hard drive, then, must be in fine working order, with files optimized for easy access by Windows.

NOTE If you have a solid-state drive (SSD), you can still enhance performance by working through this chapter, even though the technology is vastly different from that of a traditional spinning drive. Solid-state drives (often found in new netbooks) are becoming more popular and more affordable every year.

You've already begun to optimize your hard drive. You started when you began deleting unnecessary files and uninstalling unused programs, disabling programs from booting when the computer boots, running Disk Cleanup, and running Disk Defragmenter. You helped even more when you degunked the Notification area and stopped programs you use occasionally from running in the background all the time. You may have even consolidated or reorganized partitions on your hard drive to enhance your hard drive's performance. However, there's even more you can do. This is "advanced degunking," and it includes using NTFS, using system diagnostic tools, and tweaking system properties for enhancing system performance. If you dare, it can also include tweaking the Registry.

NTFS and FAT

NTFS (NT File System) is a, um, file system. It's one of several. It's the file system I recommend, my editor recommends, Microsoft recommends, and various other experts in the field recommend. Hopefully it's the file system you're using now.

If you aren't familiar with file systems, they are the basic machinery for managing your hard drives, and with Windows, you have the option of choosing between two types: NTFS and a version of FAT (short for File Allocation Table). NTFS is the most powerful because it offers enhanced security features over FAT, including file-level security, compression, and auditing. It also works much better with large disks than other file system configurations do; NTFS supports various file storage solutions, including RAID (Redundant Array of Independent Disks), among other things. None of this may mean much to you right now, and perhaps it might not ever, but suffice it to say that NTFS is the preferred option. I suggest that you find out what file system your computer is configured with, and if it's not NTFS, that you convert it.

TIP   If you want to learn more about NTFS, visit www.ntfs.com.

It's easy to find out what file system you use and convert it to NTFS if necessary. Once you convert to NTFS, though, you can't convert back to any version of FAT without reformatting the drive, so make sure you won't need to. Really, the only reason to keep a FAT file system is if you dual-boot with an earlier operating system like Windows 98. Otherwise, you're good to go with NTFS.

You can find out if you have drives formatted with NTFS by looking in the Computer Management window, among other places. Since I'd like you to explore this window, I'll take you via that route. Computer Management is an "Administrative Tool," along with several other available tools. To access the Computer Management window and to view other features, click Start, and in the Start Search window, type Administrative Tools and then click it in the search results to open the Administrative Tools folder. Figure 6-1 shows the resulting Administrative Tools folder.

Open the Computer Management window, and click Disk Management. You can now look at the disks listed in the Disk Management window. You may see more than one. Look for the C: drive, and ignore other drives for now (including recovery partitions, attached USB drives, and the like). Figure 6-2 shows what you may see.

If you find out that your disk drive is a version of FAT, it's in your best interest to convert to NTFS. Before you start, note in the Disk Management window the name of the disk to covert. In this case, the C: drive has the name HP.

Converting to NTFS is done from a command prompt:

1. Close any open programs.
2. Choose Start | All Programs | Accessories.
3. Right-click Command Prompt, and then click Run As Administrator.
4. If you are prompted for an administrator password, enter it.

FIGURE 6-1   The Administrative Tools folder offers several advanced system tools.

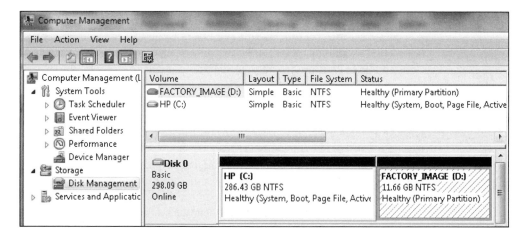

FIGURE 6-2   Look to Disk Management to find out what file system your computer uses.

5. In the Command Prompt window, type **convert *drive_letter*: /fs:ntfs**, where *drive_letter* is the letter of the drive you want to convert (likely C), and then press ENTER. For example, convert C: /fs:ntfs would convert drive C to the NTFS format.
6. Type the name of the volume you want to convert, and then press ENTER.
7. Reboot if prompted.

NOTE   If you get an error during the conversion, your hard drive might be full. I doubt it if you've been degunking in the order presented in this book, but it's worth mentioning.

GunkBuster's Notebook: Revisit the Startup Process

There's a Startup folder in the Start | All Programs list. Items in the Startup folder start when you boot your computer. You've probably already cleaned that up in Chapter 5, but it never hurts to revisit things to double-check. If you have items in the Startup folder that you no longer want to start automatically, remove them by following these steps:

1. Choose Start | All Programs | Startup, and take a look at the entries.
2. To delete an entry, right-click and choose Delete. This will not delete the program; it will only remove the shortcut from the Startup folder.

You can also *add* entries to the Startup folder. This may appeal to you if you open the same programs every time you boot your PC and you have to open them manually. For instance, if you always open Outlook, Photoshop, Windows Live Messenger, and Microsoft Office, you can put shortcuts to those items in the Startup folder. Since those programs can take a while to open and initiate, you can boot your PC in the morning (if you ever turn it off), make coffee and pour yourself a cup, and upon your return, all the programs you need to use will be open and ready to go. This is degunking finesse, because you don't have to open manually the programs you want and then wait around for them to initiate!

To add entries to the Startup folder, right-click the program icon (which may be in the All Programs menu, in a folder, or on the Desktop, among other places) and drag it to Start | All Programs, hover over the Startup folder until it opens, and then drop it in the Startup folder. Choose Create Shortcut Here. When you drag and drop an EXE file, the program will start automatically on bootup. You can also drag and drop files and folders, among other things. You can test it by moving Notepad there; on bootup, Notepad will open automatically.

Get Rid of Unsigned Drivers

Signed device drivers and files have been tested by Microsoft and are deemed safe and compatible with the Windows 7 operating system. Those that are not signed might not be safe and might not be compatible. Unsigned device drivers and files associated with incompatible hardware and software is another area that can cause a computer to have a slow boot process, have a slow reaction time, or generally have unexpected performance errors (like a failure to come out of hibernation). This incompatibility can cause major problems, including unexpected shutdowns of applications, hardware that sometimes works and sometimes doesn't, and hard-to-diagnose problems with the shutdown process (including the inability of the computer to shut down at all).

Use File Signature Verification

You can see what unsigned files (including drivers) are installed on your system by using the File Signature Verification utility. If you find unsigned drivers, you can try to find updated drivers or uninstall the hardware or software associated with them. Once that's complete, you can do a little preventive maintenance by telling Windows you don't want to ever install unsigned drivers once these are uninstalled or updated.

Here are the steps to follow to scan for files and programs that do not have valid digital signatures:

1. Click Start, and in the Start Search window, type **Sigverif**.
2. Click Sigverif in the results to start the program.
3. When prompted, click Start.

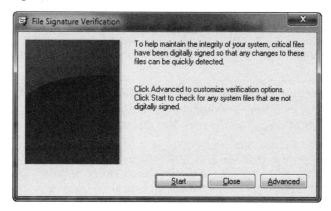

4. If you are prompted that all files are signed, click OK and then Close. If not:
   a. Make a list of unsigned filenames. A sample list is shown in Figure 6-3.
   b. Google the file and/or folder name to see what it is most often associated with.

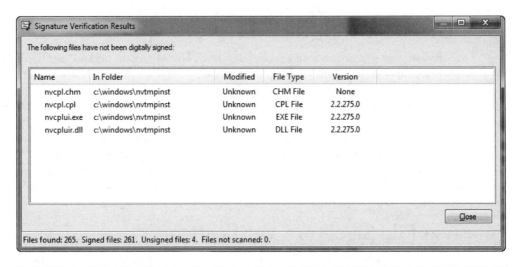

FIGURE 6-3   You may find that you have several filenames associated with one unsigned driver or file.

NOTE   You may find that you cannot access the folder that contains the unsigned files you see listed. You may find that the file relates to a sound or video card, a program, or some other item on your computer that can be updated. You'll have to decide, after researching, whether you can do anything about what you've uncovered.

    c. If you find that the unsigned driver is related to hardware inside your system, such as a sound or video card, open Device Manager and see if you can update the driver. If it's software-related, uninstall or update the program.

TIP   Don't panic! (Should I credit Douglas Adams' *The Hitchhiker's Guide to the Galaxy* here?) Although the unsigned drivers you find *can* cause system instability, that doesn't mean that they do. Take a deep breath.

If you've uncovered a piece of hardware with an unsigned driver, you can use Device Manager to update the device driver easily. You can also use Device Manager to uncover unknown problems with devices and their drivers. Here are the steps to follow:

1. Click Start, and in the Start Search window, type **Device Manager**.
2. Click Device Manager in the results to open it.
3. If you notice any items with a red *X* or a yellow exclamation point, that particular piece of equipment has problems with either the driver or the hardware itself. Double-click the item to see what the problem is.
4. To update a driver, click the Driver tab, and click Update Driver.
5. Let Windows try to locate a driver.

TIP   If the new driver doesn't work as planned, use Device Driver Rollback. However, don't install a different driver before rolling back to the old one. Device Driver Rollback only remembers the last driver installed, and no further back in time than that.

If Windows can't find a driver, you can try to locate one on the Internet. If Windows doesn't know about it, though, it likely is unsigned. In addition to installing a newer driver, you can disable a device from Device Manager. If you are positive a specific device is lousing up the system and causing performance problems, disable it for a while and see if the problem goes away.

Set Driver Signing Properties

You can tell Windows 7 to be more careful about installing unsigned drivers from here on out, but only if you're running Windows 7 Ultimate, Enterprise, or Professional (not Home Premium). Yes, that's very disappointing, but that's the way it is.

If you have the required edition of Windows 7, in the Start Search window, type **gpedit.msc** and click OK. In the Local Group Policy Editor, under User Configuration, drill down into Administrative Templates, System, and Driver Installation. In the right panel, double-click Code Signing for Device Drivers. Enable code signing, and under When Windows 7 Detects a Driver File Without a Digital Signature, select Ignore, Warn, or Block.

Enhance Performance

There are many other ways to enhance the performance of your hard drive, including checking it for bad sectors, running performance tests to see where your computer is lacking, configuring system performance options, and even using system utilities regularly and on a schedule, like Disk Cleanup. Let's start with a disk check; I'm betting you've never done this!

Run Check Disk

Your hard disk won't run optimally if there are bad sectors on it. *Sectors* are where data is stored, and if any sectors are damaged and you try to write data to them, you're going to run into problems. To scan for bad sectors on the hard drive, use the Check Disk error-checking tool:

1. Click Start | Computer.
2. Right-click the root (C:) drive and click Properties.
3. Click the Tools tab.
4. Under Error Checking, click Check Now. See Figure 6-4.

FIGURE 6-4   Although you can type chkdsk at the Run line or in the Search window, running Check Disk from here is best.

5. In the Check Disk dialog box, check Automatically Fix File System Errors and Scan For and Attempt Recovery of Bad Sectors.
6. Click Start.
7. You'll most likely be prompted to schedule the check. Click Schedule disk check.
8. Click OK.
9. Reboot the computer and let the disk check commence.

After the computer boots up, the Check Disk utility will run. Wait while Windows finds and fixes the hard disk problems. This might take a while, or it might take no time at all, and your computer will be unavailable during this process.

Run Performance Tests

Windows enables you to easily run a performance test on your computer to see where its weaknesses are. When it's finished, you can view your options for enhancing performance. This feature isn't hidden anywhere, and it's not rocket science. It's just a simple test available from Control Panel, called Performance Information and Tools.

To run an assessment test:

1. Click Start, and in the Start Search window, type **Performance**.
2. Click Performance Information and Tools in the results.
3. Click Rerun the Assessment (even if the data shows your assessment is up to date). Wait while the test completes, as shown in Figure 6-5.
4. Currently, the highest score a computer can have in any category is 7.9, and the lowest is 1.0. Review the settings for your computer and then click What Do These Numbers Mean? to learn more.
5. Close the Help window that was opened in step 4, and click Tips for Improving Your Computer's Performance. Close this window when desired.
6. Note the options on the right side of the Performance Information and Tools window. You'll use these tools to tweak performance shortly, so leave this window open.

Tweak Features and Use Advanced Tools to Enhance System Performance

Keeping in mind that entire books could be written on enhancing performance using the tools available in various versions of Windows 7, let's go over the basics of the basics. Starting from where we left off in the last section (in the Performance Information and Tools window), let's start from the top. Click Adjust Visual Effects in the left pane.

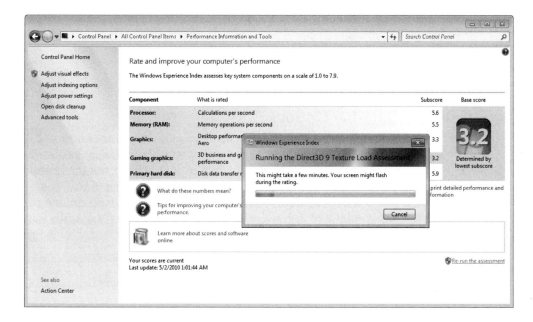

FIGURE 6-5   Run a fresh assessment of your computer to see its strengths and weaknesses.

Change Visual Effects

When you click Adjust Visual Effects in the Performance Information and Tools window, the Performance Options dialog box opens. Here, you can choose Let Windows Choose What's Best for My Computer. That's the default, but it can be changed. For instance, if you're interested in getting the best appearance from your computer, select Adjust for Best Appearance; if you want best performance, choose Adjust for Best Performance. You can also select Custom and check or uncheck anything you desire.

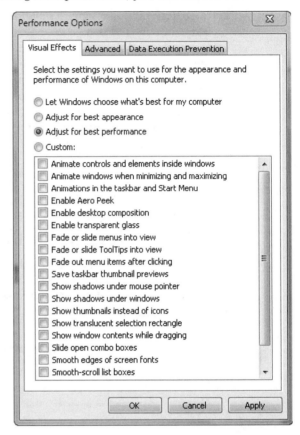

Although adjusting the PC for best performance may seem like the best answer to getting the best performance, and it probably is, the problem with this setting is lack of appearance features! No fading or sliding of menus, no smooth screen fonts, no visual styles on windows and buttons, as you can see in the illustration. Your best bet for enhancing performance is to choose Custom and uncheck as many boxes as you're comfortable with. Go ahead and do this, and then click OK.

Improve Indexing Options

Windows uses an *index* to search for files on your computer, sort of how you'd use a book's index to find something in it. You can look in a book's index, locate what you want, and then go there quickly. This certainly beats starting from the beginning and reading line by line until you find what you want, or trying to scan the pages for a particular word or idea. Similarly, the Windows index on your computer provides a faster way for Windows to find what it wants. If you want a specific file, Windows looks to its index, locates it, and then uses that information to find the file for you.

NOTE The Indexing Options dialog box is accessed from the Performance Information and Tools window by clicking Adjust Visual Effects in the left pane.

By default, Windows "indexes" the most common areas of your hard drive, and when you ask for something, it knows where to look, and this includes everything in your libraries. If you frequently store data in folders that aren't included in your libraries, though, you should add them to the index. You do this by clicking Modify in the Indexing Options dialog box, browsing to the folder you want to add, as shown in Figure 6-6, and then clicking OK.

Now, you might think that if adding some folders is good, adding more is better. That's not the case with most things, and it isn't the case here. If you opt to index your entire hard drive, then every time Windows searches for something, it will search unnecessary areas, such as the folders that contain program files, system tools, and other non-data-related areas of the hard disk. The search and locate task will take longer. Indexing your entire drive also creates a very large index. A larger index means there's more stuff to look though, which, again, increases the search time. Returning to our book analogy, you can certainly appreciate that you do not need entries in the index for things you have no use for, and a longer index simply means there's more to search through to find what you want.

Access Advanced Tools to Uncover Problems

Back at the Performance Information and Tools window, click Advanced Tools. These are, indeed, fairly advanced tools. You may or may not need them, or have any need to tweak your computer using them. If you're what used to be called a "power user," though, I'd be remiss if I did not point out these tools.

The one thing to look for here is anything listed under Performance Issues. If you see "No issues reported," you're doing great. If you see anything else listed, click it to see a solution for resolving it. After all of this degunking, you probably won't see much.

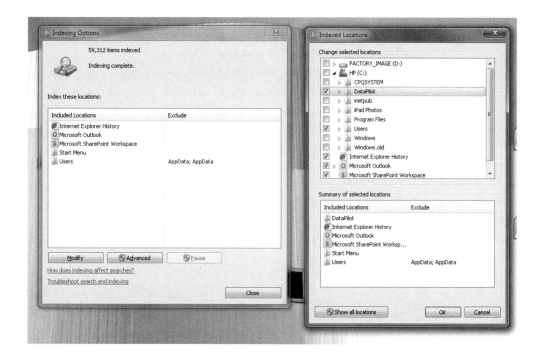

FIGURE 6-6   Add to the index folders that you access often that aren't in any library. Note you can also delete items from the index.

For now, explore the options in the Advanced Tools list by clicking them. You may want to view advanced system information, generate a system health report, or view various logs and monitors. If you find something that interests you, take a longer look. A lot of the data you'll find is pretty cryptic, though, and is used by technicians and network administrators to uncover performance problems that must be resolved by professionals. We're in "Degunking 101, 102, 201, and 202." This is graduate work. However, you may be able to use the reports and information here to further improve the performance of your computer, if you have the inkling to. Figure 6-7 shows a "critical" issue in Event Viewer's Event Log. Note that although this is listed as "critical" I've had no critical problems that I'm aware of on this PC!

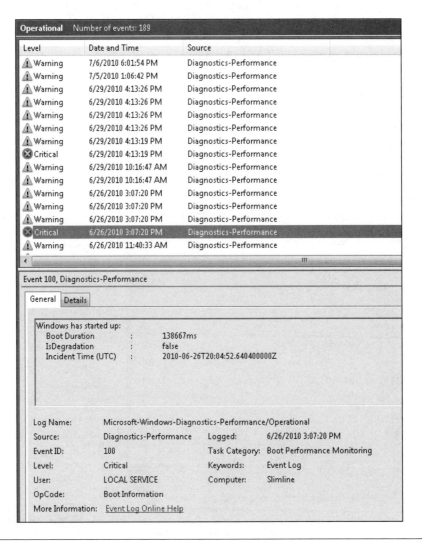

FIGURE 6-7   Event Viewer's Event Log shows problems that have recently occurred and offers cryptic messages regarding them.

Change System Settings

There's another area where you can adjust system settings. That's the System dialog box. To get there:

1. Click Start, right-click Computer, and click Properties.
2. Click Advanced System Settings.
3. On the Advanced tab of the System Properties dialog box, under Performance, click Settings.
4. In the Performance Options dialog box, click the Advanced tab.

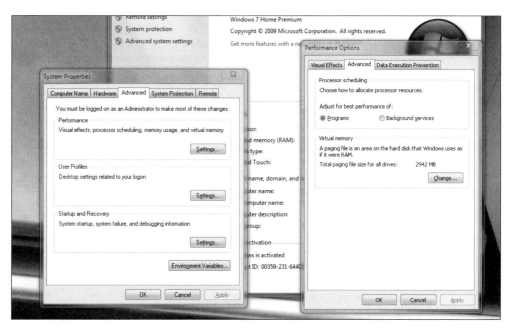

The Advanced tab of the Performance Options dialog box offers these performance tweaks:

- The Processor Scheduling setting can be configured to use a greater share of process time either for programs or for background services. By default, the computer uses a greater share of its resources on running programs, but if you'd rather have Windows 7 focus its attention on running background services, you can change the default. Generally, the default is fine.
- The Virtual Memory setting can be configured for the paging file. The computer uses a specific area of the hard disk as if it were RAM, and Windows 7 sets a default paging file size. If you need to, you can click Change and set this manually, although I think the default settings are fine.

Schedule Disk Cleanup

Some tasks run on a schedule by default, unless something happened to cause them not to. You may have opted out of getting Windows Updates when you set up Windows 7, or you could have installed your own antiadware and antimalware software, thus causing Windows Defender to be disabled. Hopefully, Disk Defragmenter runs regularly, and Windows Firewall is enabled and protecting your computer. One thing that likely should run on a schedule does not, though, and that's Disk Cleanup.

If you recall from Chapter 3, Disk Cleanup enables you to safely remove lots of unwanted files, empty the Recycle Bin, and perform other maintenance tasks quickly. I think that this is so important that you should configure it to run automatically too, and on a schedule.

To configure Disk Cleanup to run regularly and on a schedule:

1. Click Start, and in the Start Search window, type **Task Scheduler**.
2. In the results, under Programs, click Task Scheduler.
3. In the Task Scheduler window, shown in Figure 6-8, click Action | Create Basic Task. (You can also click Create Basic Task in the Actions pane on the right.)
4. For the name, type **Disk Cleanup**. If desired, type an optional description. Click Next.
5. In the next wizard pane, click Weekly, and then click Next.

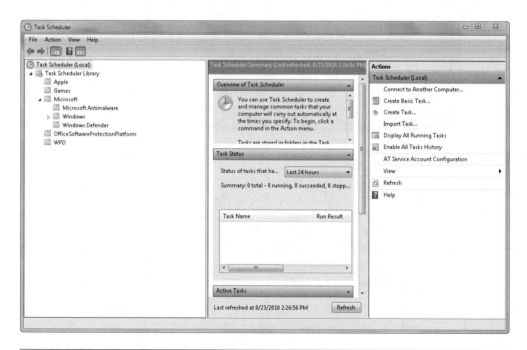

FIGURE 6-8   Disk Cleanup is a basic task.

6. Specify the schedule you want to use, and then click Next.
7. Click Start a Program, and then click Next.
8. Click Browse, type **cleanmgr.exe** in the File Name box, click Open, and then click Next.
9. Click Finish.

Clean Up the Registry

The Registry plays a very critical role in Windows. It also is a critical component that needs to be cleaned periodically to keep your computer running in top form. The Registry can easily get gunked up because Windows applications often store data in it but don't always clean up after themselves as they should. Unfortunately, the Registry is one of those Windows features that everyone is constantly warning you about, which deters most people from ever exploring it or trying to manage it. Many Windows users (and even power users) are afraid of it because they don't fully understand what it does and how it works. But in order to really degunk your PC, you really do need to, at some point, invest in a good, reliable, and trusted Registry cleaner.

Inside the Registry

Windows used to have simple configuration files (called INI files) that stored important configuration information the operating system needed to perform critical tasks, such as starting up and loading programs, keeping track of program preferences, and storing and loading system settings for the Desktop. If you have been using Windows for a while, you probably remember these pesky INI files.

When Windows NT was born, these configuration files disappeared and were replaced by the mighty Registry. The Registry is essentially a big relational database that stores information needed by Windows, such as operating system configuration data, application settings, hardware settings, networking settings, and much more. This information is stored in a hierarchical format, much like your Desktop file folder system.

As an example, let's say that you are using Microsoft Word to edit a file. During your editing session, you resize your main document window. When you quit Word, the document window size settings will be saved in the Registry so that the next time you use Word, it will open just as it was when you last left it. And you thought Windows did stuff like this by magic!

Because so much information is stored in the Registry, the Registry can easily get gunked up over time. Many of the applications you use on a regular basis will write to the Registry, and Windows itself is always storing information there. Most applications write to the Registry properly, but some don't—and the Registry is a favorite target of adware, spyware, viruses, and worms. This can leave you with a Registry that has incomplete data and extraneous data, which in turn makes your computer run more slowly.

What makes the Registry so critical and complex is that it touches just about everything that Windows does. To manage all the tasks that take place within the Registry, Windows fortunately provides built-in tools that help to keep the Registry working properly. But as with any component of Windows, gunk will seep into the Registry, and it can cause a lot of problems, such as slow performance and system crashes.

Explore the Registry with Regedit

You should at least view the Registry one time so you know what's there. You'll be fine as long as you don't make any changes. The Registry Editor (Regedit) tool is available from the Start Search window; just type **regedit**, and click it in the results. From there, and *be careful not to make any changes*:

TIP   If you're uncomfortable doing this procedure, it's okay to simply take a look at Figure 6-9.

---

1. Notice the top-level keys, also called *hives*. There are five, outlined in Table 6-1. Each hive stores all of the values that represent individual system settings.
2. Double-click any top-level hive to see its contents. Try HKEY_USERS, the fourth hive. (Table 6-1 offers additional information about the hives, or keys, listed there.)

TABLE 6-1   Top-Level Windows Registry Keys

Hive	Description
HKEY_CLASSES_ROOT	This hive stores information about all file extensions, descriptions, icons, associations, shortcuts, automation, class IDs, and more.
HKEY_CURRENT_USER	This hive serves as a link to the currently logged-in user's key stored in HKEY_USERS.
HKEY_LOCAL_MACHINE	This hive stores all software, hardware, network, security, and Windows system information. This is the area where most of the Registry keys and values are located.
HKEY_USERS	This hive stores all of the information about all users and their individual settings. The setting values include environment variables, color schemes, fonts, icons, Desktop configuration, Start menu items, network, and more. Each time a new user logs on, a new key is created based on a default key.
HKEY_CURRENT_CONFIG	This hive is actually a link that points to the currently selected hardware profile stored in HKEY_LOCAL_MACHINE.

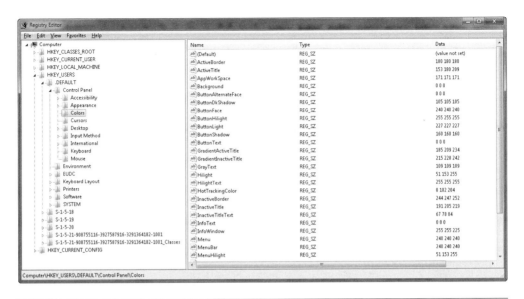

FIGURE 6-9   The Registry holds settings related to everything "computer."

3. Double-click any second-level hive to see its contents. In HKEY_USERS, try .DEFAULT.
4. Understand that each of the entries here holds your settings, including settings related to the Desktop, cursors, color schemes, and more. See Figure 6-9.
5. Close the Registry window.

TIP   If you accidentally do something to cause damage to the Registry, which in turn causes your computer to go wonky, restart the computer, and during bootup press F8. Click Last Known Good.

Know Why You Should Clean the Registry

Because the Registry is like the central control system of your computer, whenever you install, uninstall, or reinstall software, changes will be made to Registry keys. Usually the programs you install and uninstall will do a good job of setting themselves up and cleaning up after themselves; however, not all programs work with the Registry properly. Some applications simply don't remove all traces of themselves when you uninstall them. In addition, you might have programs that you simply deleted from your computer without running the proper uninstall procedures. (Now you know why you should not just delete a program by placing it in the trash. You actually need to run its associated uninstall program.) Finally, adware and spyware often leave unauthorized keys in the Registry that are not always removed with the spyware itself.

Over time, the Registry can get gunked up, and Registry gunk can cause problems such as these:

- Your computer may boot very slowly.
- Your programs may not launch properly.
- Your computer could crash unexpectedly.
- Your programs might have problems performing some operations, such as saving files to the proper directories, launching properly with the correct settings, and so on.

The more you do on your computer (if you install and remove lots of programs, for example), the more cluttered and bloated the Registry can become. In fact, if you followed the instructions in previous chapters and removed the extra programs that you don't need, it's likely that you've contributed to the clutter in the Registry. But help is on the way! However, you'll need to purchase, install, and run Registry cleaning software.

Choose Registry Cleaning Software

Cleaning the Registry manually can be an enormous task. As you saw earlier, there are hundreds of keys to work with and potentially clean up. You could seriously damage the Registry if you are not extremely careful (or if you don't know what you're doing). Instead of trying to explain how to clean the Registry manually, then, which is nearly impossible, I'll go another route. I'll suggest that you use a third-party Windows Registry cleaning tool.

There are many Registry cleaning tools to choose from, which is both good news and bad news. I'll venture to say that many of the programs available are likely to do more harm than good, too. The only thing I can suggest is that you go with a tried and true company, one that has had Registry cleaning software on the market for many years, or that you purchase the program from a reputable web site that has positive reviews of the product written by users.

Since there's no sure-fire way to pick a Registry cleaner, and because there are new cleaners added to the market regularly, I suggest you purchase one from a web site like Amazon.com, where buyers write reviews of each product. Currently on Amazon there is one that stands out: WinCleaner OneClick. For about $20, this program claims to safely clean, repair, and optimize the Registry. With a slew of four- and five-star reviews, I'm pretty confident you can trust it.

You might also try visiting your local computer store, such as Best Buy or Fry's. Talk to the people in the repair department, making sure you don't let them talk you into using their services to do something you can do yourself! Ask them what they'd use. They may even tell you that a Registry cleaner isn't necessary if your computer is fairly new. It'll ultimately be up to you. Finally, ask anyone you think may have used such software, including the network administrator where you work, your adult children, or even your children's computer science teachers.

CAUTION
Poorly written Registry cleaners can damage your computer. Worse, they can contain adware or spyware. Make sure that if you purchase one, you purchase a well-known, highly acclaimed cleaner from a reputable company. Do not let any company on the Internet run any Registry cleaner remotely, and do not buy anything online from any company you have not thoroughly researched. Again, it's really best to go to Amazon or a big-box store.

Summing Up

The main idea behind optimizing the hard drive is to get Windows 7 to boot faster, to get it to run faster, and to enhance the general performance of the computer. You can enhance the hard drive's performance by using NTFS, being aware of system errors and fixing them, detecting errors caused by unsigned device drivers or incompatible hardware, and finding physical problems with the hard drive itself. By repairing existing problems and configuring Windows 7 to run efficiently, you can improve performance dramatically.

7

Clean Up and Secure Internet Explorer 8

Degunking Checklist:

- ☑ Use Compatibility View
- ☑ Remove toolbars
- ☑ Improve performance with rarely used tweaks
- ☑ Manage add-ons and disable those you don't use
- ☑ Review privacy and security settings
- ☑ Delete cookies, temporary Internet files, AutoFill data, and more
- ☑ Explore InPrivate Browsing
- ☑ Organize Favorites
- ☑ Explore alternative browsers

Windows 7 comes with Internet Explorer included, and most Windows 7 users will use it to surf the Web. In fact, it's the most popular browser in the world. Internet Explorer 8 has lots of security features with cryptic names, including Cross-Site Scripting (XSS) Filter, SmartScreen, click-jacking prevention, and Data Execution Prevention (among others). There's no need to understand what all of these things do; they are running in the background, protecting you and your computer from all kinds of threats—from phishing, to malware, to preventing web sites from tricking you into clicking malicious links.

What's more important than defining each feature (at least those that run behind the scenes and don't require any input from you) is making sure you know how to use what's available to you to improve performance, improve security, and to degunk what you've added to Internet Explorer yourself (like Favorites, temporary files, cookies, form data, and toolbars). There are a few things you'll want to explore beyond the degunking, though, such as Compatibility View, privacy and security settings and options, and InPrivate Browsing. These help you surf the Web smarter and safer, which is certainly something to take notice of. And while I think that Internet Explorer is a fine browser, I'll help you explore other browser options. I'd like to impress upon you, though, that while a new browser may help you surf the Web faster initially (and have that fresh, new car smell), it will eventually bog down like IE has (or will). You'll end up with the same problems you have now. In comparisons and side-by-side tests, performance differences are unnoticeable to the human eye, so the browser you choose is really personal preference.

TIP Call your Internet service provider (ISP) and ask them to run a few tests to see just how fast your Internet connection really is. Tell them that performance is degrading, and you'd like to make sure that you're getting the signal and bandwidth you're paying for. Make sure you mention you'd like to see the results and review the data yourself, too.

Improve Performance

Degunking has several components, but they generally fall into one of only a few areas: you want to increase performance, be better organized, or be safer and more secure. In this chapter, we'll cover them all. You can improve IE's performance quickly by removing toolbars and managing add-ons, and you can use Compatibility View when a web site isn't working the way you think it should. You can improve security by clearing form data and using InPrivate Browsing. And you can be more organized by culling that long list of Favorites or possibly choosing another browser that is sleeker and cleaner. Let's start with performance.

TIP If Ethernet cables are crimped, Wi-Fi access points are positioned incorrectly, or the coax cable that brings the signal from the wall to your cable modem is damaged, you won't be getting all the bandwidth you deserve.

Use Compatibility View

Internet Explorer 8 is a pretty new technology, and is quite a bit different from the technology used in IE7 and earlier versions. IE8 offers new features like Web Slices, enhanced tab browsing, Accelerators, and various security features that web sites designed for earlier versions of IE might not be ready for. If there's incompatibility between a web site and IE8, you may see misaligned text boxes, misplaced text, or images that don't appear as they should. When this happens, click the Compatibility View button on the Address Bar. See Figure 7-1.

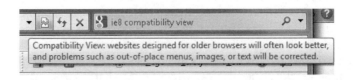

FIGURE 7-1 Use Compatibility View if a web site has display problems.

TIP   When you close and reopen any web page you've assigned Compatibility View to, it will reopen in that view automatically. Click the Compatibility View button to return to the default view.

Remove or Disable Toolbars and Add-ons

When Internet Explorer 8 was new, it was "clean." It was just IE8 and it did not contain any toolbars or add-ons that could slow it down. You're probably familiar with toolbars, at least, and you may have several: Windows Live Toolbar, Google Toolbar, Yahoo! Toolbar, and even a shopping toolbar. Each time you add something like this to IE8, it increases the "load time," and thus slows down your Internet experience. To degunk Internet Explorer, you need to see what items you have attached to IE8 and choose to disable them, uninstall them, or keep them. You may have already uninstalled some toolbars in Chapter 3 using Control Panel.

To see what toolbars and add-ons you have installed and how much these items are hurting load time, follow these steps:

1. Open Internet Explorer.
2. Click Tools | Manage Add-ons.
3. In the bottom-left corner, verify Currently Loaded Add-ons is selected. See Figure 7-2.
4. Position the titles at the top of the window so you can see the load times.

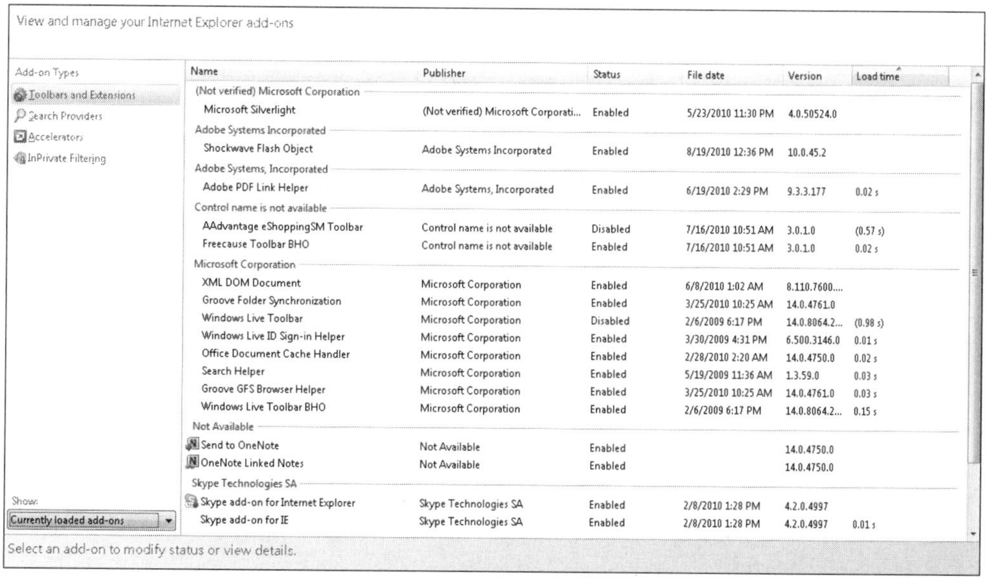

FIGURE 7-2   You'll see lots of currently loaded add-ons, but many of them won't increase load time.

FIGURE 7-3 Disable add-ons you don't use.

5. Review each add-on that's enabled. Note their load times. For each add-on, consider the following questions:
   - Should I disable this? Do I use it each day?
   - Should I research this? Do I even know what it is?
6. Select any add-on that is enabled that you do not use daily. Click Disable. See Figure 7-3.
7. Continue disabling add-ons as desired.

TIP Disabling Accelerators you no longer use will also improve performance. Click Accelerators in the left pane and disable any as needed.

8. Click Close.

GunkBuster's Notebook: Mystery Tweak from the Experts

I'm reluctant to post this tweak, but I can verify that it works even though there's no explanation for it. I'd like to credit Ed Bott for this, which is a little trick he published while running benchmark tests for ZDNet. It involves re-registering a DLL file that should have been registered when IE8 was installed, so there's no harm in trying it even if it doesn't work! With the file properly registered, IE8 may just run faster!

Here's the mystery tweak:

1. Type **cmd** in the Start Search box.
2. Right-click cmd in the search results and click Run as Administrator.
3. Type **regsvr32 actxprxy.dll.**
4. Press ENTER.
5. Restart your computer.
6. Restart IE.

NOTE   Even though load times such as .02 second don't seem like much, if you have several, before you know it you've added two to three seconds to your load time.

Improve Security

The default IE security settings help you to avoid malicious programs taking over your computer and making it run slow. Changing some of the settings on the Advanced tab can help avoid having gunk interrupt your browsing experience. While many of the security features work in the background, over which you have no control, there are some you can control to enhance security even more. For example, you can increase or decrease your privacy and security settings, manage your AutoFill data and cookies, delete your browsing history, and even surf the Web in private, without leaving traces of where you've been on the computer's hard drive. These are all good things to check and to do when you're using a computer that doesn't belong to you, or if you share a computer with someone else (and that someone else does not have their own user account).

Review Privacy and Security Settings

There are plenty of settings you can control in the Internet Options dialog box. For security, there are two tabs to explore in depth: Security and Privacy. To see the options:

1. In Internet Explorer, click Tools.
2. Click Internet Options.
3. Click the Security tab.
4. Click, if applicable, Reset All Zones to Default Level, shown in Figure 7-4.

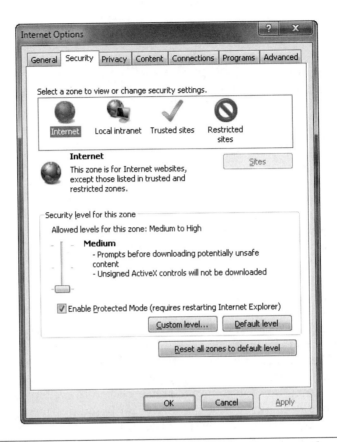

FIGURE 7-4 If you've previously tweaked Security settings, reset them.

5. Check, if applicable, Enable Protected Mode.
6. Medium-High is a good setting, and is the default. To see how these settings are configured, click Custom Level.
7. In the Security Settings – Internet Zone dialog box, review each setting, and change a setting only if you are sure you know what you're doing and why.
8. Click OK.
9. Click the Privacy tab.
10. Verify the Privacy setting is at Medium.

11. Verify the three items underneath this are checked, as shown in the illustration.

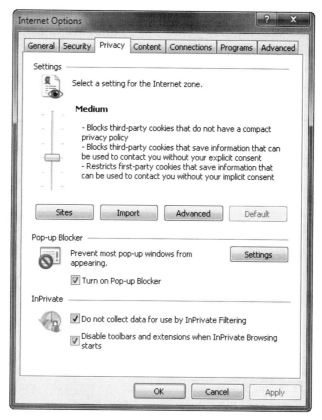

12. Click OK.

The default settings are generally the best, but you can tweak these settings. For instance, if you do not want to allow file or font downloads, which are enabled by default, you can disable them in the Security Settings – Internet Zone dialog box (step 7). You can also use that dialog box to disable the ability to drag and drop content or copy and paste data. And, if you're tired of seeing the prompt that says something to the effect "do you want to allow this web site access to your computer's clipboard," you can allow clipboard access.

You may also want to review the settings in the Internet Options window under the Advanced tab. There are some options you may want to enable or disable, including, but not limited to, the following under the Browsing, Multimedia, and Security categories:

- **Display a notification about every script error (Browsing)**   Yes, this does get annoying. If you're receiving notifications about scripts gone wrong, deselect this.
- **Notify when downloads complete (Browsing)**   You may or may not need this notification. *My feeling is, the fewer notifications and interruptions, the better.*

- **Play sounds in web pages (Multimedia)** I believe there's nothing quite as annoying as going to a web page and being bombarded with background music. Ugh. If this bothers you, disable it.
- **Empty Temporary Internet Files folder when browser is closed (Security)** If you're concerned about the temporary files you leave hanging around after a surfing session, enable this check box. All temporary files will be deleted when you close IE. This will prevent nosy people from looking through your temporary files to see just what you've been doing on the Internet in your spare time. (Or you could secure your computer with a password and log off when you're finished surfing.)
- **Warn if changing between secure and not secure mode (Security)** This is not enabled by default, but if you'd like to know, you can be notified.

Delete Cookies, Temporary Internet Files, and AutoFill Data

Cookies are small text files that web sites place on your computer so that they can recognize you and your preferences the next time you visit their web site. It's a convenience. However, cookies can also save login information, which could be a security issue for you, and they can be used by a snoopy spouse to prove you've visited a site. Deleting cookies clears this information from your computer, which means that anyone who uses your computer and accesses web pages that you've been to won't be greeted with Hello < *your name* >. While this does increase your privacy, it's an inconvenience too; you will have to tell the web site who you are (often by logging in) the next time you visit it, provided you want personalized service.

Temporary Internet files are copies of web pages, web page images, and even media that are stored on your computer so that the next time you visit a page, it can load faster. It's quicker for IE to pull the icon for Facebook off of your computer's hard drive than it is to download it each time from the web page. Again, it's a convenience for you and helps speed up your web surfing. However, temporary files can build up over time and cause minor problems, such as loading old information instead of new information. The items in the Temporary Files folder can also become corrupt over time. If you never delete temporary files and bog down the folder, other problems could occur. Beyond that, though, anyone who has access to your computer can access these files to see what you've been doing online. It's in your best interest to delete these temporary files regularly.

AutoFill data is the data that you have typed into forms. IE remembers much of this data, again, as a convenience, but, again, it's a potential security threat. History shows a list of web sites you've recently visited. As with cookies and temporary files, this can cause privacy and security problems.

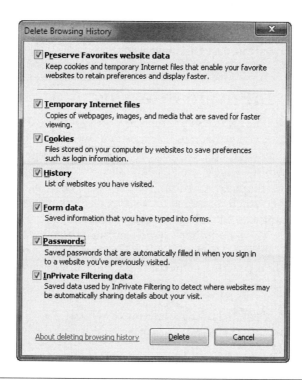

FIGURE 7-5   Delete this information often to help keep your computer secure and running smoothly.

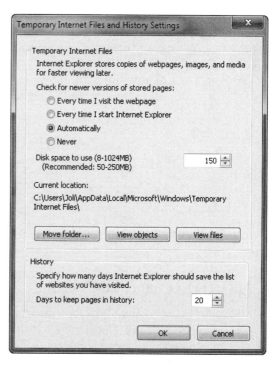

You can delete these items as well as others by clicking Safety | Delete Browsing History. Simply select the items to delete and click Delete, as shown in Figure 7-5.

You can also configure settings for temporary files, History, and the like. Click Tools | Internet Options. On the General, under Browsing History, click Settings. As shown here, you can view temporary files (click View Files), change how often IE checks for new versions of stored pages, and even specify how much disk space to use to store the information. You can experiment with the settings to see what works for you.

TIP You can override default Cookies settings in the Internet Options dialog box, under the Privacy tab. Just click Advanced.

Explore InPrivate Browsing

There may be times when you intend to visit a web site that you don't want anyone to discover later you've been to. Perhaps you intend to shop for a birthday gift online and you suspect your tech-savvy spouse will peek at your History or temporary Internet files to see where you've been. Maybe you're at an Internet café and are using a public computer, and don't want to leave any traces on it for the next user to uncover. Maybe you're planning on visiting a site that would upset others if they knew you've visited it, like a car dealership that sells only Ferraris, a church of a different denomination, or, well, perhaps some web site with a host of pretty women on it!

Whatever the case, InPrivate Browsing allows you to browse privately and discretely. When you initiate an InPrivate Browsing session, none of the following are recorded by IE:

- Browsing history (the web sites you've visited)
- Temporary Internet files
- Form data
- Cookies
- Usernames
- Passwords
- Searches
- Web page visits

To start an InPrivate Browsing session, do either of the following:

- Click Safety | InPrivate Browsing
- Open a new, blank tab and click Open an InPrivate Browsing Window

Browse with InPrivate
Browse the web without storing data about your browsing session.

Open an InPrivate Browsing window

TIP To close an InPrivate Browsing session, simply close the IE window.

Organize Favorites

It's so easy to gunk up a Favorites list! Reluctantly, mine is shown in Figure 7-6. Yes, even I have gunk. Worse though is that this isn't even the entire list. Sure, I've had a go at organizing it by creating folders, and yes, there's stuff in them. But look at all that gunk!

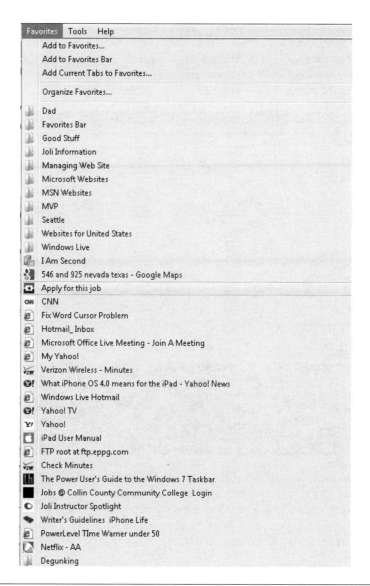

FIGURE 7-6   If your Favorites list looks like this, I can empathize.

TIP   Don't see the Favorites, Tools, and Help menus that are shown in Figure 7-6? Press ALT on the keyboard and you'll see these along with File, Edit, and View.

While you can organize these using the Favorites menu's Organize Favorites command, I prefer to use the Favorites folder. It's more familiar, you can select multiple Favorites quickly and move them, and you can even drag Favorites you no longer want to the Recycle Bin. Your Favorites folder is in your personal folder: just click Start, and then click the folder with your name on it.

To organize the folder, treat it as you would a folder that holds photos or documents. Create subfolders with titles that are representative of the content you have, and then move the data into them. Delete anything you no longer want. If you position the Favorites window so that it doesn't take up the entire screen, you can drag unwanted items to the Recycle Bin easily, as shown in the illustration.

Once you've organized the first level of gunk, drill into the second level. This requires you to open each subfolder you've created and consider organizing what's there into even more subfolders. Once you've completed this task, your Favorites list should look quite a bit better and be easier to manage. My own, shown in the illustration, certainly is improved.

Explore Alternative Browsers

There are lots of alternative browsers available, and they are (dare I say) all free. People who use alternative browsers are quite adamant about them, and insist they are faster, more secure, and just downright better than Internet Explorer. Some of this may be true. Although I've yet to see that one browser is noticeably faster than another, I can say that these alternative browsers are probably more secure than IE. I say this only because hackers (the people trying to get your personal information, track your keystrokes, and write viruses and malware) want to affect as many people as possible with their "work." Since IE is the most popular browser, they certainly plan to spend their time writing code to affect those users. This is the same phenomenon that makes Apple computers "safer" than Windows PCs. It's not that they are safer, per se, there are simply fewer hackers attacking them. Hackers would rather write code to target PC users, because there are simply more of them. The same holds true for IE.

That said, if you're really concerned about this, don't like IE, or simply want to assess your options, you can try the following web browsers, which are listed in order of popularity following IE (as I see it, anyway). Make sure you uninstall them, though, if you decide you don't want them. Each is a simple download and doesn't require much of a learning curve to use.

- **Firefox**   Created and distributed by Mozilla, which claims that Firefox is faster than IE, that Mozilla addresses security threats faster than Microsoft, and that Firefox is easier to use and more customizable. Firefox is popular for a reason: it is a great alternative to IE and does have a lot of nice features, including private browsing, password manager, antiphishing and antimalware, one-click bookmarking, tabs, and more.
- **Chrome**   Created and distributed by Google, which claims that Chrome is designed to be fast in every way, is clean and streamlined, is secure, and offers many useful features. It is sleek, I'll give it that.
- **Safari**   Created and distributed by Apple, which claims that Safari has an elegant design, does things no other browser has done before, has "blazing speed," and that security is assured. I'd be much more impressed with Safari if Apple's web site wasn't so slow to load and Safari didn't continually prompt me to install updates, but Safari is very innovative and is easy to use. Safari is shown in Figure 7-7.
- **Opera**   Created and distributed by Opera Software, which claims Opera to be "lightning fast," safe and secure, easy to use, and innovative and powerful. It does have a lot of nice features, including Widgets, Opera Unite, Content Blocking, Speed Dial, Zoom, and more. You'll have to explore.

FIGURE 7-7   Safari is quite innovative, and probably more secure than other browsers simply because fewer people use it, and thus, hackers tend to leave it alone.

Summing Up

The speed of your Internet service and the condition of your equipment often has more to do with Internet performance than your browser does. However, a browser bogged down with toolbars, add-ons, and unnecessary files and data will cause problems. You have to manage what Internet Explorer has attached to it, and disable unwanted items. You also need to manage temporary Internet files, cookies, and other data you collect over time, as well as manage Favorites. You can make IE run faster; I can certainly vouch that my Internet browsing is noticeably faster after writing this chapter!

8

Clean Up Your E-Mail

Degunking Checklist:

☑ Organize the e-mail you want to keep and get rid of the rest
☑ Create a folder hierarchy complete with parent and child folders
☑ Manage attachments
☑ Explore filtering options
☑ Learn how to avoid spam
☑ Manage the spam you get
☑ Back up e-mail data

Most households have something (usually in the kitchen) affectionately called a "junk drawer." It's the drawer where stuff gathers that doesn't fall into any of the other major stuff categories. If it's not pots, pans, silverware, or kitchen gadgets, well... throw it in the junk drawer. The junk drawer is the place originally intended to hold just a few things: scissors, a ruler, a screwdriver, and maybe a little box of rubber bands. Over the years, however, people end up tossing in wine corks with clever designs, 17 promotional beer openers gathered at home-and-garden shows, coupons, poker chips that Mom found under the refrigerator, Dad's spare sunglasses, old toothbrushes used to scrub grout, loose screws that fell out of something, and on and on and on. Eventually you have to dig hard just to find the scissors—assuming they're still in there somewhere.

Without realizing it, most people have allowed their e-mail Inboxes to become junk drawers too. As with any kind of gunk, messages accumulate for many reasons, but they do accumulate, and before you know it you have hundreds, if not thousands, of messages sitting around. The oldest are forgotten, and it doesn't take long for any single message to pass "under the fold" (that is, scroll off the bottom of the display) and quickly slip your mind, perhaps for good.

Beyond the junk you keep, though, there's spam to deal with too, as well as attachments. Spam is more than a nuisance; it's gunk! Attachments can become gunk too, because they are often stored in multiple places, causing duplicates and complicating the situation even more. Think about it: you may have an e-mail message with a large attachment in your Inbox and in your Sent Items folders, and you may have even saved the attachment itself to your hard drive. You need to take control!

Finally, and I can't stress it enough, you need a plan for regularly backing up your e-mail data. What would happen, right now, if your computer crashed, was stolen, or floated out into the hallway in a hot water heater breakdown? What if it melted in a fire? Are you prepared? How recent is your last backup? Have you *ever* backed up your e-mail?

Manage Your Inbox

Your Inbox is the proverbial junk drawer. It's where stuff collects, and it needs to be managed. The best way to manage your Inbox is to eliminate the gunk you have now, and then create a plan to prevent it from piling up again. This requires that you think hard about each message you currently have in your Inbox and decide what to do with it, and after that, think about each message as it comes in and do something with it immediately, whenever possible.

In general, any e-mail message falls into one of three categories:

- Mail with lasting value, which should be retained indefinitely
- Mail associated with a current project or otherwise limited by a calendar date that needs to be held for a period of time and then either archived or deleted
- Mail that can be dealt with right now and then deleted immediately

These three categories of mail require action that you could characterize as "keep," "hold," or "pitch." Each time you look at a message entering your Inbox, you should keep these three words in mind. In case you need a little more guidance, the next section will help you along.

Keep, Hold, or Pitch?

Deciding which messages to keep and which to pitch is really a matter of psychology rather than technology. You have to make those decisions sometime, and although technology can make some of those decisions easier, it can't make all of them for you. It's very easy to convince yourself that almost any message needs to be saved forever. Who knows whether it'll become useful in the future? Well, nobody—and that's what judgment is all about.

If you're really nervous about nuking messages, you can always consider the extra work of archiving them onto a CD or DVD so that they're not irretrievably lost. But actually, that's kind of difficult. Almost certainly better is to develop the discipline of just letting them go. Time is precious these days—almost no one goes back and reads old e-mail "just for fun." Unless it has an objectively identifiable value for the future—financial or legal records, family history discussions, unique technical advice, or content that you can refer back to and use, things like that—steel yourself to just let it go.

Here are some pointers to keep in mind when the fate of an e-mail message hangs in the balance:

- *Is it relevant to legal or tax matters?* Most tax records need to be kept for seven years. E-mail invoices for business expenses, correspondence with your accountant, or anything you would need to either file a tax return or defend yourself in an audit should be retained for at least those seven years. Keep these things in a folder called Taxes.
- *Does it really contain factual information?* Even if a message seems to be in a "keep" category, look closely. Does the message really contain factual information? Or does it simply say, "Got it! Looks good! Thanks!"

TIP   If you can't tell what a message is by looking at the Subject line, but after opening it and reading you see it is important and should be kept and filed, forward the message to yourself, and change the Subject line to something more recognizable before clicking Send. Delete the old message and keep the new one—in a folder or subfolder, of course, not in your Inbox.

- *Does the message stand alone?* Ask yourself whether the message can be understood by itself or must be read with other messages in a "thread" to be understood. Some e-mail clients can link separate messages into a thread, but many cannot, and you must fish out related messages by hand. If you have not retained earlier messages in the thread, an orphaned member of that thread may become cryptic, ambiguous, or simply useless. Dump the orphan, even if you regret having dumped the rest of the thread. Wishing won't bring it back.
- *Does it duplicate information you already have elsewhere?* If you subscribe to several related e-mail lists, sometimes members will "cross-post" a message to all of those several lists, and you may end up with three or four separate copies of the very same message. This is a particular problem when you create filters to autosort messages from e-mail lists into a separate folder, where duplicates can be easily forgotten. Sometimes e-mail messages were sent to you solely to convey a single web link. You may already have that link recorded in your web browser bookmarks. If so, you can dump the message without regret. Also, messages are sometimes sent with attachments, and the messages themselves say little more than, "Here it is! Have fun!" If you've saved the attachment file to an appropriate place, such messages become just more gunk.
- *Could you pitch the message after an appropriate, simple action?* If a correspondent sends you contact information, see if you've already copied it to your address book. If so, the message is unnecessary. If not, copy the information to your address book and delete the message.
- *Has time and history rendered the message useless or misleading?* Messages, like bad wine, can spoil. New information can render old information obsolete. Old information can be found to be false. A message may say, "Your PR contact at SurlySoft is Helena Handbasket, at 000-000-0000." If you've learned that Helena has moved on to another firm, delete the message. If a message makes your antennas twitch as no longer being true, do a quick check and dump it. If someone has sent you a draft of a document and then later sends you the final copy, the draft may contain errors or omissions that could trip you up if you mistake the draft for the final item. Nuke it, too!

NOTE Every time you send a message to someone, a copy of it is saved in your Sent Items folder—and if you don't delete or move messages out of Sent Items, they remain there forever. (At least, that's the default setting. You could have changed that.) People who have used e-mail for a number of years are often surprised to find that thousands of messages have accumulated in their Sent Items folder. Manage your Sent Items folder by deleting the items in it often (or at least the older items).

Create Folders and Subfolders and Move E-Mail

The single biggest secret to keeping your mailbase (a word I use to describe all e-mail data, including contacts, calendar events, Inbox, Sent Items, and other folders) manageable is to create a suitable hierarchy for folders in which to store your messages. Most e-mail clients come to you with just a few folders: Inbox, Outbox, Deleted Items, and Drafts. You may have others named Unread Mail or Search Folders, but these won't help you organize things. These folders are the ones through which your daily mail passes. They are not for storing mail over the long haul. For those "keep" and "hold" messages, you need to create folders.

Nearly all e-mail clients allow you to create folders and incorporate them with the folders already created. Most clients allow a folder hierarchy as well—that is, folders that contain subfolders—and this makes organizing a very large mailbase pretty easy. It's not uncommon to find medical, legal, or technology professionals with tens of thousands of messages in their mailbases, and for people like that, a good many folders may be required to make sense of it all and allow individual messages to be found quickly when needed.

The key to creating a folder hierarchy is to not have so many folders in the left margin that you forget you have them. The way to do that is to limit your folders to a single screen's worth. The rule of thumb is this: if you have to scroll a list of folders up and down, you have too many. If you feel you absolutely need more folders than will fit in a single screen, nest related folders together under a parent folder.

Deciding what folders to create (like deciding when to nuke a message) is more psychology than technology. Think hard about how you use e-mail, not so much in terms of whom you exchange messages with but rather what the messages are about. When at some point in the future you want to refer back to a message, you may recall who sent it, but primarily what you'll be looking for is the message's topic. Folders should thus be about topics and not people. Here are some examples of mail for which you could create folders:

- Mail relating to your job
- Mail relating to your church or civic groups (such as Lions, Chamber of Commerce, neighborhood association, PTA)
- Mail relating to your hobbies and interests (such as programming, model railroading, kite flying, ham radio)
- Mail relating to projects or research you're undertaking (such as research on a medical condition or for an article you're writing)

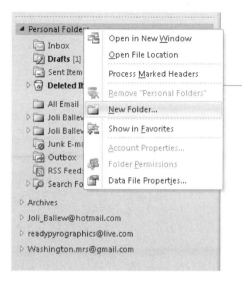

FIGURE 8-1   Often you can right-click and choose New Folder to create an organizational folder in an e-mail client.

Generally, you can create a folder by right-clicking the parent folder in the left navigation pane of an e-mail client. Figure 8-1 shows how it's done in Microsoft Office Outlook 2010. Once folders are created, you simply drag e-mail you'd like to keep into them.

Figure 8-2 shows two parent folders: Joli Ballew – Personal and Joli Ballew – Projects. Each of these folders contains subfolders to hold data I need to keep. You could create a similar hierarchy. When creating your structure, limit yourself to two folders deep. If you go three deep or more, eventually you will forget about one or more of those deeply buried folders. Watch that little plus sign or triangle in front of a folder name. If you see either of these symbols, that means a child folder lies beneath the surface and should be visited now and then!

You should also create folders for short-term projects, with the intention of deleting the folder and its contents when the project is complete and signed off on. For instance, if you're doing a kitchen remodel, you'll have e-mail from suppliers and from the contractors, among others. After the project is done, though, the mail in the folder is no longer especially useful, and it certainly won't be referred to on a daily basis, as it was during the project's execution. You can likely, after a few months, delete this folder completely.

TIP   If any e-mail contains warranty, insurance, or estimate information, print it and file it in a physical file for safe keeping.

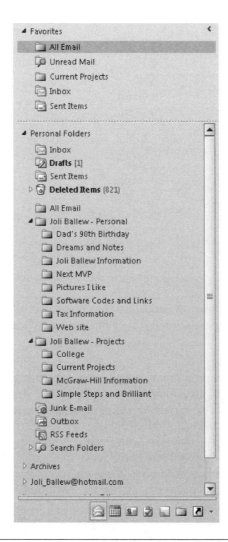

FIGURE 8-2 Consider the folder structure you need, and then create it.

Manage Attachments

E-mail attachments are separate files that "ride along" on an e-mail message. Attachments can be any sort of file, but often they are files that contain content other than text, like images, videos, or sound files. This means that they are often very large—sometimes megabytes in size—and if you accumulate enough of them, they can become a huge source of e-mail gunk.

An associate of mine tells the story of a clueless employee at his firm who was sent a humorous video and decided to send it to every single person in the company.

The video was 6MB in size, and when multiplied by the hundred-odd people in the company, and incorporating how many times they sent it to others, well, it completely filled the company's already-strapped mail server. (This was some years ago, before 100GB hard drives were commonplace.) And of course, not many people deleted that from their Inbox after viewing it, creating even more gunk.

Getting back to my point: how you want to handle the attachments you get depends on what you receive, what you really think you want to keep, and where you keep it. Remember the Keep, Hold, and Pitch rules. Additionally, here are some guidelines for dealing specifically with attachments:

- *Assess each attachment before saving it to your hard drive.* Can you find it again on YouTube should you want to view it again? Is it on your company's internal servers? Do you really need to save it to your hard drive, move it to a folder, or send it to others?
- *Do not use your mailbase as a storehouse for attached files.* When a message arrives with an attachment, immediately save the attachment to a separate location on your hard drive if it is to be retained. Otherwise, delete it. This is an especially important point to remember if your mail server has a retention policy that deletes attachments after a certain amount of time.
- *Do not open an attachment unless you know what it is.* If a message arrives with an attachment and you are not absolutely sure of what it is or who it came from, don't open it to see what it is! This is how viruses propagate. Be particularly wary of files with the extensions .exe, .com, .scr, and .pif. Remember that under Windows, opening an executable file runs it! This is idiotic, but it's a fact of life. "Opening" should mean "looking at" rather than "running," but we must deal with Windows as it is.
- *Protect your computer.* Keep an antivirus utility running and up to date. Many antivirus products include a context menu item that allows the scan of a single highlighted file. If your antivirus product includes this option, you can right-click an attachment file, select Scan for Viruses (or something close to that; see your antivirus product documentation), and your antivirus utility will scan the highlighted file. This is quick insurance. Get in the habit and you'll be at much less risk from viruses and worms! (Of course, you can also configure your antivirus software to automatically scan all files, which is even better!)
- *Enable the full display of file extensions in Windows Explorer.* Most Windows installations default to hiding the file extension, which is a very bad idea. Why? A Windows filename can legally have more than one period character in it. A virus can send a copy of itself with the name ParisHilton.jpg.exe. If your Windows installation is hiding file extensions, the filename of the virus will appear as ParisHilton.jpg. Double-click it in an attempt to view the "picture" and the virus has you by the hindquarters. To disable hiding of file extensions, click Tools | Folder Options in Windows Explorer. Click the View tab and uncheck the item marked Hide Extensions for Known File Types. Then click OK. See Figure 8-3.

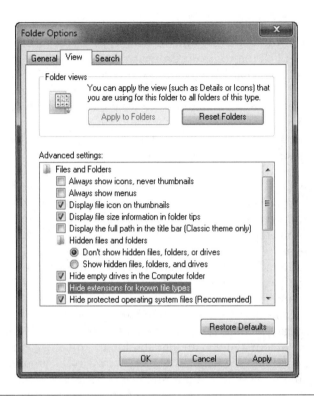

FIGURE 8-3   Opt to view filename extensions.

- *Watch out for attachments in your Sent Items folder!* If you send messages with attachments to other people, most e-mail clients will save a copy of that message and the attachments in your Sent Items folder. If those attachments are large (say, a video, song, or multiple images), you may have hundreds of megabytes of gunk cluttering up your mailbase in your Sent Items folder. This is almost certainly needless duplicate storage because you had to have a copy of each attachment file stored elsewhere to attach it to a message to begin with. The solution? Sort your Sent Items folder by message size and nuke every message containing an attachment. (Do the same in your Deleted Items folder, while you're at it.)

To explore the attachments you already have saved, see if your e-mail client has a column (most do) for an attachment icon (this is typically a paper clip). If so, make sure that column is displayed. You can also sort messages in a folder by size: the larger messages will almost certainly be carrying attachments. See Figure 8-4.

Explore Filtering Options

Most e-mail clients have built-in general-purpose filtering machinery. With a little cleverness, you can create a filter to move incoming mail out of your Inbox

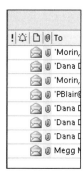

FIGURE 8-4   You can almost always sort mail by attachments to see what you can delete.

automatically, assuming you have someplace else to put it. Most people think of e-mail filters in connection with spam, but filters have other uses.

For example, many people belong to e-mail *lists*, perhaps to get an e-mail about late-breaking news, health alerts, or the latest updates on a new technology. E-mail lists can also be devoted to hobbies; for instance, people who fly radio-controlled model airplanes or climb tall mountains may belong to an e-mail list dedicated to it. Many of these lists have a lot of members who generate a great deal of e-mail, and these messages can gunk up your Inbox very quickly. A filter can be created to look for some characteristic element in e-mail coming from that list and automatically move messages that satisfy the filter to a folder created specifically for that list traffic.

Start by looking for a tag. Many mailing lists add a tag to the beginning of the Subject line of messages sent out. For example, the tag [RC-Airmodels] might be added to the beginning of the Subject line of mail sent from a radio-controlled model airplane e-mail community. You can set up a filter to look for "[RC-Airmodels]" and move all messages bearing that tag to a folder you create for them.

This may sound useful, but it's a two-edged sword. Out of sight, out of mind, it's true—but "out of sight, forever in your mailbase" can be just as true. If you don't diligently classify and cull mail as it comes in, you run the risk of having huge quantities of mail piling up in a folder somewhere. Some of that may be worth keeping, but a lot may be irrelevant chatter, and if you use autosorting to put off the necessary decision making until later, you may be faced with having to read and judge hundreds of messages in one sitting. This, of course, would make anyone cross-eyed, and after a while it may drive you to simply nuke everything in a fury of frustration.

There's always another side to it, though, isn't there? Filtering is available for a reason, and it works if you use it as it is intended. If you really do want to read the mail that comes from a source you can create a filter for, by all means, do it. Not only will it keep your Inbox clean, but it will limit how often you're interrupted while you're trying to work. Just make sure you set aside time each weekend to clean it out, and you should be okay.

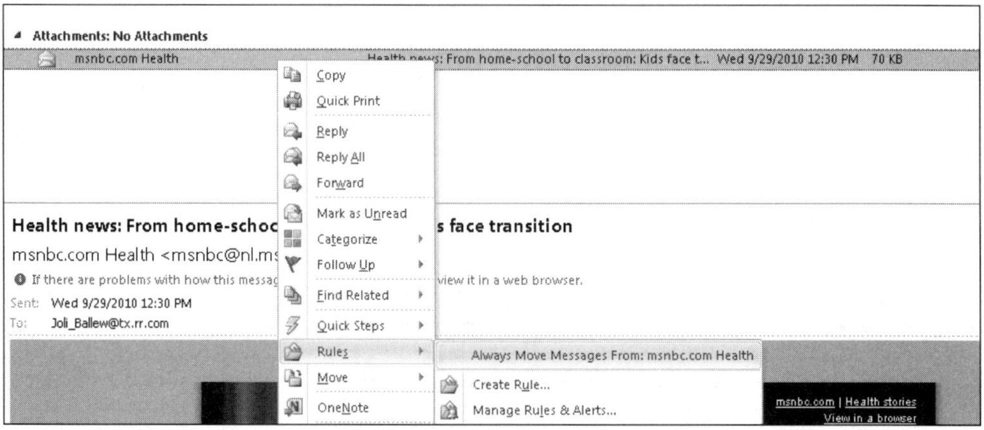

FIGURE 8-5   Right-click a message to see if options for creating rules exist.

For the most part, configuring e-mail to sort itself out automatically requires creating rules. In Microsoft Outlook 2010, you can right-click the message to access the option to create a rule. You can start from scratch, or use the option shown in Figure 8-5: Always Move Messages From. When you click this, you have the option to tell Outlook to move all messages from the sender (in this case, MSNBC Health) to a folder that you name (such as Health News). You'll have to explore your specific program to see if rules are available and how to use them.

GunkBuster's Notebook: Spring Cleaning

If you send and receive any significant quantity of e-mail—and especially if you have a complicated folder hierarchy to store it in—you should budget one day a year for "spring cleaning" to make sure gunk isn't quietly accumulating in the far corners of your e-mail machinery. As with all e-mail management, it's less technology than psychology. The hardest part is simply deciding to do it and then following through. Here's a simple checklist for your annual e-mail spring cleaning:

1. Schedule a couple of hours for it. Egad...! Who's got extra hours to spare? Well, if you let your mailbase get away from you and gunk up, you will spend a lot more time than that over the coming year straightening things out and looking for lost messages in the morass.

2. Get an estimate for the number of messages in your mailbase. No e-mail client that I know of will give you a single figure totaling your stored messages, but you can take a pocket calculator, go down your list of folders, and add them up. Prepare to be surprised! (And if you're a good record keeper, try to keep a record of the size of your mailbase over time. If it's significantly bigger each time you check, you've got some serious degunking to do!)

3. Begin with your Sent Items folder. It keeps a copy of every single message you send, and few of those are worth keeping. Keep nothing in Sent Items that's more than 90 days old. Older messages should be either deleted or (if they're important enough to keep) moved to a folder where related messages (say, for tax matters, discussions on genealogy, and so on) are kept. Repeat with Deleted Items.

4. Go through your Inbox and either delete or classify anything beyond your 25 most recent arrivals. Pay particular attention to that murky area "beyond the space beyond the fold," where messages have been lying fallow for a month or more. Force yourself to deal with anything unpleasant or difficult that's been awaiting action. If you're convinced you can't bring it down under, oh, 30–40 messages, you're fooling yourself. See if you need to add a folder or two for new interests or topics that have generated e-mail that doesn't quite fit anywhere else.

5. This is the hard part. Pour yourself a cup of strong coffee, start at the top of your folder list, and see what you no longer need to keep in each folder. No longer interested in radio-controlled models, sold your plane, and haven't flown it since last April? First, unsubscribe from the mailing list. Then, archive or delete the whole folder. Sometimes a message that looked like a keeper last year doesn't look quite as essential this year. Let it go. Sometimes messages that you thought were forever are really time limited. Be ruthless. It's the only way to stay ahead of your mailbase. Depending on what you've got going on there, you may have to set aside another couple of hours.

6. This is pure psychology, but it works: When you're done, count up the messages in your mailbase to see how many you've eliminated. Keep a record somewhere (a short text file in your mailbase folder will do) indicating how large your mailbase is this time. It helps make it all seem worthwhile to know that you're actually staying ahead of things. You don't necessarily have to *shrink* your mailbase (unless it had gotten out of control to begin with), but you sure don't want it to grow like a fungus!

Reduce Spam

E-mail is the glue that holds your personal and business computing efforts together. But, as you well know by now, careless use of e-mail will attract gunk. Unfortunately, only a little carelessness will attract an almost *unimaginable* amount of gunk, in the form of spam. Spam is one of those phenomena for which prevention is the very best cure. Here, I'll show you how to avoid gunk on your PC by preventing spam from entering your Inbox in the first place, and then we'll focus on managing what you get.

You probably are aware that spam is unwanted commercial e-mail, unless you've been living in a refrigerator box for the past decade (or two). It is generally sent from companies that you have never had dealings with and want no part of. Much or even most spam is fraudulent—get-rich quick schemes, Nigerian scams, phony (ahem) enlargement pills, controlled drugs without a prescription, and so on. Most people agree that when they want to buy online, *they* will go looking for products. They do *not* want products to come looking for them in the form of spam.

Know How Spam Works

Nearly all spam these days is formatted as HTML, which allows the embedding of images in text. A spam beacon consists of an image embedded in an HTML e-mail message. This image (which can be part of the message's art or advertising pitch, or even a single white pixel lurking in a corner of the message as a tiny "invisible" image) has a name that is uniquely coded to your e-mail address. The image's name doesn't have to *contain* your e-mail address, but it may contain a long string of numbers or characters that is linked, in the spammer's database, to your e-mail address.

When you open or preview a spam message, any images in the message's HTML are requested and downloaded from the spammer's image server. The server's log records which images are downloaded, and then the spammer's database program builds a list of e-mail addresses from which the beacon image was downloaded. *Shazam!* The spammer knows that the message arrived at your Inbox intact and was opened for display. Thus, it's found a viable e-mail address for future spam.

The key to avoiding spam beacons is to avoid downloading images embedded in HTML-formatted messages. One way to do this is never to open a spam message. Some messages, however, are carefully crafted so that you can't easily tell whether it's spam or not. Besides, clicking a message once "opens" it, making it difficult to get around anyway. Deceptive message subject headers like "In response to your recent message" may prompt you to open yet another stupid pitch for enlargement pills as well. Whatever the case, even if you can smell spam a mile away, you will ultimately click and open spam. This will get your e-mail address on yet another list of "preferred" addresses.

To avoid this deception and disable this spammer "loop hole," disable the automatic downloading of images and configure other, similar, options. Outlook 2003 and greater allow you to do this. Outlook Express and earlier versions of Outlook do not. If you don't use Outlook, look around for something like what's shown in Figure 8-6 in your own e-mail client; you want the option to disable automatic downloading of images in an e-mail, among other things. These settings are here to protect your e-mail address from those nasty spam beacons.

NOTE To access what you see in Figure 8-6 in Outlook 2010, click the File tab | Options | Trust Center | Trust Center Settings.

You can also get suckered in to spam (or worse) if you click a link in an e-mail. While the e-mail may look legitimate and contain the official logo from your bank or mortgage company, it very likely is not. It's probably a phishing e-mail and will take you to a web site that will ask you to verify some personal data (like your bank account number or social security number). It's important to note here that no legitimate company would ask you to do this, first and foremost. Thus, it's a good idea to verify that a link is going where it says it's going before you click it. You do this by hovering the mouse over the link first. Once you do that, you can see the underlying URL for the link before you click it. If it's supposed to take you to www.chase.com, but the link that appears when you hover the mouse over it says www.1234reloadchasegotcha.com, you're being scammed.

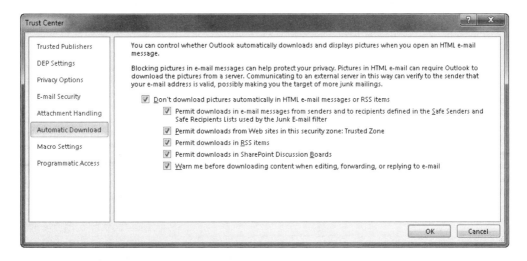

FIGURE 8-6   Outlook 2010 has these settings for reducing spam; your e-mail client may have similar options.

Use Multiple E-Mail Addresses

Spam prevention also involves your e-mail address. Smart and serious e-mail users have more than one address to minimize their encounters with spam. There are three general categories of e-mail address that you should set up:

- **Primary e-mail address**   The e-mail address on your business card. You give it to your friends and business associates. It's the address that you want the world to use. It's also the one where you'll be fighting most of your spam battles. Your primary e-mail address should be accessible from anywhere; from a computer at your house, from your smart phone, and from any computer that's connected to the Internet.
- **Backup e-mail address**   A second e-mail account obtained from a separate e-mail hosting company that is not tied to your primary address. Just in case you need it. This e-mail address will be invaluable should your small hosting company's servers go down, go out of business unexpectedly, or get hacked into (none of which is very likely, but possible). It can also be used to create a separate online identity for Facebook, Amazon, Flickr, and other web sites that require a unique e-mail address to create a profile. (You can't use your e-mail address to create two separate profiles on Facebook for instance, and you may need to. You may want to create one profile to communicate your goings-on with your friends, and another for your mother and father, or children!)
- **Disposable e-mail addresses**   Those that you use knowing that you can cancel them at any point and lose nothing. Use these for online commerce and registering at web sites.

Nearly all e-mail clients of any consequence can support multiple e-mail accounts, with one e-mail address per account. Here are the steps to follow in your e-mail client:

1. Set up a separate account for each address you use.
2. Click the check mail button, and the client will check for e-mail in every account configured and deposit all the mail from any of the several accounts in your Inbox.
3. Create a filter that will deposit all the mail sent to a disposable address (say, one devoted to use with a single e-commerce retailer) into a specific mail folder. Creating filters can be an advanced topic, and it's always very specific to a particular mail client. Whatever mail client you use, read your documentation and give it a try. Filtering can be very useful, even though it takes some practice to get it right.

So far I've been discussing e-mail addresses you use in a computer-based e-mail program, such as Microsoft Office Outlook 2010. It's what I prefer. I want complete control over my e-mail. However, you don't have to go this route. You can use a web-based e-mail server, and keep all of your mail, data, contacts, and calendar information online.

Third party web-based e-mail clients include Gmail from Google and Live Mail from Microsoft. There's also Yahoo!, AOL, and others. There are disadvantages to this choice, of course, one being lack of control over your own data. The advantages include being able to get your mail from anywhere and from virtually any Internet-enabled device and having the power of built-in spam filtering, powered by the millions of other users who mark spam as, well, spam. This reporting enhances spam filtering, and is quite effective. If you need easy access to e-mail from anywhere, want to access e-mail on a smart phone, and don't care about having complete control over your own data, this option might be for you.

Protect Your Primary E-Mail Account

If you're not careful about what you do with your primary e-mail address, nothing else matters. Once spammers lay their hands on your primary e-mail address, they will send you spam forever. Verifying to spammers that your e-mail address is "live" and working (as explained in the previous section) definitely makes things worse, but as best we in the industry can tell, addresses never "time out," and experiments have shown that spam will be sent for years to an address picked up by spammers only once.

The following sections explain what *not* to do with your e-mail address, and why. None of this is any guarantee against ever getting spam in your Inbox. Use an address long enough and spam happens. In general, you can't tell how a spammer gets your address, so trying to figure it out after it happens is pointless.

Never "Unsubscribe" from a Spammer Mailing List

Ever find it funny that a spam message (and here I'm talking about those that make no sense, only contain gibberish, or those that want to sell you enlargement drugs) rarely gives any crisp information concerning who and where the spammer is, but almost always includes a link to "unsubscribe"? That's because unsubscribing from a spammer's mailing list is almost *always* a hoax and a lie. The whole purpose of that unsubscribe link is to verify that your e-mail address is "live" and functional and that whoever it belongs to pays enough attention to their e-mail to attempt to get off of a spammer's list. That tags you not only as a live address but as a good prospect, one that the spammer can sell to other spammers for a good deal of money.

This is not the case with legitimate companies, though. Legitimate companies like Amazon, Apple, Microsoft, and the like actually do offer true-to-life unsubscribe options that work. They don't want to spam you if it's going to upset you enough that you'd no longer want to purchase products from them. In these cases, I think it's okay to click Unsubscribe if you're familiar with the e-mails and the company. See Figure 8-7.

However, and put this mental note in long-term memory: be extremely vigilant to avoid phishing e-mails that spoof real sites like Amazon, PayPal, Chase, and so on. In fact, my editor says it's probably best *never* to click on links from unsolicited e-mails, just because you can never be totally sure where you'll be taken. Greg (my tech editor) says that you can always log on to the company's web site directly to change any subscribe options.

Never Post (or Let Others Post) Your E-Mail Address on the Web

Getting new addresses to spam is one of a spammer's highest priorities, and they go to great technological lengths to snag them. In the late 1990s, spammers took a hint from web search engines and created "web crawlers," or "spiders," that simply pulled down web page after web page, 24/7, and searched for that telltale @ symbol. If your e-mail address (which contains one of those @ symbols) happened to be in one of those web pages, you were hosed, er, spammed.

The lesson is plain: do *not* post your e-mail address in "naked" form on your web page. The spam spiders are still out there, crawling day and night, even if they're called something else now. Furthermore, make it clear to your friends and other contacts that they cannot post your e-mail address on the web. This is a problem for

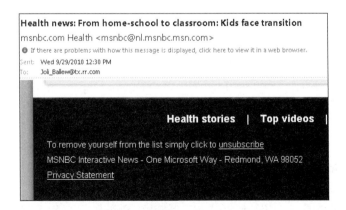

FIGURE 8-7 Many e-mails do offer a legitimate unsubscribe option, as does this MSNBC Health newsletter.

people who are publicly known for some reason and people who serve on nonprofit boards and other things for which web contacts are useful. And in this day and age of getting rewards for "referring" a contact by offering their e-mail address, it's best to make your preferences known.

Obfuscate Your E-Mail Address on Newsgroups and Discussion Boards

Just as there are spam spiders that crawl the Web searching for e-mail addresses to spam, there are spiders that download and scan newsgroups and web discussion board postings for e-mail addresses. Postings to newsgroups and discussion boards often require the entry of an e-mail address of some kind. Some people who post anonymously simply make up a phony address, but if you want people to be able to reach you apart from the newsgroup or discussion board, obfuscating an address is necessary.

The idea is to create an address that is "broken" in a way that a spider cannot fix but that any reasonably intelligent human being can. For example, here are a couple of obfuscated forms of Andy Stanton's (this is a guy we just made up!) e-mail address, rugster@stantonservices.com:

- rugster@stantonNOSPAMservices.com
- rugster@stantonPULLTHISservices.com

As given, these addresses will bounce, unless you delete the "NOSPAM" or "PULLTHIS" text.

This system worked well for many years, but spammers (to whom such mechanisms are a terrible affront) have created ever more sophisticated spiders. These days, spiders are regularly searching for blocks of uppercase letters within an address that is otherwise completely in lowercase and stripping out anything in uppercase.

The current solution (current for how long, I'm not sure) is to mix cases in an obfuscation, like this:

rugster@stantonPuLLThISservices.com

It takes a little more thought to remove the obfuscation, but most people (especially those used to the conventions of newsgroups and discussion boards) will catch on quickly.

By the way, it's now unwise to use the word "spam" in an obfuscation, whether in upper- or lowercase. Some people have tried spelling it backward, but "MAPS" has other meanings and can be confusing to newcomers.

Take Matters into Your Own Hands

Just about any e-mail program will give you some options to manage spam on your own. Microsoft Outlook 2010, for instance, enables you to apply a Junk E-mail filter, block senders, and create your own rules. Windows Live Mail enables you to easily

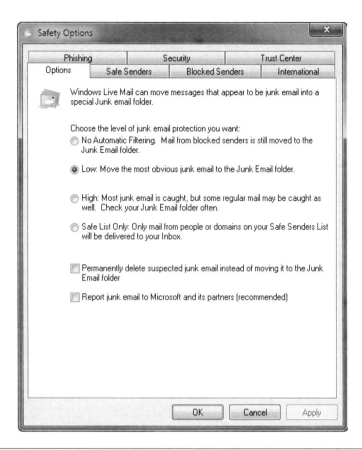

FIGURE 8-8   Junk e-mail filters are available in almost any e-mail client.

configure Junk E-mail options, shown in Figure 8-8. Here you can see the Junk E-mail options as well as the items currently in the Junk E-mail folder.

TIP   If you set the Junk E-mail filter to High, check the Junk E-mail folder often for mail that has been improperly classified as junk.

In addition to junk e-mail filters you can configure, by default, safeguards are often in place to protect you from potential harmful attachments and to block images in e-mails. If you decide the e-mail is legitimate and want to view the images, you have that option, shown in Figure 8-9.

FIGURE 8-9   In most e-mail clients, images and potentially harmful data are blocked by default, and you can easily block a sender.

You may be able to create rules that toss any e-mail with specific words in it straight into the Deleted Items folder. This enables you to create rules for words like Viagra, V!Agra, vIAGrah, and the like, to minimize that type of e-mail.

When creating a rule, note that the word may come in the body of an e-mail as a picture, in which case your e-mail client won't be able to read it. In this case, there's no reason to create a rule to search the body of the e-mail. However, words in a Subject line can't be covered up in that manner. When creating your own rules, then, try to opt for a word you'll see in the Subject line, and create the rule accordingly.

NOTE The next section, about avoiding other people's spam filters, may give you more ideas for creating rules of your own.

You'll want to spend some time now and explore the options for your particular e-mail client. Explore the menus (if you don't see any menus, try pressing the ALT key on the keyboard). Check out menus named Safety, Options, and similar titles. Safety options for Windows Live Mail are shown in Figure 8-10. Here, the Security tab is selected.

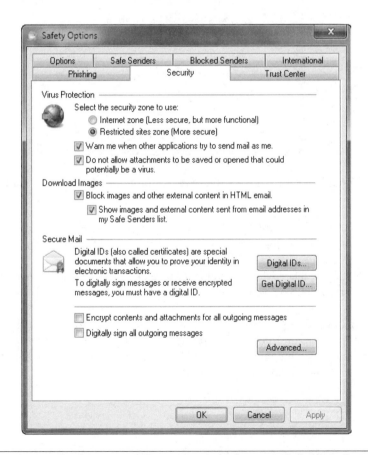

FIGURE 8-10 Locate the settings for your particular e-mail client and configure them to protect you from spam as best as the client can manage.

Avoid Triggering Other People's Spam Filters

While keeping spam out of your own Inbox is probably much on your mind these days, keeping the messages that you send out of *other* people's spam filters is something you should also be thinking about. Here are a few tips to help you keep your mail from "looking like" spam:

- *Avoid putting certain words in the subject header.* These include "free," "insurance," "mortgage," "enlargement," "refinance," and the names of many popular drugs, including Viagra, Xanax, Vicodin, Ambien, Hydrocodone, Lortabs, Valium, Levitra, and so on. Watch the spam that comes into your own Inbox and avoid the distinctive words used in their subject headers. If you work in a field that uses certain spam-favored terms like "mortgage," "refinance," or "meds," try to keep them out of your Subject line if possible.

- *Avoid using certain words in the body of your message.* Phrases like "limited time," "great deals," and so on will trigger a lot of spam filters, as will any verbiage that comes from the gutter or can be mistaken for gutter talk by a spam filter.

- *Avoid including images in your e-mail.* Many people have become so desperate to filter spam (much of which uses images) that they filter on the HTML < IMG > tag and consign any message containing an < IMG > tag to the trash folder. If you have a need to send an image to someone and you know they have a tight filter in place, it might make more sense to direct them to your Facebook account (if you have one), to Flickr, or to My Space. You could also tell them in a separate e-mail that you're sending an image so that they can watch their spam folder.

- *Send your e-mail as plain text rather than HTML.* Spam is most often sent as text formatted with HTML because many spammer tricks depend on HTML tags and comments. If you send plain text rather than HTML, many filters will be more inclined to consider your note as legitimate.

- *Make sure your PC's system clock is correct.* This is an odd one, but for reasons unclear (and spammers *always* have reasons!), much spam is sent with incorrect dates and times in the "time sent" field. I have heard reports of spam being sent that allegedly is two or three years old—and more than a few that are from several years in the future! (It is as easy to forge dates in the Sent field as it is to forge anything else in e-mail headers.) Major e-mail systems have begun to tag such misdated mail as spam. So if your PC thinks it's running in the year 2000, your e-mail will be sent with a 2000 date on it—and other people's mail servers may call it spam.

Know How to Back Up E-Mail Data

You'll be a better degunker if you're comfortable with your backups. You'll know that you can restore from backups if you delete anything you decide you want to keep later. There are many options for backing up your data, including using a built-in backup utility, purchasing a third-party utility, backing up data to an Internet server, manually locating and copying files to a flash drive, syncing data to a mobile device, and exporting data from inside an e-mail client, like Microsoft Outlook. You can even opt to leave mail on your e-mail server until you delete it or manage your e-mail using an online entity like Gmail. For now, we'll stick with what you have available to you, without having to purchase anything new or any service or web space.

All Microsoft operating systems offer an easy way to back up your data regularly. The backup utility with your operating system can be run and configured via a wizard, or you can run it in *advanced* mode (if available). If you can configure your own preferences instead of letting Windows decide, you'll be better off because advanced mode offers so many more choices and allows you to really personalize your backups. Figure 8-11 shows what you'll see in Windows 7. You can see that everything of importance is going to be backed up in this scenario.

Don't rely on one type of backup, though, especially an automatic one. You should combine this type of backup with backups you create manually. If you use Outlook or something similar, you can export the data using built-in tools made specifically for this purpose. You'll have to refer to your particular e-mail client for instructions on doing this, but I'll give you some pointers at the end of this section.

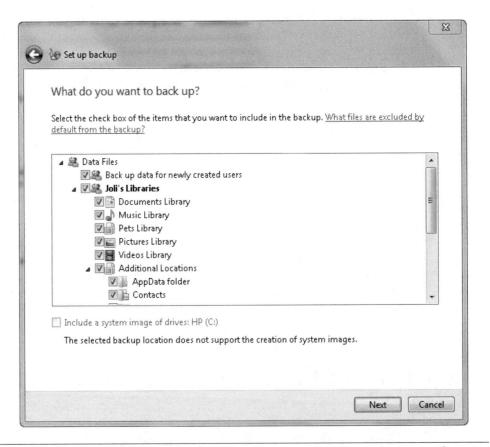

FIGURE 8-11   With a backup utility, you can choose what data to back up, where to back it up, when to back it up, and how often to back it up.

You can also locate the data yourself and copy it, bypassing any internal wizard or feature, and then paste the data somewhere safe, such as an external drive, network drive, or even a flash drive. In Windows Live Mail, for example, you can locate the Store folder (see Figure 8-12) and manually copy the data in it to back it up.

Where you store these backups is just as crucial as actually creating them. There's no point in creating a backup of your data only to store it on the same hard drive as the original data! If something happens to the computer, both your original data and your backups will be gone. Similarly, storing a backup on an external drive that sits on top of your computer tower is equally dangerous. If a flood or fire destroys the computer or a thief steals it, the external hard drive will likely be gone too. To that effect, you should save your backups offsite (or at least in another room). Save them to a flash drive, network drive, Internet server, company server, or somewhere else; just make sure to save them somewhere safe!

To really protect yourself, you could also (and I think you should) sync a mobile device with your computer and e-mail client. I use an iPad and Microsoft Office Outlook 2010, and the combination does a pretty good job. No matter what happens to my computer, I'll still have my e-mail on my iPad. Likewise, if something happens to the iPad, I still have the data on my computer.

Now, syncing data to an iPad, iPhone, BlackBerry, Android, or other mobile device isn't always straightforward, and everything doesn't always get synced (backed up, in our case). Additionally, the data may be in various places on the device. On my iPad, for instance, my Inbox is synced, but not the folders and subfolders I created in Outlook. That's a problem, so it's imperative to have another backup option in place. However, my contacts are available in the iPad's Contacts app, my calendar events and appointments are in the iPad's Calendar app, and even my photos, videos, music, audiobooks, and other data have a second home in related iPad apps. Of course, mail does arrive in the Mail app, even though at the current time I have no option to create folders or sync the ones I've created in Outlook.

And there's one more option. You can configure your mail client to leave mail on the server until you delete it. This way it's immediately accessible from any other computer if you need to view your e-mail at another location. This is also a necessary setting if you use other devices to check for new mail throughout the day. If you opt to actually work from a web-based program, like Gmail, you can also create folders there, store mail there, and otherwise manage e-mail from anywhere. Of course, this option keeps a nice backup for you, too. (Gmail syncs nicely with iPads, too, offering yet another backup option should you desire one.)

FIGURE 8-12   By locating the Store folder, you can easily copy your e-mail data.

Because I cannot account for your particular system and backup options, I'll encourage you to explore this particular option first on your computer. This option is to use the built-in backup program:

1. Click Start | Control Panel.
2. Locate Back Up Your Computer, shown in Figure 8-13, and click it.
3. Follow the prompts to set up regular, recurring, and all-encompassing backups, making sure your e-mail data is included. If you aren't sure, locate the Store folder, detailed later, and manually select that folder to be backed up here.

Once you've done that, perform a few manual backups using information available in your e-mail client. If you're using Microsoft Outlook:

1. In earlier versions of Outlook, click File | Import and Export. For Outlook 2010, click File | Open | Import.
2. Look for the Export to a File option, as shown selected in Figure 8-14.
3. Click Next and click Outlook Data File (.pst).

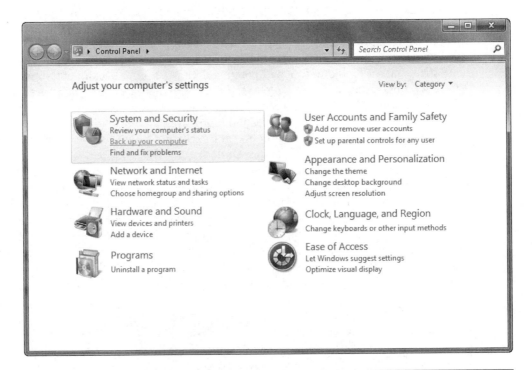

FIGURE 8-13   Locate your backup program. All Windows operating systems come with a backup program.

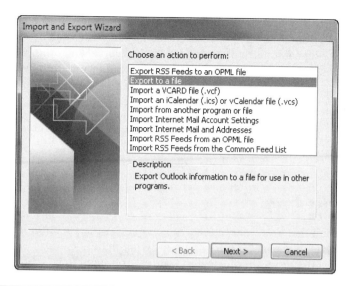

FIGURE 8-14 In Outlook you can use a wizard to help you export data (which means to copy it) to a file you can use as a backup.

4. Click Next and choose Personal Folders. Verify the Include Subfolders check box is selected. See Figure 8-15.
5. Click Next, and select Replace Duplicates with Items Exported.
6. Click Browse.
7. Locate a place to save the backup.
8. Click Finish.

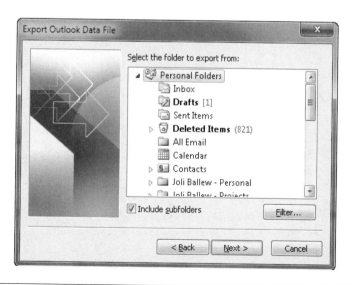

FIGURE 8-15 Choose what folders to back up; be sure to enable Include subfolders.

Repeat these steps, but this time, in step 3, choose Comma Separated Values (Windows), and in step 6, choose Contacts. This will enable you to back up only contacts. Repeat to back up Calendar, Tasks, Notes, and other Outlook data.

If you're using Windows Live Mail or a similar program, you can also back up your data. With these simpler e-mail clients, you have to know where the Store folder is located or you have to learn, on your own, how to back up your data in another way. When in doubt, check the Help files. Because third-programs are updated often and because there are so many programs to choose from, it is impossible to show you how to find your Store folder here or how to back up in every instance.

Summing Up

The e-mail that you *want* to receive is no better than spam if it turns into gunk on your PC. Unlike spam, however, your own e-mail responds better to psychological measures than to technological measures. You need to be ready to deal with e-mail *as it arrives*—and become an ace at deciding when to keep a message, when to hold it for a limited time, when to pitch it, or when to deal with it (read it or reply) right now.

You also need to know how to prevent and deal with junk e-mail. Most e-mail programs have built-in spam filters, and an option to create rules, block senders, or both. Explore these features and use them regularly. At every turn, protect your e-mail addresses too. Don't post them on web pages, give them to people who you think might spam you, or use them willy-nilly in newsgroups or for registering for web sites.

Finally, learn how to back up your e-mail data, and do it regularly. It's important to have a plan. I suggest three strategies: using the backup program that came with your PC, using the backup wizard in your e-mail client or copying and pasting the Store folder (as applicable), and using a mobile device to sync calendars, contacts, and mail daily.

9

Secure Your Computer

Degunking Checklist:

☑ Keep out intruders by using user accounts

☑ Thwart prying eyes with a password-protected screen saver

☑ Resolve errors with the Action Center

☑ Protect your computer with Windows Update, Windows Defender, and Windows Firewall

☑ Get important updates and review optional ones

☑ Obtain, configure, and use antivirus, antimalware, and antiadware software

Securing your PC is just as important as enhancing its performance, and that's what we're going to discuss in this chapter. It doesn't do any good to clean up, maintain, and organize your home or garage if you're going to leave the door unlocked and the alarm turned off while you're away, allowing anyone and everyone to drop in and take or use what they want (or do or see what they want). Upon your return, your home or garage may be in a state of chaos. The same is true of your PC. Don't go to all the trouble of getting it running efficiently, organizing all its files, and performing scheduled maintenance only to leave a door open to prying eyes, nosy coworkers and kids, hackers, viruses, worms, and adware or spyware programs. Intrusions, just like data, can really gunk up your machine.

Use, er, User Accounts

When you turn on your computer or awaken it from sleep, do you have to input a password? If you don't, then anyone can turn it on and use it. This includes your kids, parents, coworkers, a cleaning crew, and guests in your home. And yes, it also includes the thief that obtains your laptop because you left it on the plane, in an unlocked car, or at Starbucks. Think of all the damage any of these people could do! They could send an e-mail from your account and pretend to be you, they could update the status on your Facebook page, or they could send instant messages to your contacts. Beyond what they can do to your reputation, though, consider the sensitive documents, files,

151

spreadsheets, and pictures you store on your computer. What about the usernames and passwords you've saved in Internet Explorer to log you in automatically to web sites? Is there anything on your computer you wouldn't want others to see?

Um, probably.

To protect your computer from some of these threats, you can create a user account (and apply a password) for yourself and anyone else who uses it. When user accounts are in place, and when each user logs on and logs off when they need access to the computer, personal data stays secure. As an additional perk, with user accounts, each user then has their own settings, their own data folders, and their own preferences. And better than all of that, if you configure your computer and all the other computers on your network with user accounts and passwords, you should never have a problem (or certainly you will lessen the problems you have or resolve them completely) accessing the data on other computers on your network. Windows 7 and previous Windows OSs prefer that you have user accounts and passwords, and will play nicely with other PCs if those things are in place.

NOTE It won't do any good to create a user account and password if you don't use them.

You can configure user accounts and passwords all day, but if you leave your computer unattended and do not take advantage of them, your computer is still at risk. A disgruntled employee could easily change your Facebook status to "I am the worst boss in the world and I play Farmville for 6 hours a day" while you're at the soda machine picking out a diet cola. An unhappy mother-in-law could browse your photos. An angry child could send e-mails to everyone in your address book, use your credit card online, or access your bank account. Thus, you *must* do one of the following *on a regular basis*:

- Log off from your computer when you're finished using it.
- Set the computer to sleep after a few minutes of inactivity.
- Apply a screen saver after a specified amount of time and protect it with a password.
- Turn the computer off when you're finished using it.

TIP You have a user account on your Windows 7 PC, but you may not have a password. You should apply a password to that account as soon as possible.

Create User Accounts (or Apply a Password to Yours)

Now that you are convinced that you must do more than create user accounts and passwords, and that you actually have to use them, let's get on to the business of creating them. You start from Control Panel, shown in Figure 9-1. Here, to further secure your computer, under User Accounts and Family Safety, you can create new user accounts for others who use your PC, apply a password to your own account, or even create a secondary account you can use that is not an administrator account.

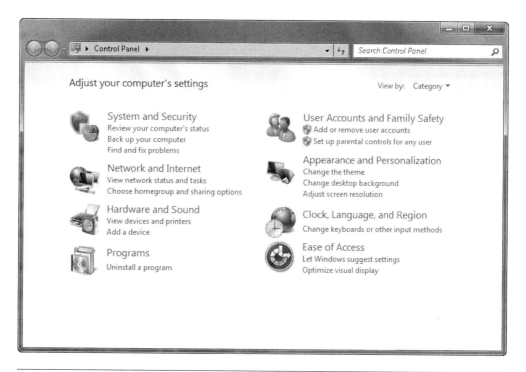

FIGURE 9-1   Control Panel is your starting place for creating user accounts or applying a password to your own.

When creating an account, you have two options: Administrator or Standard User. Ideally, a computer should have only one administrator account and the rest should be standard user accounts. (There's a hidden administrator account, but you're supposed to ignore that.) Administrators can do just about anything, including installing software and hardware, creating other user accounts, changing security settings, and accessing the system files on the computer. Standard users can't do any of this without administrator's credentials.

To create a new user account in Windows 7:

1. Click Start | Control Panel.
2. Click Add or Remove User Accounts (under the User Accounts and Family Safety category).
3. Click Create a New Account.
4. Type the new account name, select Standard User or Administrator, and click Create Account (see Figure 9-2).

NOTE   By default, no password is created during account creation. Refer to the next section to apply a password to each account on your computer, even if there's only one, yours.

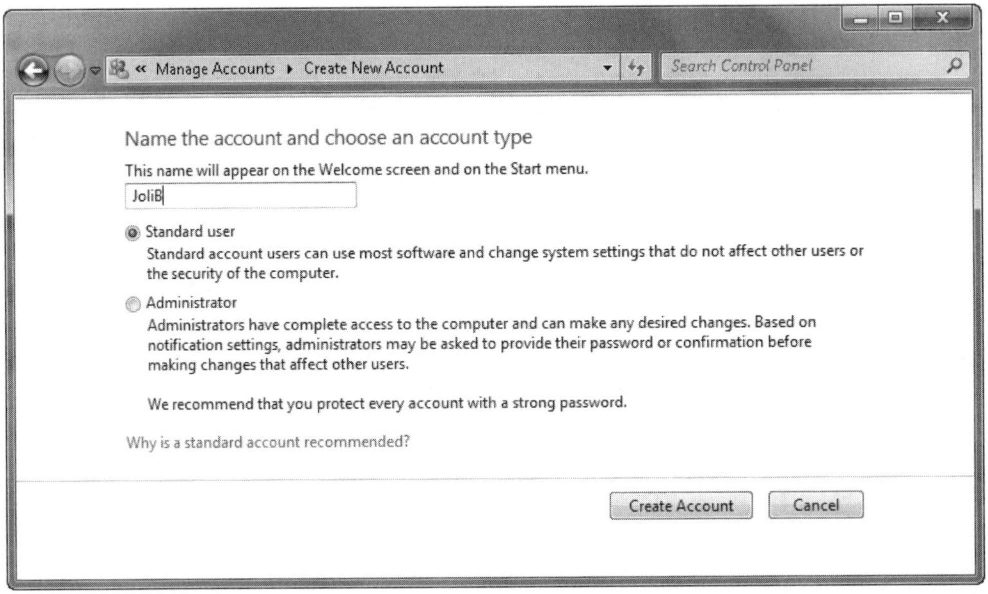

FIGURE 9-2   Create a new account, preferably a standard user account, for any new user.

GunkBuster's Notebook: Change Your User Account from Administrator to Standard User

Do you know that your user account is likely an administrator account? Yes, it's true, and you may be aware that using an administrator account all of the time is a potential security risk. You can, if you desire, create a standard user account for yourself and log on with that most of the time. Of course, this presents problems; you'd have to first create the account, and then move your files and folders, move your bookmarks and contacts, and reconfigure your settings and preferences, among other things. Additionally, you must have at least one administrator account, so you can't just downgrade yours to a standard user account. What a nightmare.

There's a way around this. First, create a new administrator account. Name it **Admin**. Now your computer will have two administrator accounts, yours and the new one. Work through the process to apply a password to the new Admin account. Write the password down and store it somewhere safe. Next, select your own account and click Change Your Account Type. Change the account from Administrator to Standard User. Make sure a password is applied to that account as well.

Now, you will use a standard user account all the time, and input the administrator account's credentials (Admin, and your password) when you need to make system-wide changes to the computer.

As you know, there's no option to create a password during user account creation. That's a separate step. And it doesn't do any good to create a user account if you do not assign a password to it and to all the other accounts on your computer (which implies that the user-account-creation design isn't as effective as it could be). It also isn't effective to create a user account and set the password to your pet's name, one of your kids' names, your birthday, or something else that hackers will automatically try, like password, abcde, or 123. You need to set a strong password, preferably one with mixed-case letters, a few numbers, and maybe even a symbol.

To apply a password to an existing account:

1. From Control Panel, click Add or Remove User Accounts.
2. Click the user account for which you want to create a password.
3. Click Create a Password (see Figure 9-3).
4. Type the password, type it again to verify it, and type a password hint.
5. Click Create Password.

Use a Guest Account

If you're planning on having guests and know they will need access to a computer to check e-mail, surf the Web, print documents, or write letters home (who does *that* anymore?), you'll want to enable a Guest account. A Guest account is the perfect way to give visitors the computer and Internet access they need while still keeping the computer and your personal files safe and secure. You can easily configure the Guest account to show on the Welcome screen so that guests have easy access to it.

FIGURE 9-3   You have to create a password as a secondary step to creating user accounts.

Once configured, the Guest account has the following properties:

- Guests have access to the computer, and that access is protected.
- Guests cannot install software or hardware.
- Guests have access to installed hardware and software.
- Guests cannot upgrade an account to Administrator or join any group that has more privileges.
- Guests have access to items in the Public folders.

Once you've decided you need a Guest account, it's extremely easy to enable the default one. When your guests leave, though, you should disable the account immediately. An enabled Guest account is considered a liability and is not a good long-term security configuration.

To enable and configure the Guest account, follow these steps:

1. Open Control Panel, and click Add or Remove User Accounts.
2. Click the Guest account icon.
3. Click Turn On.

NOTE   It is extremely important to the health of your computer and the security of your data and personal information that all user accounts have passwords and that all users are required to log off when they are finished using the PC.

Protect Your Computer with Built-In Windows 7 Features

Windows 7 comes with lots of ways to protect your computer automatically. For instance, during setup, you're prompted to accept recommended settings for installing Windows Updates. And by default, Windows Defender and Windows Firewall are enabled. Additionally, the Action Center will look for solutions to problems your computer has encountered, and offer suggestions for you.

While all of this sounds peachy, you may get the sense that some of this activity may be gunking up your machine. You may ask, for instance, are all of those updates really necessary? What is the Action Center really doing, and when does it do it? What if you've purchased a third-party spyware utility or a third-party firewall utility? Are any of these things slowing your computer down and creating gunk?

For the most part, your concerns are *not* justified. Generally, these tools are protecting you, and protection is not normally considered gunk. However, you can tweak these tools for the best performance possible, and verify you're in control.

There are other Windows 7 features to help you protect your computer that aren't enabled by default. One is to apply a screen saver and require a password to disable it once it's running. You can also use Windows Defender to run a manual scan for spyware if you think you're infected, and you can choose what Windows Updates to install (versus the alternative of installing them all). These things and others are quite important, and warrant a special look. On that note, let's start with the password-protected screen saver, which is very important indeed. Later we'll look at what Windows 7 is doing in the background to protect you!

Apply a Screen Saver Password

A screen saver is a moving animation or a set of images that appears after a period of inactivity, the length of which you set. Generally, the best screen savers are those that don't use too many system resources, came with Windows 7, and hide your Desktop. The Bubbles screen saver is cool, for instance, but it does not serve the latter purpose. You can see what's on the screen even when the screen saver is enabled (see Figure 9-4).

NOTE   The original purpose of a screen saver was to prevent monitor "burn-in" of the image on the screen, but that is no longer a concern with modern computers. Now screen savers are used aesthetically, to secure the computer by hiding the data on the screen, and/or to require a password when the screen saver is disabled and the computer is brought out of screen saver mode.

A screen saver is disabled when you move the mouse or press a key on the keyboard. You can, while configuring the screen saver, opt to require a password before the screen saver can be disabled and access to the screen is offered. This is an awesome security feature, and you should apply it.

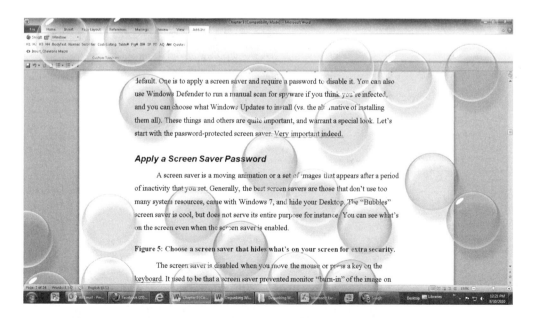

FIGURE 9-4   Choose a screen saver that hides what's on your screen, for extra security.

TIP   If you'd rather not wait for a screen saver or even apply one, just press Windows Key+L to lock your computer when you step away from it. If you can make this a habit, it'll protect your computer better than a screen saver.

To apply a password-protected screen saver:

1. Click Start, and in the Start Search window, type **Change Screen Saver**.
2. Click Change Screen Saver in the results.
3. In the Screen Saver Settings dialog box (see Figure 9-5), select a screen saver from the list.
4. Check the On Resume, Display Logon Screen check box.
5. If desired, click Settings and apply settings as desired.
6. Click OK.

NOTE   You must have a password applied to your account to make this a secure screen saver and to require a password on wakeup.

FIGURE 9-5   Choose a screen saver that will hide what's on the screen and password-protect it.

Use the Action Center to Resolve Known Security Issues

Ugh. You're going to see pop-up messages (aka "pop-ups") from Windows. It's only because Windows 7 is trying to take care of your PC and your data; it's not because Microsoft is trying to annoy you. You'll see a pop-up if your antivirus software is out of date (or not installed), if you don't have the proper security settings configured, or if Windows Update or Windows Firewall is disabled, among other things. Oddly, you won't see a pop-up if your computer is not password protected, which is a huge security risk.

When you see a pop-up, you should check it out. Maybe it's nothing; maybe it requires your attention. You check it out in the Action Center (see Figure 9-6). If you see anything in the Action Center that's denoted with red or yellow, click the down arrow (if necessary) to see a description of the problem. You can click the button that's offered, perhaps Check for solutions or Options, to view the resolution and/or perform the task. This is shown in Figure 9-6.

When you opt to check for solutions, the Action Center will go online, look for solutions to problems it's been amassing, and offer various options for resolving those problems. What it looks for and finds isn't relegated to only Windows operating system missteps, though. The Action Center may suggest that a new video driver is available, for instance.

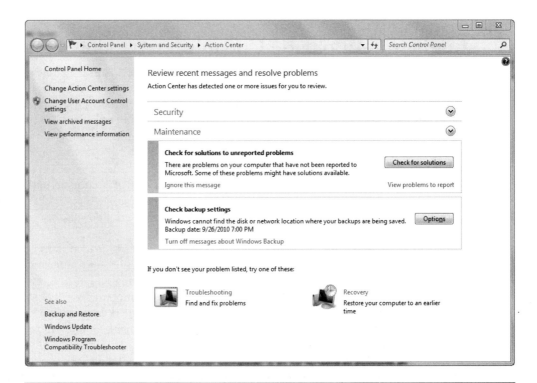

FIGURE 9-6   The Action Center offers a wealth of information regarding the health of your computer.

If you haven't done so, then, click Start, type **Action Center** in the Start Search window, and click Action Center in the results to open it. Work through the information to see if anything needs urgent attention. The most common complaint by the Action Center is lack of antivirus software. If you see that is the case, consider using Microsoft Security Essentials, detailed later in this chapter.

While you're in the Action Center, click the down arrow beside Security. You'll have an opportunity to review all of your security settings. Be careful here—don't just enable everything because you think you should! For instance, you may see that Network Access Protection is not enabled. Don't enable it just because you want to. Know this first:

Network Access Protection (NAP) is a platform that network administrators can use to help protect the security of a network. When you connect to a corporate network that uses NAP, your computer is checked to make sure that it has the required software and settings, and that the software and settings are up to date. If anything is missing or outdated, your computer can be automatically updated. Your network access might be limited during that time, but usually this process happens quickly, after which full network access is restored.

You probably do not want to enable this. You can learn more about any disabled item by clicking the link below it. Then you can decide if you want to enable it or not.

Configure Automatic Updates for Windows 7

Windows Update is the easiest and most efficient way to keep your computer safe and sound and up to date. Windows Update is Microsoft's way of making available all of the security patches, fixes, software updates, and other important items that your computer needs to stay in good working order. It's extremely important that you either visit the Windows Update web site regularly or configure Windows 7 to visit on its own, in the background.

NOTE   Check for updates manually for third-party programs, which is often an option from the program's Help menu. Note that some of these will automatically update themselves or offer a pop-up when an update is available for download.

Keeping your computer updated with important updates is crucial to maintaining a well-running, high-performance, and secure computing environment because without these patches and fixes, your computer is vulnerable to all of the newly found security holes to which hackers and attackers have an open door. These rogues can access your computer remotely (if they know how) and do damage in a number of ways. While some folks are a bit suspicious of the monitoring and downloading process, the information collected from your computer is not information that could personally identify you, your e-mail address, or your surfing habits (among other things). It's okay to let Windows install these "important" updates. Trust me.

I do understand your reservations, though. It indeed seems logical that using the automatic settings to download updates would slow down your machine and install a bunch of gunk, especially if the updates are downloaded in the morning when you boot your computer and you don't opt to control what's downloaded. However, Microsoft swears that the updates will be downloaded in the background and will not interfere with or slow down network activities such as Internet browsing, and by default, those downloads occur in the middle of the night anyway. (That's why some mornings you wake up to a computer that's rebooted on its own.) You can also rest assured that only the most important updates are pushed to your machine and installed automatically. Even with the highest Windows Update setting, you'll still see optional updates when you check Windows Update on your computer. As shown in Figure 9-7, important updates have been installed, but there are optional ones I can look at and decide about on my own.

To configure Windows Update or review your current settings:

1. Click Start and type **Windows Update** in the Start Search window.
2. In the results, click Windows Update.
3. Click Change Settings, shown on the left in Figure 9-7.
4. Figure 9-8 shows how my machine is configured, and I suggest you configure yours the same. Although you may get a little gunk, it's better to be safe than sorry.

TIP   You can deselect the Give Me Recommended Updates the Same Way I Receive Important Updates check box, and only important updates will be installed automatically.

FIGURE 9-7   Windows Update only installs important and recommended updates by default; you can decide whether or not you want to install updates deemed less important or optional.

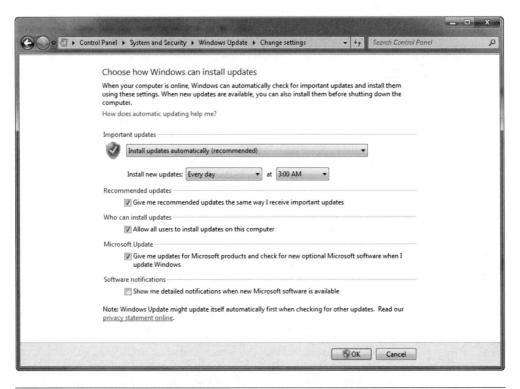

FIGURE 9-8   I prefer to get all important updates automatically, and I think you should choose that setting too.

With the important (and hopefully recommended) updates taken care of, you can now take a look at the optional ones, as shown for my computer in Figure 9-9. You'll have to use your best judgment here; I can't tell you what to install and what not to install. I have updates available for a modem, for instance, but since I never use the modem and don't plan to, there's no reason to install the update. That would indeed be gunk! You may see this update or others like it offered. Common updates include those for monitors, display drivers, audio drivers, and even storage and network controllers. Select what to install and click OK.

Perform a Scan with Windows Defender and Enable Windows Firewall

I would be doing you a disservice if I did not mention, albeit briefly, the built-in features Windows Defender and Windows Firewall. Windows Defender protects your computer against malware and similar Internet threats, and Windows Firewall watches what data

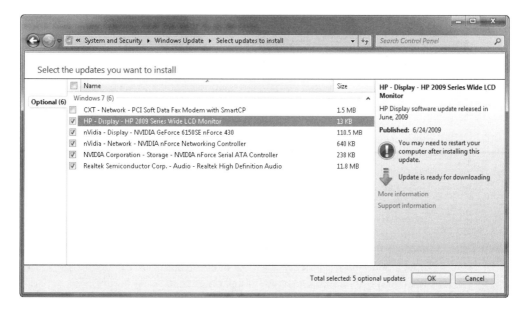

FIGURE 9-9   You can remain in control of optional updates, such as those available for modems, network controllers, and video and audio devices.

comes in and goes out via the Internet, and further protects your computer. The only thing else that needs to be said, really, is that these two options should remain enabled until you install something that replaces them. Not that you need to buy something to replace them, mind you. However, if you purchase a security suite that includes a firewall and/or antimalware, antivirus, and antispyware software, you need to disable their Windows counterparts. You never want two firewall programs running at the same time, and you never want two antivirus programs running at the same time, and you never want...well, you get the idea.

NOTE   Most all-in-one security software will automatically disable competing programs in Windows 7, including Windows Defender and Windows Firewall, if applicable.

You access Windows Defender and Windows Firewall the same way you access other tools in Windows, by searching for them from the Start Search window. Once opened, you can change their settings. With Windows Defender, you can even run a scan to check for infections.

NOTE   Firewalls protect computers from Internet intrusions, just as deadbolts on a door protect your home from intruders. Just as you would secure your home with locks and a security system, you should also secure your computer with a firewall *and* antivirus, antiadware, and antimalware software.

GunkBuster's Notebook: I Do Not Like User Account Control!

User Account Control (UAC) is what's responsible for you having to input administrator credentials every time you want to make a system-wide change to your computer. This can include downloading software from the Internet, installing a program, and possibly even accessing Device Manager. That pop-up is so annoying! You have to stop what you're doing and either input credentials or click OK, or both. It takes time; it slows you down; and after a while, it makes you want to pull your hair out. I get it.

This security measure keeps rogue entities from making changes to your computer, though; an executable file may be able to run, but it can't guess your credentials, type them in, and click OK to continue its installation! UAC is there to protect you. UAC is a good thing. However, I understand that it can work your nerves. I understand why you may want to disable UAC.

As a good leader, teacher, and role model, I must advise against this. *Strongly.* If you must, though, here's how to get rid of that pesky prompt:

1. Click Start, and in the Start Search window, type **UAC**.
2. In the results, click Change User Account Control Settings.
3. Move the slider to Never Notify, as shown here:

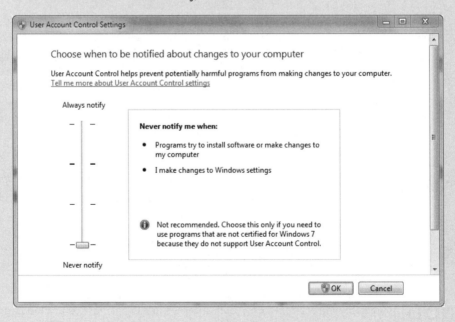

4. Click OK.

It's important to note that Windows Defender and Windows Firewall do not protect against viruses. Windows Defender does a good job of protecting against malware, and Windows Firewall does a good job of keeping out many types of Internet intrusions, but neither protects you from viruses. That's why the next section is devoted to protecting against viruses yourself.

Protect Against Viruses, Malware, and Adware

You know now that although Windows 7 comes with Windows Defender for protecting against malware and similar Internet threats and Windows Firewall for protecting against Internet intrusions, there's nothing built in for protecting against viruses. You also know that the Action Center is the part of Windows 7 that offers those pop-ups telling you that your computer's security is at risk if you don't have antivirus software. It's important to bite the bullet and get some antivirus software if you don't have it— and no, not just to squelch that annoying prompt!

Antivirus software, when kept up to date, is the easiest way to protect your computer against Internet risks like viruses and hackers. Antivirus software is fairly inexpensive, easy to install, and a snap to keep current. Antivirus software can protect against lots of different Internet threats, not just viruses and hackers, though. It can protect against unauthorized connections and privacy threats too. It can repel unwanted cookies and Java applets and scan incoming and outgoing e-mail. Many of these products also include a personal firewall, which can provide even more protection. You can also opt for an all-in-one package that also protects against adware, malware, unapproved downloads, and other things. These "ultimate" packages also often offer network monitoring, parental controls, and even antispam features.

There are lots of antivirus software manufacturers to choose from, although Symantec and McAfee likely are the most recognizable. Almost any brand-name product from a big box store can be trusted to do a good job at keeping your machine more secure, although some of the "protections" they offer can drive you a bit batty. Protections include scanning e-mail, preventing downloads that you deem safe, scanning your computer while you're trying to use it, and whatnot. Just be patient with the time it takes to protect your computer, at least for a while anyway, and if you can, tweak the program settings to perform the more resource-intensive tasks in the middle of the night (like scanning your PC for threats). Additionally, if the time it takes to say, scan outgoing e-mail works your nerves too badly, you can consider disabling that particular feature.

To expand on this, once installed, almost any protection-related software can be configured to suit your needs. Generally, the default settings are fine, but you might want to set the application to look for and download new security definitions every night (instead of the default, which is sometimes every week) if you want extra security. You can perform full system scans daily, weekly, or monthly and view reports of various activities on a schedule you prefer, too. As a rule, consider the following configuration choices for your antivirus software (or better yet, simply accept the defaults until something starts working your nerves, and change that one thing):

- Set the antivirus program to "auto-protect" and have it start each time you boot the computer. You should leave the application running in the background at all times.
- Show the software icon in the System Tray so that it is easily accessible and alerts can be viewed easily.
- Let your antivirus program automatically repair any infected files it finds. Quarantine the file if the repair is not successful.
- Perform a complete system scan at least once a week, and perhaps daily (each night) for computers that hold sensitive data.
- Enable script blocking so that malicious scripts (which can be viruses) are not run.
- Scan incoming and outgoing e-mail for viruses.
- Enable protection on any instant messaging systems you use.
- Enable automatic and scheduled downloads of new virus definitions at least weekly. If you have a continuous connection to the Internet, configure definitions to be downloaded daily, preferably at night or whenever you aren't using the computer.
- Enable protection from spyware and adware, if provided as an option, and make sure to disable any existing software that currently handles that task.
- When configuring e-mail protection, configure the application to automatically delete files that contain known viruses.

With all of these precautions in place, you should be pretty well protected against viruses, hackers, and general Internet threats.

TIP The antivirus software you select may not protect against Internet pop-ups and may not include a solution for avoiding adware and spyware. You'll need to make sure to cover all of your bases, and choose a full-protection package or mix and match antivirus, antiadware, and antimalware solutions.

Consider Free Security Software from Microsoft

If you'd rather not have to pay for software, or if you don't have the money to purchase the package you want (just yet), or you will go without protection due to monetary restraints or simply not knowing which product to choose, you do have an option. Microsoft Security Essentials will protect your computer almost seamlessly.

To get this software, simply visit www.microsoft.com/security_essentials/. Download and install the software, accepting the default settings. Once installed, you can access the application by searching for Microsoft Security Essentials in the Start menu. Figure 9-10 shows what viruses and threats on my computer have been detected and quarantined, all behind the scenes. I never knew anything about it.

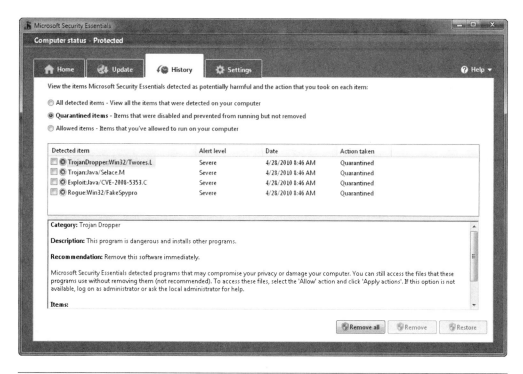

FIGURE 9-10   Microsoft Security Essentials will protect your computer for free.

Summing Up

Improving security is a multilevel task that involves creating user accounts and incorporating built-in tools like the Guest account, the Action Center, and Windows Update. It also involves installing antivirus software and protecting the PC with a password and a password-protected screen saver. However, improving security is worth the time it takes to do it; an unprotected computer can get gunked up beyond belief by a single worm or script attack—and the attack can occur scant minutes after you connect your PC to the Internet. Viruses will attempt to seize your PC and add it to "zombie" networks to do shadowy work behind your back. In fact, you might not be able to recover fully from a virus or worm without reinstalling Windows completely, along with everything else you use. As detailed in this chapter, you must enhance security to avoid getting gunked up in the first place!

10

Clean Up and Secure Your Network

Degunking Checklist:

☑ Secure your router

☑ Make sure your network is private

☑ Verify sharing is configured correctly

☑ Create a homegroup

☑ Use the available network troubleshooters to resolve network problems

☑ Remove unwanted wireless networks

When you are first notified of an available network or when you first set up a PC or laptop within range of a network, Windows 7 gives you the option to mark the network it finds as Work, Home, or Public. When you need to access a network in a library, coffee shop, hotel, and the like, you'll choose Public. If it's a network you trust, you'll choose Work or Home. I needed to get that out of the way, just in case you didn't know it. Because you've likely taken that step and are already part of a network, you need to concentrate now on degunking that network (or other networks you connect to). That's what you'll learn here.

First, you need to verify your network is secure. You need to make sure you've set up your own work or home network *hardware* correctly, and that means accessing the router settings. You may have to dig around for this information or possibly even make a phone call or three, but I'll offer tips for locating the information you need to verify that your router is secure. You also need to make sure your trusted network is marked as Work or Home. If you've inadvertently marked your network as Public, you'll have more than a few problems with regard to sharing and accessing data, and probably even seeing other computers on the network. You'll find that information and more in the Network and Sharing Center.

Second, you may need to re-create your network and/or create a homegroup. The latter is true if you have other Windows 7 PCs on your network or if you have compliant devices you want to share data with, like an Xbox 360, a media extender, a media receiver, or other, related devices. When you create a homegroup, you can more easily share data, media, music, video, and pictures, as well as perform some really cool tricks (like choosing Play To from a context menu, and then playing the media on a different device in the house!).

NOTE   Homegroups are new to Windows 7 and only work with other Windows 7 machines and compliant hardware.

Finally, you'll need to learn how to keep your network healthy and degunked. While there isn't quite as much to do here as, say, keeping your Pictures folder organized or managing the TV programs you record in Media Player, there are a few things you can do. You can cull your list of wireless networks, which you'll generally find on laptops and netbooks. Windows has to go through this list when trying to locate a network, so short and sweet is the way to go here. You'll also want to manage the cables, routers, devices, and wireless access points you use to create your network. Cables can get crimped under desks and chairs, hardware devices can become unnecessary, and wireless access points can be moved, for instance. All of these can cause problems that are difficult to diagnose. On occasion you'll even need to reboot the entire network—router, cable modem, and all. There's a trick to that, and if you don't do it right, you'll have headaches!

Verify Your Network Is Secure

Your network likely has a router that you initially set up so you could share your Internet connection with other computers you own. For the most part, that's the way it goes; you get a cable, DSL, or satellite modem, you connect a computer to it, and then, when you add a second, third, or fourth PC to the home or business, you add a router to share your single connection to the Internet with all of them. That router may be "wired" so that you have to plug each computer into it using an Ethernet cable, it may be wireless (no cables), or it may support both. You may have set up the router even when you had only one computer in the house, for security reasons. (You don't really want to plug a PC directly into a cable modem without going through a router for extra protection.) Whatever the case, it's probably true that you have three things: a modem that connects to the Internet, a router to share that connection or provide security (or both), and some computers and network devices.

Unfortunately, you may not have known what you were doing when you set up your router. You may not have set it up correctly, and your network may be open to everyone that comes within range of it! Your router needs to be configured with a password or passphrase, a network name, and perhaps secured with some sort of encryption or other available safeguards.

NOTE   If you set up your network years ago and used a switch or hub, you have an outdated system. If this is the case, purchase a router and set it up. When that's done, continue here. I know, that's a pretty tall order.

Secure Your Router

To secure your router, you must access a specific web site through a wired connection. If you have the router documentation, drag it out and mull through it to find out what web site that is. This documentation may also offer credentials for logging on the first time (or information about some utility you need to install). The most common way to verify your router settings is by visiting the web site the router manufacturer provides. Once there, usually you have to enter a login name of Admin or Administrator and enter a password to get in. Often the password is "password"! You're supposed to change that name and password the first time you log in. If you can't find your router's documentation, open a web browser, and in the address bar type **http://192.168.1.1**. This might get you in. If you know your username and password, type them in, as shown in Figure 10-1.

If you can't find your router booklet and/or your login information, look at your router and call the technical assistance number on it. You may have to use Google to find the login page if you can't find a support number. Whatever trouble you have to go to, though, you need to find out if your router is secure and is protected with a password and other security options.

Once you're in, you'll see something similar to what's shown in Figure 10-2. Browse the available options, verifying that security is in place.

In Figure 10-2, security is applied. If None were selected, then anyone in the vicinity could probably access that network. Locate your options and verify your router's security options are set to something other than None. Generally, you also should avoid WEP. Although it can protect against casual access, it's easily compromised using software that's all too easy for more determined snoops to download. On a side

FIGURE 10-1   Type the username and password for your router after navigating to http://192.168.1.1.

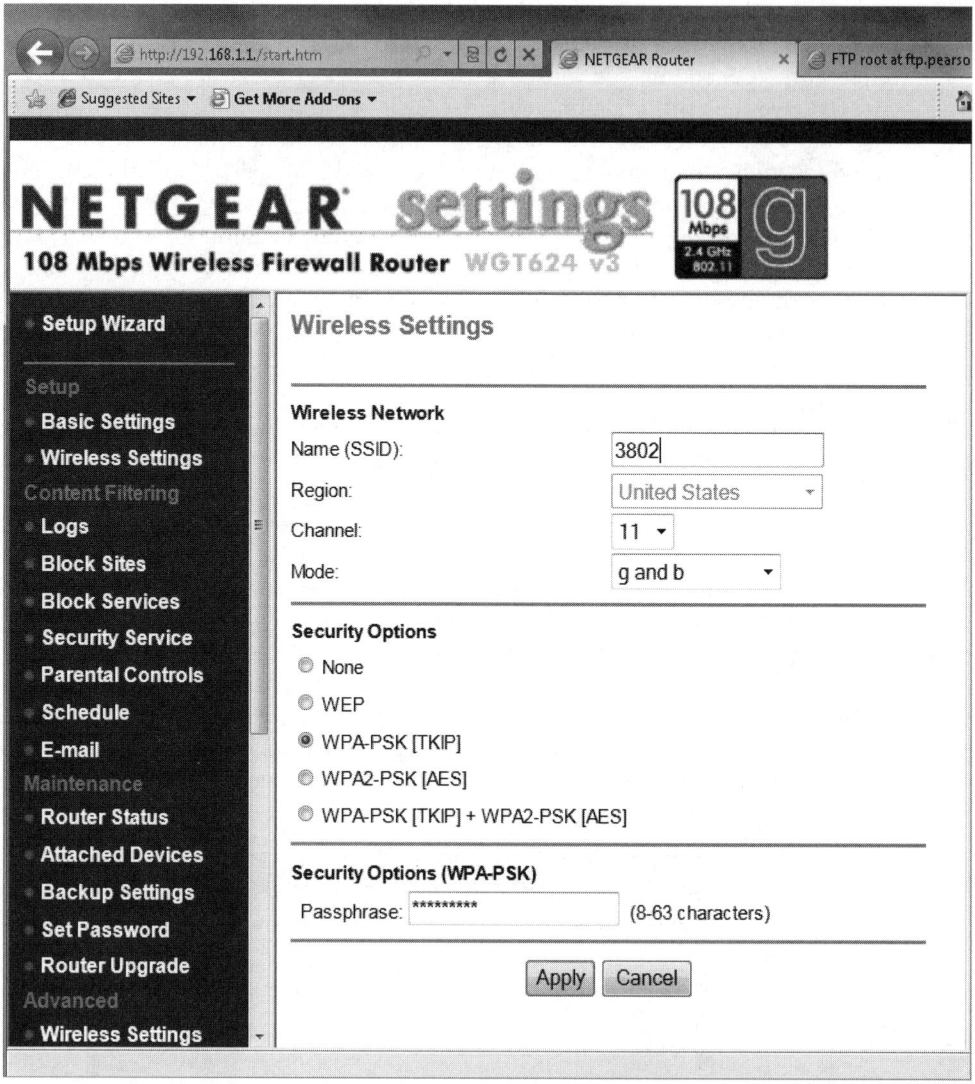

FIGURE 10-2   Once you've logged in to your router settings page, browse the information to see how security is configured.

note, generally, the least secure option is listed first and the most secure is listed last. In Figure 10-2, for instance, None is the least secure, followed by WEP, while WPA-PSK [TKIP] + WPA2-PSK [AES] is the most secure. Detailing what all of these security options stand for or mean or provide is beyond the scope of this discussion. Most of the time, that information is offered in a sidebar of your router's configuration page anyway. If you have questions, refer there.

CAUTION   I've chosen WPA-PSK [TKIP] here because I have an older netbook on my network that does not support the higher security settings. You may have similar limitations.

With that done, verify you've set a password or passcode. It should be a strong password that you can set or have the router software set for you. If you aren't sure what your router's passcode or passphrase is, reset it and write it down. Finally, note the network name. It should not be your street address, your last name, or any other identifiable information. Make the desired changes before continuing.

Make Sure Your Network Is "Private"

If it's been several years since you set up your router, you may have run some sort of "network wizard" on one of your computers. Back then, you selected the computer you wanted to be "in charge of stuff," which was often the computer you deemed fastest or most powerful, and you told it to set up a network workgroup for you. These old network wizards allowed you to create a workgroup that the local computers could join to share files, folders, and media. You got to pick the name for the workgroup, but aside from that most of the security settings were configured for you. Beyond the headaches involved in tweaking those settings by creating user accounts, passwords, and sharing folders, it was pretty effective.

Um, so what exactly does this have to do with degunking?

The problem is that you could have set up your network years ago with an old Windows XP machine! Heck, your router may be that old! As you added and removed computers from your network, you probably didn't make any changes, either. Your Windows 7 machine may simply be an add on—an afterthought—and you probably didn't configure that Windows 7 machine to "be in charge of stuff" or even review the settings! Therefore, there's no telling what sharing configuration you're working with, and there's no telling, without looking of course, what security settings are configured for your personal network. Your network could be severely out of date. That's where you may find gunk.

Lucky for you, it's possible to take control of those settings and sharing configurations from the Windows 7 Network and Sharing Center. That's what you'll do here.

Verify Sharing Is Configured Correctly

As you know, there are three network types: Home, Work, and Public. Windows 7 treats Home and Work networks the same; having two names is only there for your convenience. When you take a look at sharing settings, then, you'll notice the first "section" is called Home or Work (current profile). This is shown in Figure 10-3 along with the first few options for the sharing configuration. If you scroll down, you'll see an option for Public. We'll be mostly concerned with the Home and Work profiles, since these are the settings configured for your local area network.

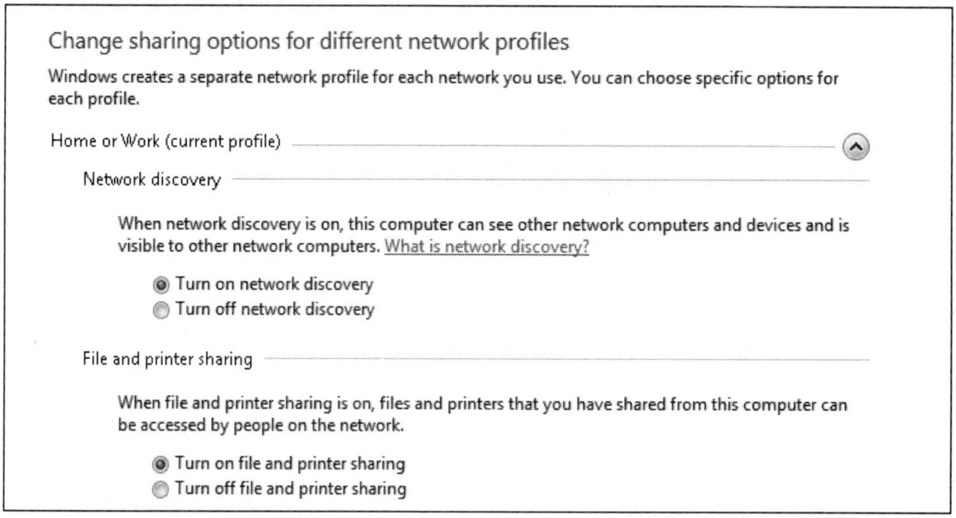

Change sharing options for different network profiles

Windows creates a separate network profile for each network you use. You can choose specific options for each profile.

Home or Work (current profile) ————————————————————————————————— ⌃

   Network discovery ————————————————————————————

      When network discovery is on, this computer can see other network computers and devices and is
      visible to other network computers. What is network discovery?

         ◉ Turn on network discovery
         ◯ Turn off network discovery

   File and printer sharing ————————————————————————————

      When file and printer sharing is on, files and printers that you have shared from this computer can
      be accessed by people on the network.

         ◉ Turn on file and printer sharing
         ◯ Turn off file and printer sharing

FIGURE 10-3   Home and Work network profiles are the same; Public is
something else.

Open the Network and Sharing Center and review your sharing and security
settings:

1. Click the network icon on the Taskbar.
2. Click Open Network and Sharing Center, shown in Figure 10-4.
3. Verify that the Network setting is Home Network (or Work Network), as shown
   in Figure 10-5. The only time you should see Public Network is when you're
   connected to someone else's network, likely from a laptop. If the setting is not
   correct, click it, then:
   a. Select the proper network type, as shown in Figure 10-6.
   b. Click Close.
4. In the left pane, click Change Advanced Sharing Settings.

FIGURE 10-4   Although there are several ways to open the Network and Sharing
Center, this requires the least amount of clicks.

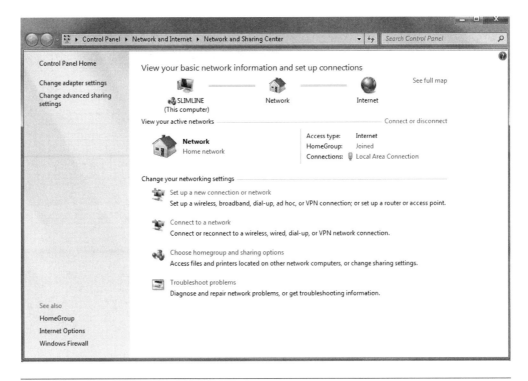

FIGURE 10-5 Get to know all parts of the Network and Sharing Center. Here, the network type is Home Network.

5. Make changes as applicable. Here are some guidelines:
   a. Network Discovery needs to be enabled for your computer to find and connect to networks.
   b. File and Printer Sharing needs to be enabled if you want to share files and printers that are connected to or stored on this computer.
   c. Public Folder Sharing needs to be enabled if you want to share the data you keep on this computer with others on the network.
   d. Media Streaming needs to be enabled if you want to, well, stream media to other network devices. There's a whole chapter on this coming up next.
   e. File Sharing Connections lets you change file sharing settings. Don't change this unless you have problem sharing with devices on your network.
   f. Password Protected Sharing needs to be enabled if you want to grant access to data on your computer to people who have a user account and password on the computer. This can be a real pain, and I suggest turning this off unless you really want to create user accounts and passwords for everyone who may need access to the data on your computer and the hardware attached to it.
   g. HomeGroup Connections are configured such that Windows 7 manages them. You'll learn about Homegroups next. For now, leave Allow Windows to Manage Homegroup Connections (Recommended) selected.
6. Click the arrow beside Public. This is shown in Figure 10-7.

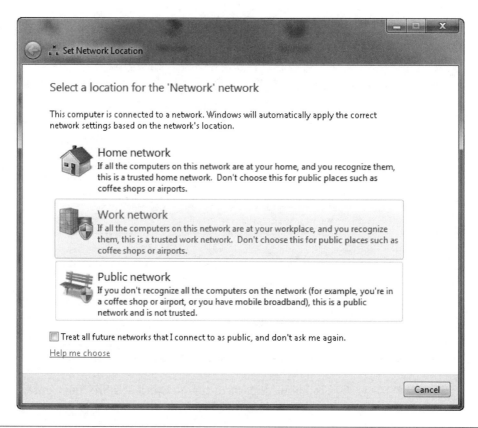

FIGURE 10-6 You can change the network type easily.

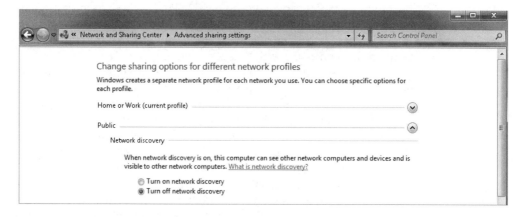

FIGURE 10-7 Public is another option in Advanced Sharing Settings.

7. Note the default settings for Public. You should not change any of these at this time, unless you're using a laptop, connect to public networks often, and know what you need to change to work effectively. For instance, if you want to stream media across a public network, you can enable this feature.

8. Click Save Changes.

Re-create Your Network and/or Create a Homegroup

I'm not a big fan of letting an old Windows XP machine remain in charge of your network and its settings. In fact, I'd actually recommend, if you find yourself in this situation, that you set up a new network from your Windows 7 computer. Let it be in charge; let Windows 7 set up security and sharing. Tear down that old network and begin again. You may find when you do this that you don't even need that XP machine anymore, or that you can use it as a backup device.

If you set up your network using a Windows Vista machine, that's actually okay. Despite the bad press, it's a pretty decent OS, and you can trust it to be in charge of your network. Still, I must say I prefer Windows 7, and I'm still going to encourage you to consider re-creating your network using Windows 7. If you want to, then, turn off that old XP machine (or Windows Vista PC) and create a new network with your shiny, new, Windows 7 PC. You can do this in the Network and Sharing Center by clicking Set Up a New Connection or Network. Make sure to create a new workgroup name so as not to confuse things. You know the drill: Connect to the Internet. Run the wizard. Add the PCs. Share the data. Stream the media.

Intro to Homegroups

But wait! What's that you say about homegroups? Shouldn't I just create one of those? Isn't that supposed to be the cure-all for every network ill? The answer to that is a resounding, yes! Provided, that is, that you have another Windows 7 PC on the network or compliant devices to enjoy it with.

Homegroups only play well with other Windows 7 computers and compatible Windows 7 devices. You can't add a Vista or XP machine to a homegroup. (If you have these devices, you'll continue to access them through your network, but not the homegroup.)

TIP   Homegroups are perfect for sharing and streaming media to compatible media extenders like the Xbox 360.

A homegroup makes sharing files and printers on a home network really easy, because the proper settings are already configured. You can automatically share pictures, music, videos, documents, and printers with other people in your homegroup easily. You can stream media. And other people can't change the files that you share, unless you give them permission to do so. You can also use the Play To context menu option with compliant devices, and thus easily play a song stored on one computer on a different one, or on a media extender or digital receiver, among other things.

NOTE | Using a homegroup is one of the easiest ways to share files and printers on a home network.

Locate an Existing Homegroup or Create a New One

You may have a homegroup available on another Windows 7 PC on your network and not know it. You may have already set up a homegroup on this computer and forgotten about it. This happens because Windows 7 automatically offers to create a homegroup the first time you start it, when you set it up. You may have done that without actually knowing you were doing it.

You can see if your PC is part of a homegroup or if one is available from the Network and Sharing Center. If you're part of a homegroup, next to HomeGroup, it'll say Joined. This was shown earlier, in Figure 10-5. You may alternately see Ready to Join. This means a homegroup has been configured on another Windows 7 PC on your network, and you can join it if you want to. You may find you are not part of any homegroup at all!

First, let's see if you have a homegroup on this computer or another computer and explore the options:

1. In the Network and Sharing Center, click Choose Homegroup and Sharing Options.
2. You'll be notified if no homegroup exists on this computer or on the network, as shown in Figure 10-8. Otherwise, you'll be asked to join an existing homegroup or have the option to change homegroup settings.

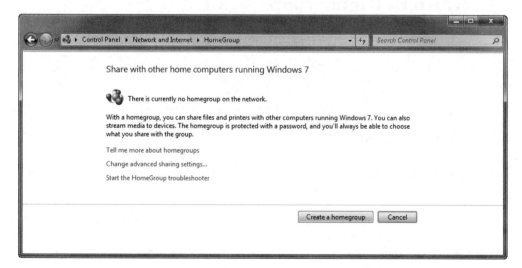

FIGURE 10-8 On this computer and network, no homegroup exists.

Creating a homegroup is simple really; you just click Create a Homegroup, and in the resulting dialog box, check the items to share. Although Documents isn't selected, I suggest you select it, provided you're secure with your network and can prevent access from unwanted sources. You're going to want to access documents from other computers, without a lot of muss and fuss, so you might as well go ahead and select to share documents now. After you've created the homegroup, you'll be given a password you can use to have other computers on the network join.

After you create or join a homegroup, you can select the libraries that you want to share, you can prevent specific files or folders from being shared, and you can share additional libraries later. You can help protect your homegroup with a password, which you can change at any time.

Tweak the Homegroup

With the homegroup created, you can now add other Windows 7 computers and compatible devices to it. You have to know the password, though, which you can obtain from the Network and Sharing Center by clicking Choose Homegroup and Sharing Options. From there, you can choose streaming media options, view the homegroup password, change the password to something you can more easily remember, change advanced sharing options, and run homegroup troubleshooters.

When you're ready to work with media and to stream it to other devices, you'll need to refer to the next chapter, but here's a carrot. Figure 10-9 shows the Play To option, available when you set up a homegroup and configure the proper sharing settings (no small feat, I might add). You can sit at one computer and play media on another. This includes compatible devices too.

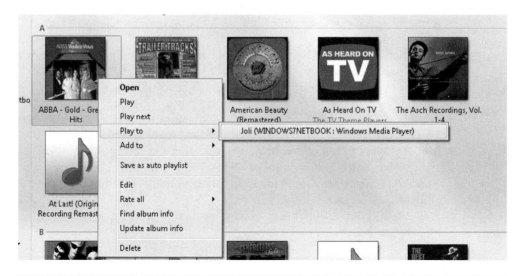

FIGURE 10-9   With a homegroup, you can perform all sorts of neat tricks, like playing media to other devices.

TIP The Network and Sharing Center offers a Network Map. Click See Full Map to see details about your network and what's connected to it.

Keep Your Network Degunked

Now that your network is healthy again (and I'm also hoping it's been reborn and is being controlled by your leanest, meanest, Windows 7 machine), it's important you learn how to keep it that way. There's not much to do here; as you know, once a network is up and running, it can go years without issues, especially if you leave it alone. It can collect gunk, though; for instance, if you connect to lots of wireless networks and have a list of them a mile long! You have to clean that up. Also, cables can get crimped; wireless access points can become repositioned; routers can get dusty; and ports can get gunked up (literally). For the most part, though, a network is pretty stable, once it's set up properly.

Resolve Network Problems

Windows 7 comes with all kinds of troubleshooters, and this includes network troubleshooters. Before you go that route, though, note that, for the most part, problems with a network typically stem from one of only a few areas:

- Your Internet service provider is at fault. Check your cable modem to see if you're connected to the Internet before you start troubleshooting, and if you need to, call the ISP's help line to see what they have to say about any outages in your area. (If you have a "standby" button, make sure it has not been inadvertently enabled.)
- Something has come unplugged. Check routers, modems, access points, and other hardware.
- An Ethernet cable has become disconnected, is crimped under a chair or desk, or otherwise busted. Fix it!
- Your wireless access point has fallen behind your desk, has been badly repositioned, or cables connecting to it have been dislodged or crimped.
- A plug, cable, or power cord has failed. Try a new plug, new cable, or new power cord.
- You may need to "reboot" your network. Generally, turn everything off, and then turn on hardware in this order, pausing a minute or two in between:
  - Cable, DSL, or satellite modem (giving it a chance to complete its startup cycle before continuing)
  - Router (giving it time to get its bearings before continuing)
  - PCs (one at a time, preferably)

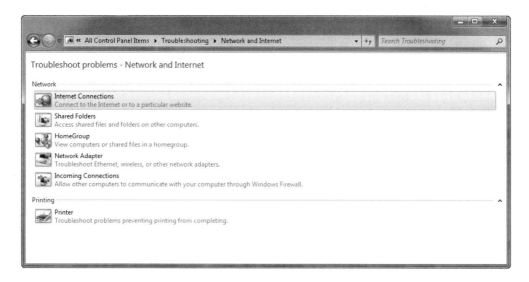

FIGURE 10-10   The troubleshooter first narrows down the type of problem you're having.

Once you're sure the problem you're having isn't related to any of these things, you can opt for a troubleshooter. It's easy: From the Network and Sharing Center, click Troubleshoot Problems. Then, choose the type of problem you are having, as shown in Figure 10-10, let the troubleshooter review the problem and offer solutions, and then try those solutions in the order they are presented.

As shown in Figure 10-11, suggestions will be made. Here, where the problem is that certain homegroup computers are not accessible, there are some suggestions, basically:

- The computers must be turned on to access the data on them (or connected via Ethernet or Wi-Fi).
- The computers must be part of the same network this computer is part of.
- The computer can't be part of a domain.

Most of the time, I'll say 99 percent of the time, following my suggestions and Windows' suggestions will fix the problem you're having.

Remove Unwanted Wireless Networks

When you use a laptop or netbook (or desktop PC) to connect to a wireless network, Windows 7 remembers the network. It puts it in a list of networks it keeps handy so that the next time you want to connect to it, the information is available. The list is ordered. Windows puts the networks you use most frequently at the top of the list,

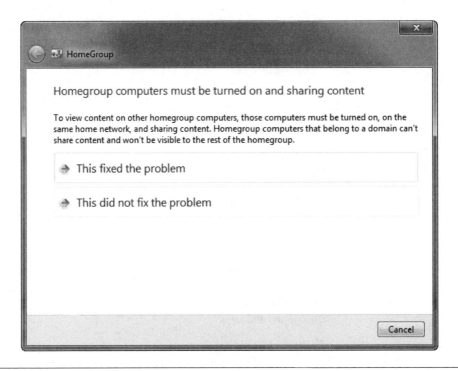

FIGURE 10-11 The troubleshooter walks you through the most common solutions first, and if they don't fix the problem, it gives you the option of trying something else.

and the rest underneath it, accordingly. When it looks for a network to connect to, it will start from the top and work its way down. And when your wireless features are enabled, it's always looking for a network.

Gunk happens when this list gets long and contains networks you'll never use again, like the one at the MotelHell you stayed at last year when you went to Vegas. You don't need Windows to look for that network ever again. No casino! Why bother? Gunk also accumulates when your laptop is looking for a wireless network to connect to, when in reality, you're not looking!

You control some of this gunk from the Network and Sharing Center. On the left side, click Manage Wireless Networks. In the ensuing window, shown in Figure 10-12, right-click any unwanted network to remove it, rename it, move it up or down in the list, or otherwise manage it.

TIP Move your most frequently accessed network to the top of the list and disable wireless capabilities when you are not interested in connecting to a network.

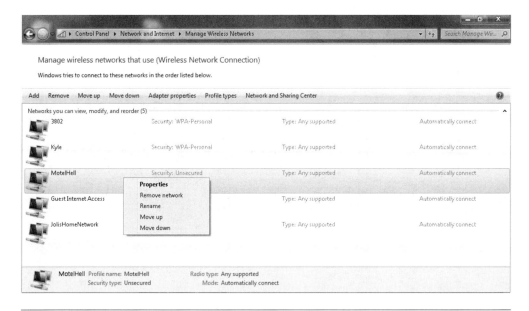

FIGURE 10-12 Right-click to manage the wireless networks you've amassed.

Regarding the unnecessary searching of networks, most laptops and netbooks have a switch on the outside to disable this. Additionally, some have a key combination. Windows 7 also offers the Mobility Center, which you can use to disable wireless capabilities, as shown in Figure 10-13.

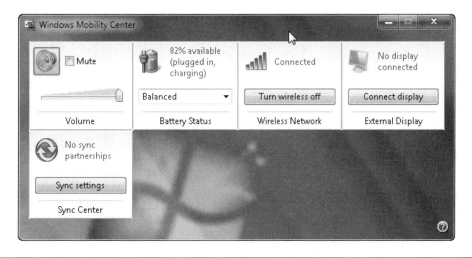

FIGURE 10-13 The Mobility Center lets you disable Wi-Fi capabilities quickly.

Summing Up

In this chapter, you learned how to secure your router, how to secure network settings, and how to troubleshoot network problems. Most of the time, gunk that occurs on a network is due to crimped cables, improperly placed wireless access points, improper sharing settings, too many wireless networks in a list, and the failure to make the most of homegroups. Networks should be secured from the router up—through Windows 7—and topped off with sharing.

11

Fix Problems with Media

Degunking Checklist:

☑ Get updates for all of your media players

☑ Get rid of media players you don't use

☑ Review and clean up your playlists

☑ Create useful auto playlists

☑ Back up media and/or media licenses

☑ Authorize or deauthorize computers to play media

☑ Troubleshoot Play To

☑ Review what you're recording in Windows Media Center

☑ Degunk Windows Media Center

You've already organized your media files into folders and subfolders, looked for duplicate files, learned how to place media to avoid duplicates, and incorporated Public folders for sharing (Chapter 4). You've deleted unwanted and unnecessary media data (Chapter 3). You've learned how to configure sharing over your network, how to secure that network, and how to create a homegroup (Chapter 10). We're not going to go over all of that again here, so if you're skipping around (shame on you!), you'll have to review those chapters to see what you missed; we don't want to rehash all of that. What we want to do here is degunk the media *programs* you use and resolve the problems that occur while using them.

You are painfully aware of the problems you have. Some files won't play in a particular media player because they are not the right "format." For instance, you can't play the movie *Avatar*, which you purchased from iTunes, using Zune or Windows Media Player. Some files are "protected" because you rented them from a third party via a subscription service, and won't play, period, because you no longer subscribe to that service (although this is becoming a less common problem lately). You have too many playlists or not enough. You have too many computers authorized to play media you've obtained online and are unable to add your new Windows 7 PC to the list. You have not backed up your media properly. You're worried about "media rights" and "licenses" and don't know where yours are or what would happen if you lost them. You've set up a homegroup and enabled media streaming, but you still can't get Play To to work. You don't have all of your album art. You've filled up your entire hard drive with 30 recordings of *Star Trek* when you really only intended to record one. Ugh.

Media programs created mostly to play music get no props from me for being "smart." They do not manage themselves by looking for duplicates and suggesting what they are, where they are, or why you have them (much less what to do about them); they show the same album twice if they've found it both on the network and in your personal folder (see Figure 11-1). They may not obtain album art automatically. They seem to resist you even harder when you aren't online.

It's not just music-based programs like Windows Media Player, Zune, or iTunes that you'll have trouble with. You'll likely have issues with Windows Media Center too, if you use it to record TV. The default record settings are to record everything, even reruns. You have to dig deep into the settings to tell Media Center how much space you're willing to allot to it, how to record your shows, and how long to keep them. Although there's more to Media Center than TV, for the most part, this is where the gunk is. Once you're there, though, you'll find other places to degunk, and I'll help get you started. You'll want to go through all of the settings there to take control of Media Center, including how much hard drive space to allot to recordings, where to save those recordings, and more.

NOTE   There are less common issues you'll encounter that we don't have space to address. These can involve codecs (software used to encode and decode compressed media files) and undecipherable error messages that seemingly appear out of nowhere, among other things. When you encounter these rare problems, perform a web search for answers.

FIGURE 11-1   Music players including Zune, Media Player, Media Center, and iTunes will show duplicates in your media library without even noticing them.

General Media Degunking

When you purchase software, you can always expect an update sooner or later. Some applications require updates regularly, like antivirus and antispyware software, while others require updates only a few times a year (or less). You should get these updates when they are offered, for several reasons: they make the software more secure, repair known problems, and oftentimes offer a new interface and/or new features. This is certainly the case with Media Player updates, although iTunes updates seem to be less dramatic. One of the first things involved in general degunking is to check for these updates.

You also need to uninstall media players you don't use or don't like. If you tried iTunes but don't like it, why fight all of those pop-ups about updates? Why bother with making sure it doesn't start when Windows does, or that it isn't hogging disk space or system resources? You can uninstall it, along with anything else that tagged along with it, like Safari or Mobile Me.

After you are sure you have the latest version of your media player(s) and only the one(s) you want to use available, you'll want to review things you've created, specifically, playlists. Some playlists may no longer be needed, such as the one you created simply to burn an audio CD for your car. You'll be surprised how many playlists you have that you no longer need. With fewer playlists, your interface will appear sleeker and cleaner, and you'll be able to find what you want, faster.

And finally, you'll want to back up your media licenses and understand how to restore them if needed, and how to deauthorize computers you no longer use and authorize only the ones that you do use. These things only apply if you purchase media online.

Get Updates for All of Your Media Players

You may have multiple media players. You may use Windows Media Player or Windows Media Center; both of these come with Windows 7. You may have iTunes or Zune if you have their compatible devices. Beyond that, you may have something like what's shown in Figure 11-2, a media player just for managing audiobooks. This one is from Audible. Notice I've pulled up the Options dialog box to show that you can use the Audible interface to manage your audiobooks, but if you'd rather, you can opt to play those books using Windows Media Player. Most media players, even simple ones, offer some way to configure at least a few settings.

To see if you have the latest version of any media player, locate a Help tab or menu, and then look for something like Check for Player Updates or Check for Updates. If you don't see any tabs, press the ALT key on the keyboard. Sometimes, this offers familiar options, as shown in Figure 11-3. If you can't find an update option under a Help menu, check Settings or something similar. Alternately, you may have to go to the manufacturer's web site to obtain updates.

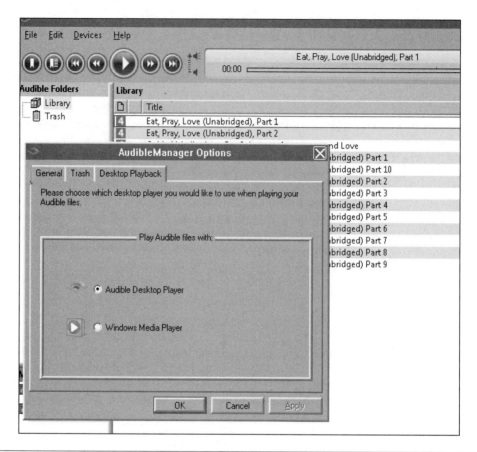

FIGURE 11-2   Think outside the box to determine all of the media players you use.

You can also update your player to include album art. If you aren't seeing album art (or you aren't seeing much of it), you need to tell the player to get it. One way to update an album is to right-click it and tell the player to update the file. Figure 11-4 shows an example using Windows Media Player. Figure 11-5 shows the option using Zune software. (Oddly, on my computer, the album art is missing from Windows Media Player but available from the Zune software.)

Of course, you'll find options to get album art and other data automatically in the player's settings or options dialog boxes. In iTunes, click Advanced | Get Album Artwork. In Windows Media Player, press ALT on the keyboard, click Tools | Options, click the Privacy tab, and check the desired options. For the most part, you want to check Display Media Information from the Internet and Update Music Files by Retrieving Media Info from the Internet. While you're there, opt to download media rights and licenses automatically too.

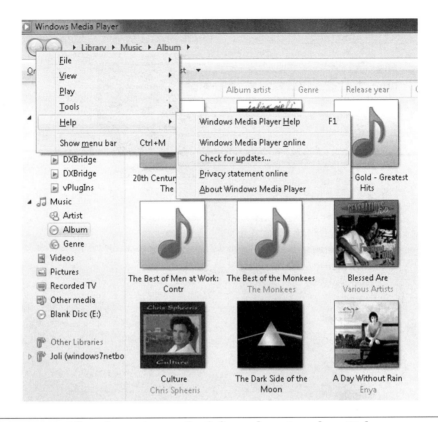

FIGURE 11-3   Often the option to check for updates is under a Help menu.

FIGURE 11-4   You can update album information by right-clicking it and selecting the appropriate option.

FIGURE 11-5   The command to get additional information about an album is almost always available with a right-click.

Get Rid of Media Players You Don't Use

You are likely aware of the problems that occur when multiple media players vie for control of your media. They're always asking if they can be the "default" player; they always want to know what types of files they should be in control of and play without prompting or permission. A specific program may open when you connect a device even if you never use that program, requiring you to close it every time you connect the device. And there are the dreaded pop-ups for updating that unused program along with other tag-along software. One way to stop these things from happening is to uninstall the software you do not use. You do this from Control Panel (see Figure 11-6).

NOTE   For more information on removing unwanted data and programs, see Chapter 3.

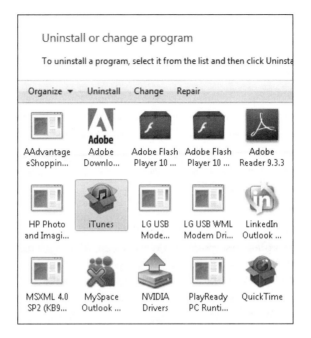

FIGURE 11-6   Uninstall media players you don't use.

TIP   Before uninstalling media players like iTunes, deauthorize the computer. Generally, you can only authorize a specific number of devices, so you always want to deauthorize those you don't need or use. In iTunes, click the Store tab. (You may find other deauthorize options under other tabs too. For instance, you deauthorize an Audible.com account in iTunes under the Advanced tab.)

Review and Clean Up Your Playlists

Now that you're down to the bare minimum player-wise, and you've already organized and managed your media in prior tasks, let's put our focus into playlists. Playlists give you control of your music. You use playlists to organize music, play music, and create music montages, including creating lists of songs you want to burn to CDs. You can create playlists based on mood, genre, artist, rating, date played, date added, and more. Unfortunately, your playlists *list* can become quite a mess. Figure 11-7 shows a few of my mostly unwanted playlists in iTunes. To delete a playlist, you generally right-click it and choose Delete.

NOTE   When you delete playlists, you don't delete the songs in them from your library. You only delete the playlist itself.

FIGURE 11-7   Watch your list of playlists and delete any playlist you no longer need.

While we're on the subject of playlists, you should be taking advantage of auto playlists. Auto playlists are a good way to quickly create playlists that match criteria you set, and that change automatically based on your listening preferences and how and when you obtain music. For instance, you can create an auto playlist that only plays songs you've listened to 100 or more times, and you could name this playlist My Favorite Tunes. Each time a new song reaches that threshold, it would be added automatically to the playlist. You can also create auto playlists based on a song's characteristics, including:

- Date added to a library
- Total count on weekdays
- Total count on weekends
- File size
- Length
- Title (and more)

To create an auto playlist in Windows Media Player, follow these steps (creating auto playlists in other players is similar):

1. In Windows Media Player, in the Music Library, click the arrow beside Create Playlist.
2. Click Create Auto Playlist.
3. Name the auto playlist accordingly (such as My Most Recent Music, as shown in Figure 11-8).
4. Under Create an Auto Playlist That Includes the Following, click Click Here to Add Criteria.
5. Select a criteria from the list. I'll opt for any music obtained in the last 30 days.
6. Configure additional attributes as desired.
7. Click OK.
8. Locate the new playlist under Auto Playlists (it should be highlighted).
9. Check out the songs in the list. Continue to edit and create new auto playlists to organize your library.

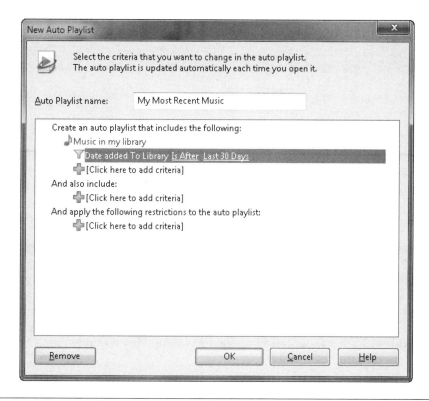

FIGURE 11-8   Auto playlists are automatically updated and are "smart."

Work with and Troubleshoot Media Licenses and/or Media

To play the music you've downloaded from legitimate sites on the Internet, you generally have to have a license for each track you want to play or you have to "authorize" the computer as one of the devices that you want to use to manage your media. In the latter case, files you download from the music store are encoded in such a way that they will only play on an authorized computer. (This is not usually true of CDs you own and copy to your PC, but is certainly true of subscription and for purchase media services.) The licenses and authorizations allow you to play the downloaded music on your PC, burn it to a CD, or copy it to a digital music player. By default, Windows Media Player and other players download these rights automatically. The option to do this in Windows Media Player is under Tools | Options, on the Privacy tab: Download Usage Rights Automatically when I Play or Sync a File. If you're having problems with rights management, make sure this is checked first.

If for some reason your media player can't find a valid license or authorization, if you never obtained the required media rights, or if you try to play media you've purchased with one program (iTunes) on another (Zune or Windows Media Player),

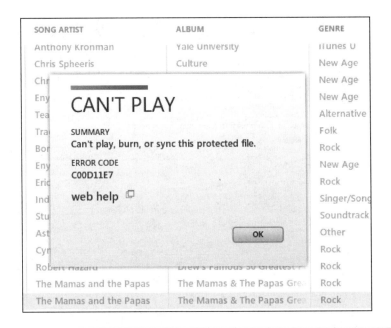

FIGURE 11-9   Zune can't play media obtained from iTunes.

you'll get an error message. Examples of this are shown in Figures 11-9 and 11-10. You'll have to make adjustments when this happens. You can opt to play the file in its native program, or try to obtain the rights, codecs, or other items necessary to play it. You may even have to convert the file to a different file format! The point is, a license is required to play media, and media obtained in iTunes plays in iTunes, music obtained from Zune Marketplace plays in Zune software, and so on.

Can you imagine what problems could occur if you lost your licenses or your media? For the most part, you can't say, "Hey, Walmart. Hey iTunes. Hey Microsoft. I lost all of my music in a computer crash, but I bought a lot of music from you. Can you restore my licenses and my music? I'd like to download it all again and make my media library as good as new." They can't and they won't. Because of this, you have to know how to back up and restore your music (which includes your licenses), should the issue ever arise.

FIGURE 11-10   Windows Media Player can't play media obtained from iTunes.

GunkBuster's Notebook: Use Third-Party Conversion Software

There are lots of third-party programs available that allow you to convert a file from one file type to another. If you really want a specific file to play in a program that's not compatible, you can almost always force it to happen.

Here's an example. You've purchased an audio book online from a third party. It won't play on your Sony Walkman MP3 player because it's not an MP3 file; it's an AA file (Audible audio book). MP3 devices won't play AA files, and thus your poor little Walkman isn't up to the task. You don't have an i-device (which can play it), and you don't want to burn it to a CD (which is an option) because you don't have a mobile CD player. You want to listen to that audio book at the gym, on your Sony Walkman, and you should be able to. You purchased the book, after all. If you really want to play that audio book on your MP3 player, you can make it happen by converting it using third-party software. Not everyone will be happy about this, mind you, particularly the audio book's digital rights owner. However, that doesn't mean it can't be done with the proper software.

And here's something else to consider. When you burn encrypted media to a CD, the music (or book or audio file) is unencrypted. Once unencrypted, you can rip the CD back to another computer. Of course, music stores have caught on to this, and only allow you to burn a track to a CD so many times, but hey, it's a workaround if you need it.

If you're interested, I suggest you visit www.amazon.com, search for digital music conversion software, and see what others are buying, what they've written about it, and how they've rated it.

Now, you used to be able to back up your *licenses* in Windows Media Player. You can't do that in Windows Media Player 11 or 12. Besides, they're called "media rights" or some such thing now anyway, and the entire backup feature is gone. Kaput.

You've never been able to back up licenses or rights in iTunes. No surprise there. And you can't redownload something you've already downloaded (without pulling out all the stops at Apple and getting permission to do it, which is nearly impossible), leaving you in a lurch should you ever lose your library. (However, you can easily back up your library from File | Library | Back Up to Disc.)

And as far as Zune is concerned: You can't back up media rights, period. You can, however, easily redownload protected songs and videos from Zune Marketplace as long as the items in question are still part of Zune Marketplace *and* either or both of the following is the case:

- Your Zune Pass subscription is active.
- You bought the media that you're restoring.

Well, good luck with that. Your best option for any of these three players or any other you use is to back up your media files manually now, and immediately after obtaining media from now on. You can always restore your media manually by copying your media back to the proper folders, and then look for some option to restore your licenses, if that exists or is necessary.

Regarding error messages and restoring media after a computer crash: if you see an error message that indicates you're missing rights for a file, and you had these rights previously, you might be able to resolve the problem by restoring your media usage rights. You have several options to do so:

- If you obtained the file from an online store, the store might offer media usage rights (license) restoration. It may not. If it does, you may need to type in a username and password and then navigate to an option to restore those rights. Look around for an option name such as computer authorization, library restoration, or license synchronization. Although other online stores are similar, here's how to restore media rights with Zune:
  1. Sign in to Zune Marketplace.
  2. Click Settings | Account.
  3. Click Purchase History or Subscription History, depending on the type of content you want to restore.
  4. Select Songs, Videos, or Music videos, as appropriate.
  5. Select the items whose rights need to be restored.
  6. Click Download for one or multiple items. Click Restore All to get them all.
- If the file you're lacking rights for is a song you ripped from a CD with the **Copy Protect Music** option turned on, you might be able to restore your usage rights by playing the file. You will be prompted to connect to a Microsoft web page that explains how to restore your rights a limited number of times.
- You may be able to do a System Restore on Windows 7 if something simply went wonky with your media. If, on Monday, all was well, and on Tuesday, all was not well, try a System Restore. It just may work.

Again, your best bet is to back up your media regularly. I back up my media to an external drive and an iPad, and back up compatible media to a Sony Walkman. There are lots of ways to back up media, though, and Chapter 14 discusses several of these ways. For now, right-click your Music folder, select everything, and then drag and drop the media to another disk drive. Choose Copy. If you've moved your music to the Public folders, back up those too. It's okay for now if your backup device is a simple flash drive; just get it backed up now.

Authorize or Deauthorize Computers to Play Media

Media services allow you to download and play media using their service on a specific number of computers and devices. When you purchase media from iTunes, for instance, you can play it on up to five computers that you choose (authorize). The media on these computers can be synced with an iPod, iPad, or iPhone (or a combination of these).

You can also sync or stream to an Apple TV. When you purchase media from Zune Marketplace, you can download and play music on up to three computers. You can then sync that with your Zune music player. When it comes to other music services, well, you'll just have to check. Rhapsody offers authorization on three PCs. Audible offers authorization of up to four computers and three portable devices.

Whatever the case (and I don't want to research all of this and list who allows what—you can figure that out), you authorize the computers you want to use, and when you no longer need a particular computer to be authorized, you deauthorize it. Some people make the mistake of authorizing too many PCs or devices, or sell a computer without deauthorizing it, and get into trouble. You can easily authorize or deauthorize devices from the program. Where that option is depends on the program. iTunes is shown in Figure 11-11.

Troubleshoot Play To

Windows 7, in combination with other Windows 7 machines and compatible devices, homegroups, and Windows Media Player, enables you to stream media throughout your home and on compatible media devices. There are some settings to configure. You can probably already tell you'll have problems setting that up; there are too many variables.

FIGURE 11-11   Always deauthorize a computer before selling it or putting it out to pasture.

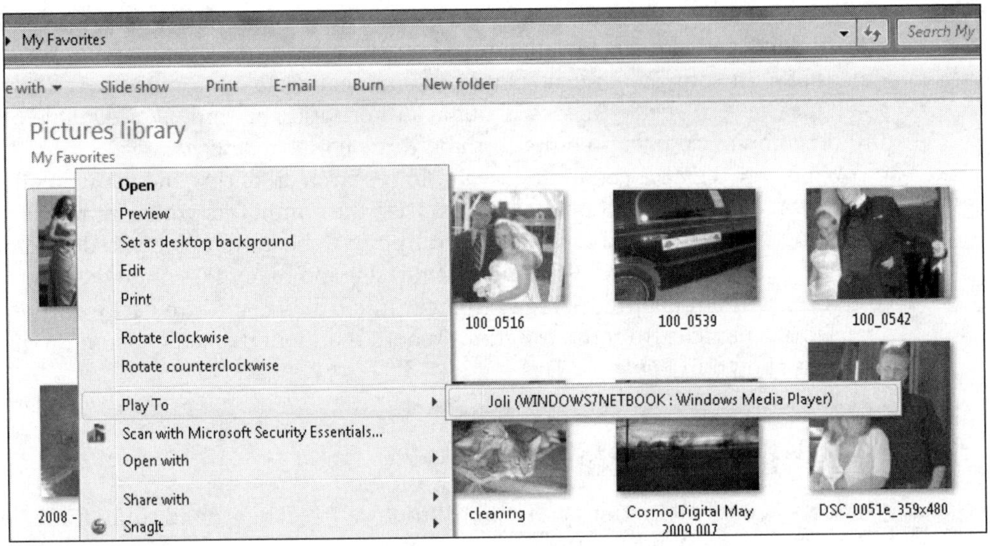

FIGURE 11-12 Play To lets you control media from one place while playing it
at another.

Once the Play To feature is set up, though, it's totally awesome. You can sit at
one computer, right-click any media, and choose Play To from the context menu.
Then, you can choose the device or computer you want to play it on. And it's not
just music and video, it's pictures too, as shown in Figure 11-12.

If you're having trouble with Play To, and most people do initially, here's a
checklist of things to do:

1. Set up a homegroup. Add your other Windows 7 PCs to it. See Chapter 10.
2. Set up media streaming:
   a. In the Network and Sharing Center, click Change Advanced Sharing Settings.
   b. Under Media Streaming, turn Media Streaming on, and then choose your
      media streaming options.
   c. Allow and configure settings for devices you want the option to stream to. See
      Figure 11-13.
   d. Click OK and then Save Changes.
3. In Windows Media Player on all devices:
   a. Click Stream and select the options to allow remote control and allow devices
      to stream media. See Figure 11-14.
   b. When prompted, opt to allow this over the local network.
4. To test the settings:
   a. Right-click any song, video, or picture.
   b. Click Play To and choose the device to play the media to. See Figure 11-15.

Choose media streaming options for computers and devices

Name your media library: Joli
Choose default settings...

Show devices on: [Local network ▼]   [Allow All]   [Block All]

Media programs on this PC and remote connections...   Customize...   [Allowed ▼]
Allowed access using default settings.

compaq   [Allowed ▼]
Allowed access using default settings.

Joli (WINDOWS7NETBOOK : Windows Media Player)   [Allowed ▼]
Allowed access using customized streaming preferences.

WINDOWS7UK   [Allowed ▼]
Allowed access using default settings.

All devices are allowed to access your shared media.

Choose homegroup and sharing options
Choose power options
Tell me more about media streaming
Read the privacy statement online

FIGURE 11-13   You are in control of what devices can receive streaming media.

Windows Media Player

◄ ► Library ► Music ► Artist ► The Allman Brothers Band

Organize ▼   Stream ▼   Create playlist ▼

Allow Internet access to home media...
✓ Allow remote control of my Player...
✓ Automatically allow devices to play my media...

Library
Playlists
   Lee   More streaming options...
   My

FIGURE 11-14   You must tell Media Player you want to stream and receive
streamed media.

Play all
Play
Play next
Play to   ►   Joli (WINDOWS7NETBOOK : Windows Media Player)
Add to   ►   Joli (WINDOWS7UK : Windows Media Player)
Edit
Rate   ►
Find album info

FIGURE 11-15   You can set up several devices to accept media streaming or to
stream it.

Degunk Windows Media Center

Media Center is Media Player's partner in crime. It's the smarter, more flexible one. It can do more and is more capable. With it and the right hardware, you can watch, record, pause, stop, rewind, and ultimately fast-forward (previously paused) live television, for instance. If you don't have a TV tuner, you can watch Internet TV. You can keep up with your favorite sports teams. You can also view all of your pictures and compatible videos, listen to all of your compatible music, and even watch movies from Netflix, among other things. Figure 11-16 shows my Instant Queue in Media Center, obtained using the Netflix feature under Movies.

If you have used Media Center before or are using it regularly, you need to see what you can do about degunking it. Its default settings are not what you'd want to choose to minimize gunk. As an example, I'm betting that when you opt to record a TV series, you don't want to record the new shows *and the reruns*, which is the default setting, shown in Figure 11-17.

If you don't change this, or if you did not change it the first time you set up a series recording, you may be in for a big surprise! You may have a hard drive full of recorded TV! Because not only will Media Center record and record and record, it will continue to record until "space is needed." And again, by default, it'll fill up your entire hard drive before it stops (see Figure 11-18). My hard drive on this machine is 286GB. You simply don't want that.

FIGURE 11-16   There's a lot to Media Center you may not have explored, like Netflix.

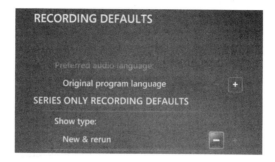

FIGURE 11-17   The default setting for recording TV is to record new shows and all reruns until space is needed.

NOTE   If you use Media Center and record lots of TV, consider a computer you can dedicate solely to it. This can be quite useful and make media easier to manage (and offer lots of space to record and keep whatever you want).

It's not just recorded television, though; there are lots of settings you need to review. Of course, you need to make changes to how television records and how much space you're willing to allot to it, but there are other areas to consider. Here are some more of the default settings:

- At midnight each night, Media Center will automatically look online for album art, Media Center data, and information about DVDs, movies, and more.

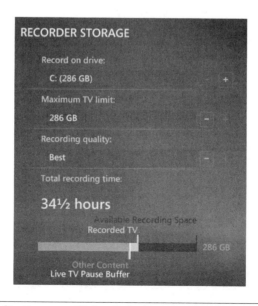

FIGURE 11-18   Media Center will, by default, continue recording until your entire hard drive is full.

- Audio settings are set automatically, but you can change them for DVDs and choose between Theater, Normal, or Night modes.
- There are no media extenders set up on your network even if you have them. You have to set them up manually.
- Media libraries only include data from common places, like your personal and Public folders. If you keep data elsewhere, you must tell Media Center about it.
- You can sync from Media Center to a portable device. You can set up syncing in Media Center after connecting the device.
- The TV "Guide" has categories you can use to search for specific shows. It's kind of hidden and you may have missed it.

Because recorded TV causes the most gunk, if you've ever recorded even a single TV show using Media Center, you absolutely must check out what you have saved. Although you can see what you've recorded by opening the Recorded TV folder, it's best to review it in Media Center, so that you can change the settings quickly if necessary:

1. In Media Center, scroll to TV and click Recorded TV.
2. Note how much is recorded already. An example is shown in Figure 11-19.
3. For any item, right-click and choose Settings.
4. In Settings, click TV. (Later you'll return here and work through the other options.)
5. Click Recorder and then Recording Defaults. Consider changing the following to degunk Media Center:
   a. Keep: If possible, choose 1 Week or Until I Watch.
   b. Quality: If you don't need the Best setting for quality, consider Better or Good. You'll be able to record more TV because the lower the quality, the smaller the file size.
   c. Show type: Do not record reruns. Consider New Only.
   d. Keep up to: Consider 2, 3, or 7 recordings to keep recorded TV from filling up your hard drive with recordings you'll never watch.
   e. Click Save.
6. Click Recorder Storage. Consider changing the following to degunk Media Center:
   a. Record on drive: If possible, connect an external drive and save media to that drive.
   b. Maximum TV limit: Change this setting so that no more than half of your hard drive can be used to store recorded TV.
   c. Recording quality: Consider Good or Better to record more shows with less hard drive space.
   d. Click Save.
7. Click Media Libraries. If you record TV on another PC and want to access that library, click Add Folders to Library. Follow the prompts to locate the folder to add. See Figure 11-20.
8. If you've found out that you are recording TV and do not want to record anything, click Clear Recording Schedule. Click Yes to confirm.

FIGURE 11-19   If you've ever recorded anything, you should check out the Recorded TV section of Media Center.

9. Click the Back button enough times to return to the main Settings screen. Repeat these steps with the other options, General, Pictures, Music, DVD, and so forth. See Figure 11-21.

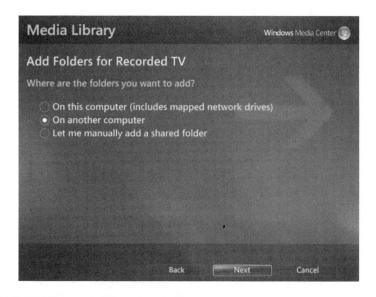

FIGURE 11-20   You can always tell Media Center to look for other libraries of data on this computer or another.

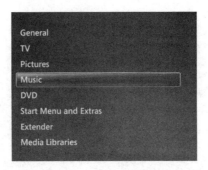

FIGURE 11-21   You can configure settings for all parts of Media Center.

As you continue to work in Media Center, exploring all of the categories, options, and features, keep degunking in mind. Delete videos, movies, pictures, and music you'll never watch or listen to, or move that data off your PC onto an external drive. Note how different Media Center is from Media Player when you do this. If you like Media Center better, make the switch. You may never have to use Media Player again if you don't want to.

Summing Up

Although there's no way I could ever address in a single chapter all of the things that could gunk up your machine with regard to media, this chapter should certainly get you off on the right foot. For the most part, you want to stay on top of the media you acquire, deleting it or archiving it when necessary and on a schedule. You should keep your media players up to date, and uninstall players you don't use.

With that done, you can organize the music you want to keep with playlists, both manual and auto. You can create playlists that change when your media does, such as the playlist I created to include only the music I've acquired in the past 30 days. That auto playlist will always be relevant.

Beyond that, you need to back up your media and licenses, and have a plan in place should something happen to either. This depends, of course, on what media player you've selected and what the rules are regarding it. Zune, iTunes, and Windows Media Player all function differently here. In that same vein, you should also remember to deauthorize any computer you don't need to manage media from an online source.

Finally, you'll want to explore Play To and Media Center. Both are great features and should be part of any media setup. Regarding Media Center, you'll have to work hard to keep it gunk-free, especially if you record TV. The settings aren't configured in the best non-gunking-up manner, and you need to change them.

12

Optimize Syncing

Degunking Checklist:

☑ Explore Device Stage

☑ Set up a sync partnership

☑ Troubleshoot sync partnerships

☑ Manually sync a generic MP3 player and review automatic sync options

☑ Troubleshoot syncing in Windows Media Player

☑ Inventory third-party sync applications

☑ Cull unwanted devices and sync software

☑ Review and degunk third-party sync settings

You have devices you connect to your computer that, once connected, depending on the device and the settings you have previously (and likely haphazardly) configured, cause various applications, dialog boxes, and windows to open. I'm betting much of this is both a nuisance and unnecessary. Gunk.

Once you've dealt with the unnecessary tasks involved with connecting devices (closing windows, applications, and/or dialog boxes, for instance), a software program may automatically open and sync the device for you (as is the case with iTunes and Zune software). What syncs may or may not be optimal, especially if your device has limited hard drive space. Data may be removed you want to keep, or things may be kept you no longer want. Gunk.

If you aren't automatically syncing devices (to avoid the hassle that seems to come along with it), you are probably dragging and dropping files, likely to add music to a generic MP3 player or flash drive. This is time consuming and ineffective, especially if you never set up automatic syncing after you've done it once. As noted in Chapter 11, you may also use a media-specific program like Audible for audiobooks, and you may complicate all of this when you use specific software to sync your mobile phone, digital camera, or video recorder. This can all add up to stress for you, especially when these programs cross paths and try to do the work of the other or constantly prompt (vie) for default status.

While I do have doubts about what you sync and how (and perhaps even why), I have no doubt that you have sync gunk. No matter how you've configured your devices so far, there's likely something you can do to improve those configurations.

Explore Device Stage

One way to reduce gunk is to see if you can use one application to sync multiple devices. Windows 7 offers a feature that you may not be familiar with yet, called Device Stage, that can help in this regard (see Figure 12-1). Device Stage shows all devices you've connected, ever. The mobile devices that you currently have connected are darker than the rest (provided Windows has decided to play nicely with them). This makes it easy to review what's available, what's been previously installed, and what you may or may no longer need.

TIP   If you want to open Device Stage now, click Start | Devices and Printers.

Here, the Apple iPad is connected but is not darkened. That's because Microsoft doesn't play well with Apple. You can't set it up to sync through Windows; you have to use iTunes. You'll have to use iTunes to sync all your iPxx hardware, so if you're trying to get rid of iPxx and iTunes gunk via Device Stage, forget about it. The Walkman is darkened and connected, as is the Canon video camera. You may see other things in the window, including phones, faxes, printers, and scanners. And, you may see problem areas, as shown in Figure 12-2.

NOTE   If you're having a problem syncing through iTunes, Zune, or some other specific device's software, refer to the directions and help files to resolve those problems. Here, we're going to focus on Windows 7 syncing and sync options.

If Device Stage recognizes your device and darkens it when you connect it, you may be able to use Device Stage and Windows 7 to perform the syncing tasks for that device. If this is possible, you can get rid of that device's software by uninstalling it.

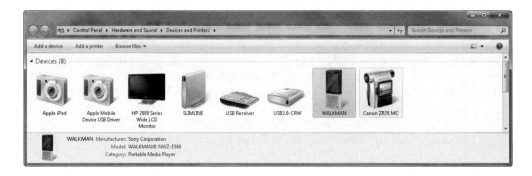

FIGURE 12-1   Device Stage is a feature of Windows 7 that lets you review your devices and manage those that are compatible with Windows 7.

Canon ZR70 MC

FIGURE 12-2   If there's a problem with a device, you'll see a yellow exclamation point.

This enables you to have one less syncing application vying for control, opening unnecessarily, or running in the background using system resources. If you can make Device Stage work for several devices, you can get rid of a lot of gunk.

Set Up a Sync Partnership in Device Stage

You can set up compatible devices to sync using resources included with Windows 7 from Device Stage. To get started, connect a device and double-click it. Figure 12-3 shows what happens when I double-click the icon for my Sony Walkman. Note the option to set up a sync partnership.

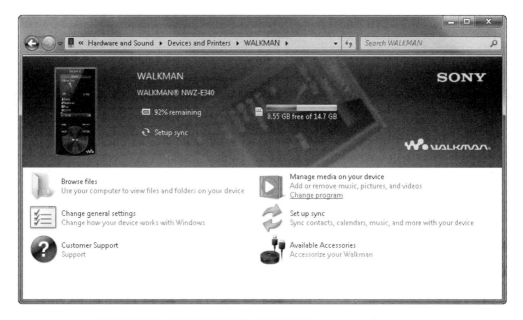

FIGURE 12-3   If your device is compatible, you can set up a sync partnership in Windows 7 and forgo any third-party software.

To set up a sync partnership using Device Stage:

1. Connect the device.
2. Close any dialog boxes or programs that open automatically.
3. Click Start | Devices and Printers.
4. Double-click the device to set up syncing with.
5. Click Set Up Sync.

CAUTION   If you double-click a device in Device Stage and you get a Properties dialog box instead of the option to set up syncing, your device isn't supported. You'll have to continue using third-party software or search for a workaround.

6. Decide what you want to sync and select it. In my case, I'll only sync music, as shown in Figure 12-4.

NOTE   What you see in Figure 12-4 depends on the type of device you're trying to sync. If it's a supported phone, you'll likely see Contacts, Calendar, and other options.

7. Click Settings.
8. You can opt to sync as much as possible, if desired. I suggest you handpick what to sync (see Figure 12-5):
   a. Click Sync with Music Folders, Playlists, or Songs That I Select.
   b. Click Add Music Folders.
   c. Click OK.
9. Click Sync Now.

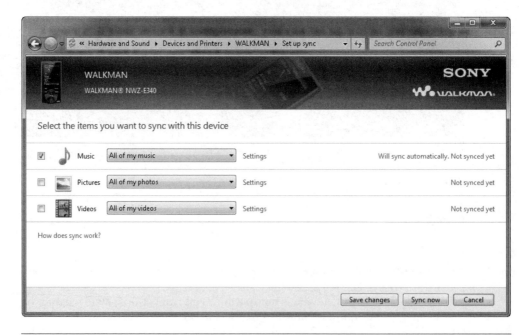

FIGURE 12-4   Decide what to sync, then click Settings.

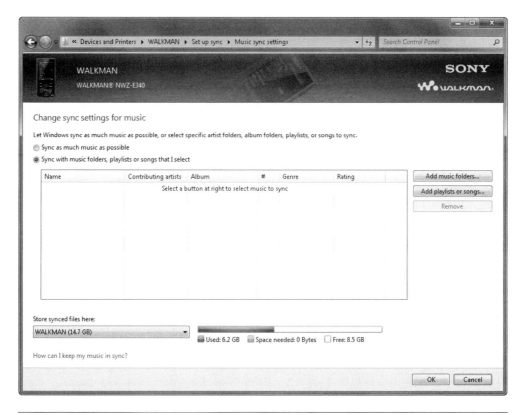

FIGURE 12-5   Handpick what to sync when you first set up a sync partnership to avoid gunk on your device.

Troubleshoot Partnerships

Device Stage is customized for each device by the manufacturer of that device, and displays different options for different devices. If you double-click a device and get a Properties dialog box, the device isn't supported. That *usually* is not Microsoft's fault; it's generally the fault of your device's manufacturer. They have not created the software necessary, have not worked through the required channels to get it approved, and/or they want to force you to use their software and no one else's.

NOTE   If you have more than one device connected to your computer, you can have more than one instance of Device Stage open at the same time.

If you've synced the device before and are now having problems, consider the following solutions (otherwise, it's probably the case that your device is not compatible):

- The device is not connected.
- The device is connected but not turned on or charged.

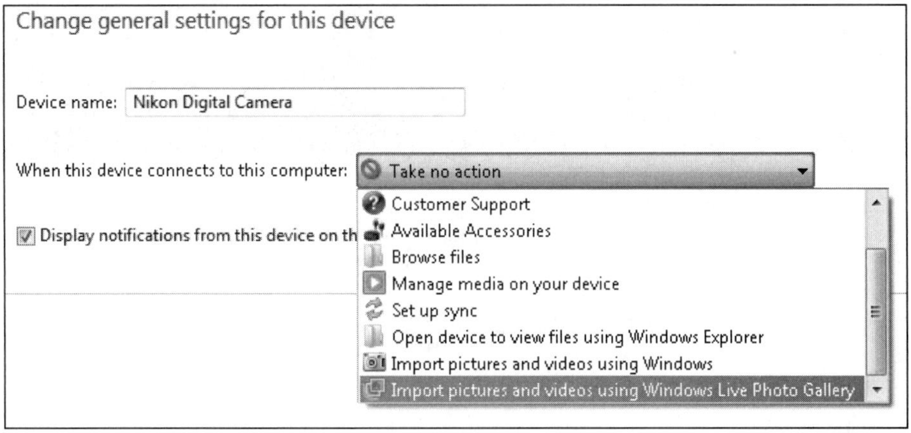

FIGURE 12-6   You can tell Device Stage what you want to happen when you connect a device.

- The device driver for the device needs to be reinstalled.
- The cable is not connected properly or the cable has been damaged.
- The general settings for the device are not set properly. See Figure 12-6. (To get here, select the device in Device Stage, and click Change General Settings.)
- You don't have the proper rights to copy the media files to a device.

NOTE   If you're experiencing a new problem, consider rebooting. If that doesn't work, try System Restore, restoring back to a time when everything worked properly.

Explore Windows Media Player

You don't have to use Device Stage to sync MP3 (and other compatible) players. You can use Windows Media Player if you'd rather. You may have noticed the Sync tab, shown in Figure 12-7. As shown here, after connecting a compatible device, you simply drag media to the Sync pane and, when ready, click Start Sync.

You can also click the small icon under the Sync tab and select Set Up Sync to configure what should sync and what should not, and to have the sync occur automatically anytime you connect the device (see Figure 12-8). You can create your own sync list, too. You can get really personal here; you can sync your favorite playlists, your most recently acquired music, music you've rated, and more. Once done, you can shuffle the media if desired, and change media priority.

FIGURE 12-7   You can use Windows Media Player to sync media.

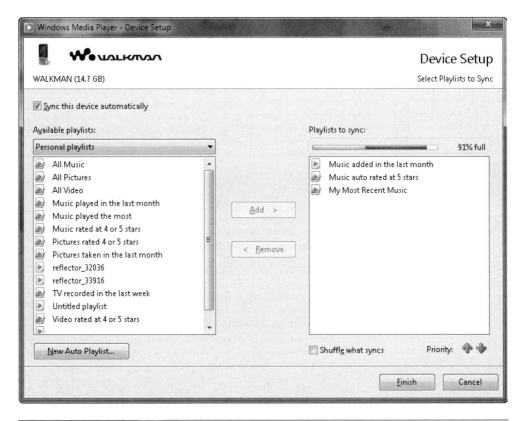

FIGURE 12-8   Media Player lets you configure how you want to sync.

GunkBuster's Notebook: Stop Windows, Dialog Boxes, and Applications from Opening when You Connect a Device

You know what happens when you connect a device (or insert media like a media card, DVD, or CD). Something always happens. A dialog box opens, an application starts, a window opens, or the CD or DVD plays. Maybe you don't want anything to happen! For instance, when I connect my iPad, I want iTunes to sync it. I don't want to view the files on it. It's aggravating for the Windows Explorer window to open, implying I can drag and drop files to my iPad, when indeed, I cannot! And every time I connect my iPad, I have to close that stupid window!

You can stop the madness. You can take control. To get started, type **AutoPlay** into the Start Search window and click AutoPlay in the results. You can then configure what you want to happen when you insert media or connect hardware. The illustration shows the options for hardware I connect.

Devices	
📷 Digital Video Device	Import video using Windows Live Photo Gallery ▼
📷 MATSUSHITA	Ask me every time ▼
📱 WALKMAN	Open Device Stage ▼
📱 Apple iPhone	Ask me every time ▼
📱 Joli's iPad	Open device to view files using Windows Explorer ▼
	📷 Import pictures and videos using Windows
Reset all defaults	📷 Import pictures and videos using Windows Live Photo Gallery
	Open device to view files using Windows Explorer
	Take no action
	❓ Ask me every time

Here, for my iPad, I'm choosing Take No Action. Whew. All of that aggravation for all of these months, gone! Work through all the options and take time now to configure them. You'll reduce the gunk.

You won't run into too many problems when syncing with Media Player. You'll have common issues as outlined earlier (including damaged cables or dead players), and you'll have the usual problems with a device not being compatible. But for the most part, syncing goes pretty smoothly. However, to cover your bases, here are a few things to consider if you run into problems:

- You can sync most audio and video files. Not all devices support all file types, though. You may have to refer to your device documentation if you're having trouble syncing a particular file type. (You may be able to convert files that aren't compatible.)

- If your device becomes full, Windows Media Player will sync what it deems your favorites, removing those you don't play often. (You can tell Media Player what your priorities are with playlists, ratings, and other settings.)
- If you have a device that supports it, you can manipulate the media on your device and sync those changes back to Media Player.
- You can sync up to 16 devices with Media Player, although your media rights may not support your copying the media you own to that many devices.
- When you delete a file from your computer, it will be deleted on the device during the next sync. If your player supports it, this works the other way too.
- Some files may have to be converted to play on the device. If that's the case, options may also become available for conversion.

Take Inventory of Third-Party Hardware and Software

If you can't set up a sync partnership in Device Stage or sync using Media Player, you'll have to rely on the third-party software that came with the device. This may be iTunes, Zune software, BlackBerry Media Sync, Verizon's V CAST Media Manager, or similar software. I wish that this were not the case and that I could give you some magical answer for simplifying your life. For the most part, I have to admit I find these programs cumbersome. It doesn't matter that it's all for the better good—media rights protections and all—what matters most is that it's a pain to use and its proprietary. I'm always extremely perturbed when I cannot drag and drop files. That's the worst.

If you're stuck with one of these devices and its related software but you have and use additional devices, you may be able to work around the problem by avoiding a specific device. For instance, if you only listen to audiobooks at the gym or only listen to music when you're jogging, you don't have to use your phone for that. You can use a compatible media player. If your problematic smartphone won't let you drag and drop files to it, upgrade to one that will, the moment your contract is up. (This will send a message to manufacturers, too: "Hey, we're simply not going to put up with this.") If you think a device isn't compatible in Device Stage because you don't have the most up-to-date drivers, get them! That may resolve your Device Stage issues.

Unfortunately, there will be times when none of these workarounds will help. When there's no other option, you have to play with the cards you're dealt. However, if you found that you could sync your mobile device with Media Player, by all means, dump the burdensome software and sell your unwanted hardware!

Dump Unwanted Hardware, Software, and Media

Look in Device Stage at all of the hardware you've connected or have connected. Take inventory. Now look around the room, in your car, in your office, and in your junk drawers. Is there anything you don't use? Anything you can recycle or sell?

Can you "trade up" to something better? If so, do it! Get rid of unwanted hardware and uninstall its resource-hogging, hard-to-use, proprietary software! Consider selling the hardware on Craig's list, donating it to a church, or giving it to your parents or kids. Just get rid of it and degunk your life. Once you've done all of that (including uninstalling the device's software, removing its cable to free up a USB port, and removing the power cable to free up an outlet), return to Device Stage, and for every item you see that you no longer have or use, right-click to delete it. Figure 12-9 shows an example. (Don't forget to remove the car charger from the glove box!)

Tweak Settings in Third-Party Media Sync Applications

I can't really address the specific problems you may have with third-party software. There are simply too many programs available for me to try to address them. Also, there are plenty of help files and user groups on the Internet to help you work through

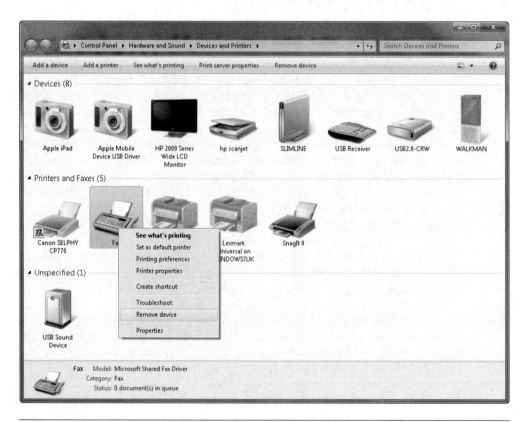

FIGURE 12-9   Delete items in Device Stage you don't need or use.

your issues. This book is about degunking anyway, so here I'd like to help you make wiser choices when you have to work with bulky software. Here are a few tips:

- Check for updates to software often. Even if the interface says no update is available, sometimes there is.
- Search the Internet for software options. If you use Roxio Media Manager, for instance, you may be able to use something else.
- Opt to sync only items you handpick. Now that your file system is organized, it should be easy to pick only the photos you want to share, the music you want to hear, and the videos you want to access on your mobile device.
- Encrypt backups when possible. Know where your backups are stored and consider making backups of your backups.
- If space is an issue, consider using standard definition videos, using lower bit rates, and rotating media you store on your device. Also, only sync calendar data if you'll actually use it. Only sync contacts if you use them. Only sync music you listen to. You get the idea.
- Create auto playlists and sync those to your mobile device. You can create playlists that contain your most recent media, your favorite songs, or other criteria you select.
- Keep your music, pictures, videos, and the like in their default folders and organized in subfolders you create. If you move your media, your software program may have a hard time finding it.
- Research your options. There is a way to use a non-Apple device with iTunes with a third-party sync application. There may be a way to use your device without its proprietary software.
- Read the user guides that came with your hardware and software.

Summing Up

I can almost guarantee you have syncing gunk. You have software and hardware you don't use, don't know how to use, don't like, or don't want. This unwanted hardware is gunking up your junk drawers and its software is gunking up your PC. You're also inundated with unwanted windows, applications, and dialog boxes when you insert media or connect hardware. You may have limited options for syncing some of your devices, and thus end up using a half-dozen programs to get the job done for everything.

You can work around some of the issues by incorporating Device Stage. If your devices are compatible, you can ditch the third-party software and use this. You can also use Windows Media Player to easily sync once, manually, or to set up sync settings for future syncs.

Finally, you can ultimately enhance how you sync by culling the programs you use, media you select, and playlists you create, and by selling or upgrading hardware you own. You may think you're stuck with proprietary, hard-to-use software, but you may not be.

13

Resolve Lingering Software and Hardware Issues

Degunking Checklist:

☑ Update software you use

☑ Get rid of unwanted update-related pop-ups

☑ Check the Action Center for solutions regularly

☑ Get rid of unwanted Action Center pop-up notifications

☑ Use Program Compatibility Mode to run an older program

☑ Check out DirectX Diagnostic Tool

☑ Troubleshoot device driver problems

☑ Upgrade hardware when you can

☑ Tweak System Restore settings

☑ Repair with the Windows 7 DVD

☑ Physically clean your PC

We're getting down to the wire here; you've been a diligent degunker and I'm proud of you. You've hung out, held on, and made some hard decisions with regard to data, programs, and security (among other things). You've cleaned the house, you've cleaned the garage, and you've taken the trash to the curb. You've organized and secured what you want to keep, and are maintaining your computer well and on a schedule. Great job!

In this last chapter on degunking (Chapter 14 is more about securing your data than degunking), you'll do some final tweaking. You'll sweep the bugs from under the rug and get rid of that nagging little bit of gunk you have yet to deal with. This is the stuff you thought would have been taken care of by now through previous degunking efforts but hasn't been; it's the dust in the corners.

You probably know what still bothers you—pop-up messages about updates to third-party software, pop-ups from the Action Center nagging you to do this or check that, older software that doesn't work quite right, hardware that isn't completely compatible, and error messages you've been unable to resolve. Don't worry; you can fix all of that. And after you finish this chapter, you can rest easy. Your only remaining task involves setting up a redundant backup system.

Finalize Software Degunking

By now, the only software you should have installed on your computer is software you use. If you still have software installed that you don't use, uninstall it now......long pause...... Did you get rid of it? Okay, with that done, you have permission to continue.

Now that you have only the programs you want installed on your computer, let's tweak those for ultimate performance. There are several options for increasing performance, many of which you've already worked through if you've followed this book from start to finish, but for a final touch, you need to update your software. Most of the problems you could potentially encounter with software can be prevented through updates, and problems you have now can often be resolved. With that done, you'll want to get rid of unwanted pop-ups about updates you don't want or need; those can get rather cumbersome and annoying.

After you've updated your software, you should check the Action Center once more (and preferably once a month or so from here on out), to see if there are any solutions to problems your computer has encountered. While you're there, you can also opt out of pop-ups from the Action Center, if they bother you. You can tell the Action Center you don't want to be bothered with notifications about Windows Update, Internet security settings, spyware, and related protection (and more), and thus reduce the remaining annoyances you have with your PC.

If software and computer updates don't resolve your problems, and you can't find a suitable replacement for a program you use often that is still causing you fits, you can opt to run the offending program in a different operating system environment (using Program Compatibility Mode). That should work out any lingering kinks with software. Finally, we'll check out a feature of Windows 7 you have probably never heard of, DirectX Diagnostic Tool (Dxdiag), and explore a few additional options there for making multimedia games and related hardware run a little better.

Update Software You Use

You can rest assured that any problem you're having with third-party software is also being experienced by hundreds if not thousands of other users. Thus, software companies know about the problems and try hard to fix them. Almost all the time, then, a software update will resolve the problems you're having with third-party software. Even if you aren't having issues, though, updates can help secure a program, offer you new features, or make the tasks you perform easier to complete.

Generally, you can check for updates using a Help tab, Help menu, Preferences tab, Settings tab, or similar option from inside a software program. Look for an option named About *Software Name*, too. This option typically shows what version of the software you have, which is useful to know when you are checking whether you have the latest software update. The Check for Updates option in Audible Download Manager is shown in Figure 13-1. There may or may not be an update available.

If you don't see an update, you should visit the software manufacturer's web site. Do this a few times a year, whatever the case. You may find that while a free update is not available, there is an update (or an upgrade) you can purchase. In many instances, especially if you use a program daily or weekly, paying for an update is a very good idea simply for access to the newest features and security options.

Deal with Unwanted Update Notifications

There's another side to the updating story. The ugly side. A single program can generate tons of pop-ups over its lifetime. These pop-ups can be incredibly annoying. What's worse is that if you simply dismiss them or don't click on them, they go away, only to return tomorrow, next week, or next month. It seems to be way too often that Adobe Reader has an update, that Java something or other has an update, that QuickTime has an update, or that printer software has an update. Often, we simply don't care because we use the program so rarely. Even if the update is

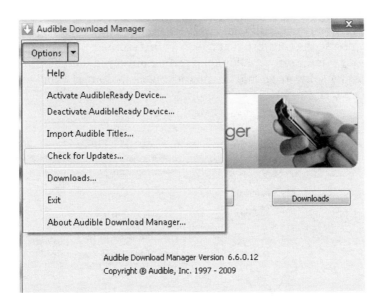

FIGURE 13-1   Look for a Help or an Options menu and see if there's an option to check for updates.

security-related, we don't care because we have antivirus software protecting us. Stop reminding me! Leave me alone! So how do you manage this inconvenience? Well, there are several ways.

CAUTION   I have a computer that is not connected to the Internet. It never has been. At one point I installed a printer on it, along with the printer software. Every six weeks, a pop-up appears telling me an update is available. Seriously, there's no way for that program to know that, having never been connected to the Internet! This is more than annoying, it's deceptive and deceitful. This makes me want to return that printer!

The first way to disable unwanted update notification pop-ups is to open the program and look for a setting you can disable regarding them. Figure 13-2 shows that setting in QuickTime.

The second way to avoid these annoying update notices is to register your product and opt out of updates from the web site. This is not an ideal solution, because registering often causes you more headaches in the form of spam, but it's worth a try if you simply can't get your printer software to stop nagging you about installing a new update now and again.

Finally, you can uninstall the update *program* from Control Panel. Some software and hardware come with this, as is shown in Figure 13-3. If you do this, you should still be able to check for updates manually, at your convenience, and avoid unwanted pop-ups. (Be diligent though; you want updates for software you use regularly!)

If none of these options works and you don't use the software, uninstall it. Not many people actually use the software that comes with a printer or a camera. (Most do use the software that comes with a scanner.) However, if you find you don't use your printer software but keep getting printer update notifications, uninstalling the printer software should do the trick. Look to Control Panel to locate unwanted software (see Chapter 3).

FIGURE 13-2   Ah, sweet relief! Opt out of unwanted software updates.

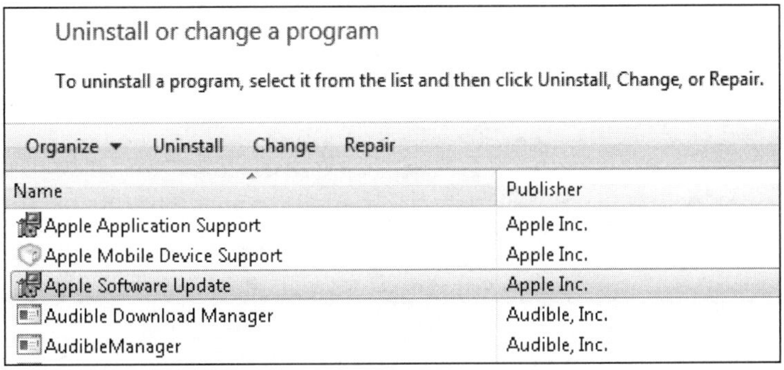

Uninstall or change a program

To uninstall a program, select it from the list and then click Uninstall, Change, or Repair.

Organize ▾ Uninstall Change Repair	
Name	Publisher
Apple Application Support	Apple Inc.
Apple Mobile Device Support	Apple Inc.
Apple Software Update	Apple Inc.
Audible Download Manager	Audible, Inc.
AudibleManager	Audible, Inc.

FIGURE 13-3   Some programs come with their own update software.

Check the Action Center Regularly

You can also resolve old problems by checking for new solutions in the Action Center. You already learned about the Action Center and how to use it in Chapter 9, but Microsoft may have a solution for you now that wasn't there the last time you checked. To find out, open the Action Center, and if you see the option to check for solutions, click it. If solutions are presented, perform them as applicable.

TIP   Make sure you check the Action Center every now and again to see if it has any suggestions for resolving the lingering problems you're having.

While in the Action Center, click Change Action Center Settings. From the window that opens, you can disable messages that the Action Center generates. Figure 13-4 shows the categories. If you're sure you don't need to see notifications about a specific item, go ahead and deselect it.

Finally, click Problem Reporting Settings at the bottom of the window shown in Figure 13-4. From there, make a choice regarding how and when to check for solutions to problems. I prefer Automatically Check for Solutions (Recommended).

Use Program Compatibility Mode

Old software can cause new problems when you install it on a computer it wasn't intended for. It can hang up, shut down, or even cause the computer to become unstable. If you've looked for an update (both free and for a price) and can't find one,

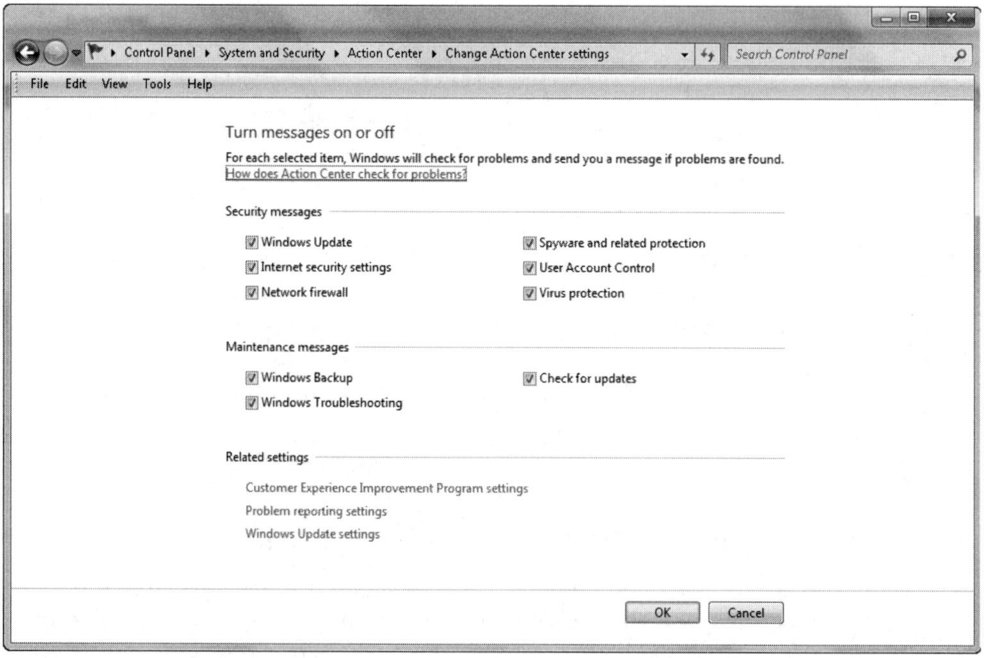

FIGURE 13-4   I prefer to leave all of these checked, just in case, but you can deselect specific items if you wish.

consider Program Compatibility Mode. Program Compatibility Mode lets you run an older program in a separate environment, like a Windows XP environment.

NOTE   If your favorite software program was created for Windows XP, no update is available, and you can't replace it or don't want to, run it in Program Compatibility Mode.

You may know that right-clicking any program icon brings up a deluge of choices. You choose Properties to see the properties for the program. From there, you can tell the program what to do when you click the shortcut icon. I like my programs to start in Maximized mode, for instance, shown in Figure 13-5. Properties is also the dialog box where you configure program compatibility.

To configure a program to run in Compatibility Mode:

1. Locate the program icon on the Desktop or the program name on the Start | All Programs menu. The program has to be one that you've installed; you can't set compatibility options for Windows 7 applications like Internet Explorer, Paint, or similar programs.

FIGURE 13-5   Right-click to access a program's Properties dialog box, where you can configure various settings for the program.

2. Right-click the program icon and choose Properties.
3. Click the Compatibility tab, check Run This Program in Compatibility Mode For, and notice that the options in the drop-down list become available.
4. Choose a mode for the program from this drop-down list. See Figure 13-6.
5. Click OK.

TIP   Don't run antivirus software in Program Compatibility Mode.

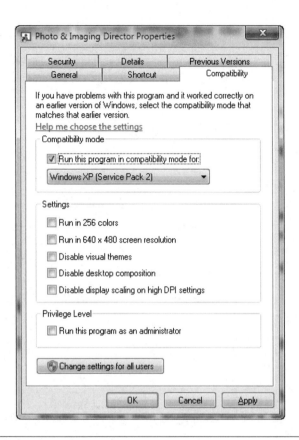

FIGURE 13-6   If a problematic program can't be upgraded or replaced, run it in the mode it was created for.

Make Multimedia Games and Software Run Better

Multimedia and games use DirectX, a tool that enhances the multimedia capabilities of your computer. DirectX enables programs to determine the hardware capabilities of your computer and then sets program parameters to match, thus making sure the program can access and use all of the high-performance options available. You can learn about DirectX and your hardware capabilities and drivers using the DirectX Diagnostic Tool: Click Start, and in the Start Search window, type **dxdiag**. Click dxdiag in the results. Figure 13-7 shows the interface.

If you are familiar with DirectX terminology and tools, or if you just want to see if there are any problems, you can work through the tabs of the dialog box. Each offers information on various problems and features. If you do find problems, click Help. There, you'll find various troubleshooters that will walk you through solving any problems you've found.

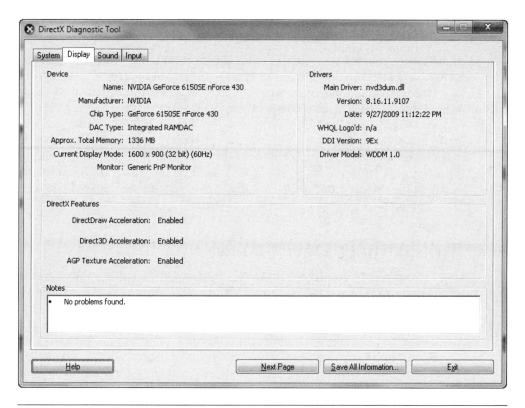

FIGURE 13-7   The DirectX Diagnostic Tool window offers options for tweaking and enhancing DirectX on your system.

GunkBuster's Notebook: So You Think You Want to Explore PowerShell?

You may have heard something about PowerShell, another new feature of Windows 7. You may think that right about now would be a good time to take a look at it. Perhaps it can help you get rid of those last, few, lingering error messages you just can't shake. Well, it's not about that, and no, it won't work. However, no book on degunking Windows 7 would be complete without at least a short description of it. In that vein, here it is:

Windows PowerShell lets you automate tasks, and consists of a command-line interface and an associated scripting language. With it, you can perform administrative tasks on both local and remote Windows computers. So, you use Windows PowerShell to automate IT tasks, not to resolve error messages. And it's highly unlikely you'll ever want to automate IT tasks on your newly, degunked, Windows 2007 PC. So back off, folks! Nothing to see here!

What, you're still here? Okay, if you really want to learn more about PowerShell, visit http://technet.microsoft.com/en-us/library/bb978526.aspx.

Finalize Hardware Degunking

Hopefully, your software is now in order. Before continuing, though, seriously consider uninstalling software that still causes error messages and purchasing something else to take its place. If the troublesome software is related to hardware, it's likely the hardware is troublesome too. The combination could be wreaking havoc.

And speaking of hardware, here are a few last-ditch efforts to degunk your peripherals. You can update their drivers, roll back drivers you try but that don't work, and replace incompatible devices. Beyond that, though, you can also upgrade your internal hardware. You can add RAM to improve overall computer performance, add a second monitor to extend your display, add an external drive to back up your data, and more.

Troubleshoot Device Drivers

You've installed device drivers. A *device driver* is software that enables an external peripheral or internal hardware to communicate with your computer. Generally a driver is included on a disc that comes with a device, but for the most part (99 percent of the time), you don't even need that disc. Windows will detect a newly connected device, locate the driver for it online, and install it. No problems. No gunk.

However, on rare occasions you have to go looking for a device driver. Perhaps an old printer won't work on your new Windows 7 machine, and Program Compatibility Mode doesn't help with the generic driver that Windows installed. Perhaps you've lost the device driver disc. Maybe you purchased the hardware from a garage sale and didn't get any drivers with it. In these cases, you have to take charge.

GunkBuster's Notebook: Wait! Don't Install That Device Driver Disc!

When you get a new hardware device, don't install the disc that comes with it! Most of the time that disc contains much, much more than a device driver. It contains unwanted software, update software, registration software, and more! It's 75 percent gunk, which you're probably going to end up uninstalling.

Instead, connect the device and turn it on. Wait to see if Windows can locate the device driver. I've never installed anything on my Windows 7 machines that Windows couldn't handle. Then, see if you can make the device work without any of the disc gunk. You may be able to use Windows Live Photo Gallery to import pictures from cameras, Windows Live Mail or Microsoft Office Outlook to e-mail those pictures, or Facebook to upload them to the Web. You may be able to use the Computer window to access the files on a device (think phones, MP3 players, and the like) or a program you already have like iTunes or Windows Media Player to manage the media you acquire with it.

The point? Don't get this far in degunking your PC only to gunk it up with unwanted software!

You can find device drivers in a number of ways:

- In Device Manager, you can opt to update any current device driver. Opt to let Windows search for the correct one.
- You can run Windows Update.
- You can check the Action Center for suggestions.
- You can add a device manually in Control Panel.
- You can search the Web for a compliant or substitute device driver, although you should be wary about drivers that you find in odd corners of the Web—stick to the manufacturer's web site if at all possible.

Unfortunately, when you go this route, you can create more problems than you already have. You can install an incompatible driver and cause the system to become unstable, for instance. The system may even completely shut down. Installing an incorrect driver for a device doesn't just affect the hardware you're installing the device for; it can affect your entire system.

If you suspect a newly installed driver has caused a system problem, you can remove that driver and replace it with a different one. You can also use the rollback feature of Windows 7 and instruct your system to use an older version of a driver. You can access Roll Back Driver in Device Manager, as shown in Figure 13-8.

FIGURE 13-8   Roll Back Driver is available in Device Manager.

To access the screen in Figure 13-8:

1. Click Start and right-click Computer.
2. Click Properties.
3. Click Device Manager.
4. Expand the applicable trees and double-click the problematic device.
5. Click the Driver tab.
6. Click Roll Back Driver. (Note that this option will be grayed out if no new drive has been installed.)

If you're having other issues, for instance, if you don't know what device is causing problems:

1. If you have recently installed more than one hardware device, such as a camera and a scanner, disconnect all the hardware devices that you have installed recently and then connect each device, one at a time, and test to see if you can find the device that is causing problems for your system.
2. Once you find the problem device, reinstall the hardware driver for it. Use the installation disc that came with the hardware device and follow the instructions carefully or use one of the other options for installing a driver, detailed earlier. It is possible that device driver files became corrupted and reinstalling them can solve your problem.
3. If this doesn't work, navigate to the web site of the company that produces the device you are reinstalling the driver for. Many companies offer driver updates for free, and their web sites are likely to have the most recent drivers. Find the driver you need, download it, and install it.
4. After you successfully install the new driver, reboot your computer to ensure that the new driver gets initialized properly.

Replace Incompatible Devices with Compatible Ones

If you have recurring and unexplainable problems with your computer, problems such as those listed here, you may have incompatible hardware (and device drivers):

- Your system crashes randomly, but you think you may see a pattern. It just might have to do with a specific piece of hardware or software.
- A program that you use regularly locks up without warning, or when you're exploring for a file, trying to scan a photo, or trying to share a document to an online entity.
- Your computer freezes up when performing tasks like printing files or produces errors or hangs when you turn a specific device on.
- A new device you've recently connected to your computer, such as a scanner or a printer, is causing your computer to lock up and exhibit other strange behavior.

These problems are obviously created by the hardware that you've added to your computer. You have three choices: you can wait it out to see if Windows Update or the manufacturer produces a solution or new driver, remembering to check often for updates; you can disconnect the device and uninstall the hardware, and find some other way to perform the task you want to perform until a new driver or solution is issued; or, you can remove the device and the software and replace it with something else. I suggest the third option if you can afford it.

NOTE You may be able to view and troubleshoot problem devices in the System Information window. Type **msinfo32** in the Start Search window, click it in the results, and expand the Components tree.

Upgrade Hardware When You Can

There are lots of types of hardware you can acquire to beef up your system, including adding RAM, additional monitors, and/or a backup device. Adding RAM (physical memory) is the way to go if you want faster performance and your computer supports it, adding a second monitor can certainly enhance productivity, and installing a backup device can obviously enhance security (if you use it).

Add Memory

Adding memory is the easiest and fastest way to speed up and improve the response time of your computer. These days, purchasing an extra 2–3GB of RAM won't break the bank, either.

NOTE RAM stands for random access memory, and it's where Windows stores data it needs or thinks it will need very soon to complete a task such as printing a document, performing a calculation, or rendering edits you've made to a photo.

RAM is an important component because it is used for the temporary storage of data and code that you need to perform a task such as cropping or recoloring an image, multitasking between programs, or using commands like Copy and Paste. RAM is fast and can be accessed much more quickly than the hard drive. When RAM gets full, though, and there's no free space left for storing data temporarily, Windows 7 sends data over to the hard drive in an area called a paging file. Obviously, this happens a lot more often when you have smaller amounts of memory in a PC. Accessing data from the paging file on a hard drive takes much longer than accessing it from RAM on the motherboard, so if you are low on RAM, you're sure to experience slower response times than you need to.

Although I could talk for quite some time about the types of RAM available, what kind of RAM you may need, how much RAM your particular computer can have installed (can support), how much each Windows 7 edition supports, and more, it's ultimately easier for you to run the Crucial System Scanner tool, which is free. It will scan your system and produce a nice, neat report with all you need to know. To get started, navigate to www.crucial.com and click Scan My System. Figure 13-9 shows Crucial's suggestions for one of my PCs.

Once you have the new RAM in hand, you'll need to install it. Your RAM should come with installation instructions, but for the most part, installing RAM is as simple as turning off your computer, unplugging it, locating the slot on the motherboard, and popping in the RAM. Some RAM sticks pop straight in, and some slide in from an angle. Laptops may require a little more work. Be careful when you install new RAM, though; you don't want to "shock" the board or the RAM stick. Make sure you touch the chassis and that the computer is unplugged before you perform any installations. Read the instructions carefully because different memory types install in different ways; however, installing RAM is generally quite simple.

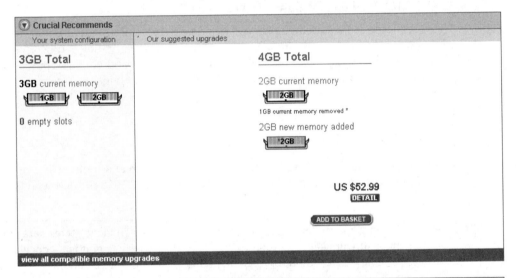

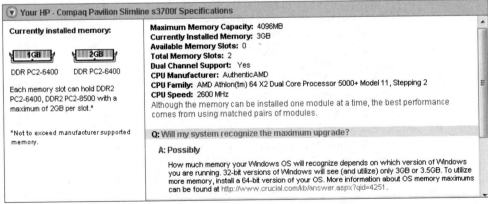

FIGURE 13-9   Let Crucial.com scan your system and suggest what and how much RAM you need.

CAUTION   It is extremely important to ground yourself properly before touching anything inside the computer case. I believe that purchasing a special grounding device is a must. Grounding bracelets only cost a couple of bucks and you can get them wherever RAM can be purchased.

GunkBuster's Notebook: Tweak Virtual Memory Settings

When RAM is full, Windows 7 sends temporary data and code to an area of the hard drive reserved for such events, and data and code are swapped back and forth between the RAM and this special area (the paging file) as needed. Because it takes longer to access data from the hard drive, you'll obviously want to have as much RAM as you can afford (assuming you are into increasing the performance of your computer)! However, no matter how much RAM you have, the data stored there will eventually be swapped, so you want to make sure that the settings configured for virtual memory are the best they can be.

Virtual memory is the imaginary memory area that makes the computer act like it has more memory (RAM) than it actually does. Virtual memory is implemented using a paging file (sometimes referred to as a swap file), which is generally located on the C: drive. You can set the size of this file manually if you'd like, or you can accept the defaults. There are two options to change, the initial file size and the maximum file size.

The Initial Size box is the area where you provide the number of megabytes for the virtual memory paging file on the selected drive, and it is where you set the initial (or beginning) size of the file. The Maximum Size box is the area where you provide the maximum number of megabytes that can be used for the file. The numbers configured here define the size of the paging file. If you want, you can leave your virtual memory settings to whatever Windows suggests, which is about one and a half times the amount of RAM on the system for the initial size of the file and about three times the amount of RAM for the maximum paging file size. However, there are a few tweaks you can make if you desire:

- If you have 1GB of RAM, leave the paging file as is, using the default settings.
- If you have lots of RAM, say, 3GB or more, set the initial paging file size to about half of the physical RAM and set the maximum size at three times the RAM.
- Keep in mind that an extremely large maximum paging file does not necessarily increase performance and may actually hinder it. You don't want to allot too much of the hard drive area to this file.
- Even if you have 4GB of RAM, don't turn off the paging file. Some programs may crash if no virtual memory is available.

(Continued)

If you'd like to tweak the virtual memory settings, here's how you set a custom paging file in Windows 7:

1. Click Start, right-click Computer, and click Properties.
2. Click Advanced System Settings.
3. On the Advanced tab, under Performance, click Settings.
4. Click the Advanced tab, and under Virtual Memory, click Change.
5. Deselect the Automatically Manage Paging File Size for All Drives check box.
6. Select the drive to manage in the Drive list.
7. Click Custom Size.
8. Input the desired settings in the Initial Size and Maximum Size fields, shown here:

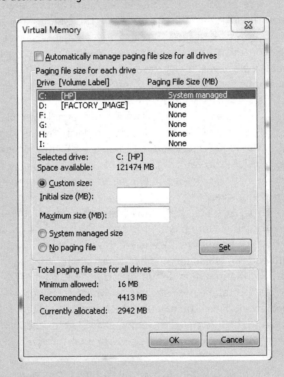

9. Click OK three times to exit.

Add a Second Monitor

If your monitor is all gunked up with running programs and you constantly have to toggle between them, consider adding another monitor. Adding a monitor can be beneficial when you use multiple programs and have to access multiple open windows, such as a day trader, programmer, or artist might need to do. Windows 7 lets you add a monitor (if you have the required hardware) and then extend your desktop to it.

That means you can add another monitor and open a couple of programs on one and a couple of programs on another, and drag items across the boundary between monitors as though both were a single device. This is a really neat feature that many users don't know about. It can quickly solve the problem of not having enough room on the screen to do what you want to do.

Adding a second monitor is easy if your computer comes with two display adapters. You simply plug in the monitor to the second adapter and extend your desktop to it using Display Options in Control Panel. Many computers don't come with this extra adapter, though. (To check, take a look at the back of your computer.) If your computer only has the one display connection, that's okay; you can purchase an external USB converter or install a new display card inside the computer, whatever your preference.

NOTE   I have a USB adapter that lets me connect my secondary monitor to a PC that came with only one display adapter. This was a nice solution for me, since I did not have to open the computer case to install one internally. However, I believe I'd be getting better monitor performance had I opted for an internal card. I am experiencing a little "lag time" on the secondary monitor. Before purchasing an adapter, talk to an expert at a computer store to make sure you purchase exactly what you need.

Once connected, open Control Panel, open Appearance and Personalization, and open Display. Click Connect to an External Display, shown in Figure 13-10, and configure the settings as desired.

NOTE   Almost all laptops support dual monitors by plugging a monitor into the external display port, and using it along with the laptop's built-in display.

Add a Backup Device

To protect yourself from disaster (a hard drive crash, a spilled cup of coffee, or a lighting strike, for instance), you'll want to back up your data regularly. While Chapter 14 (next) is all about backing up your files, here I'd like to talk a little about selecting and adding a physical backup device.

My favorite backup device is the external hard drive (I'm not real fond of the software that comes with these devices, though, as I'll explain later). External backup devices can hold *huge* amounts of data. I really never have to worry about running out of space in the middle of a backup. And, because I can connect it to a computer, do a backup, connect it to another computer, do another backup, and then unplug it and store it in a safe place until the next backup is needed, it meets almost all of my backup criteria.

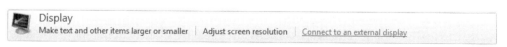

FIGURE 13-10   Windows 7 has built-in support for secondary displays; just connect and extend!

NOTE   It's important to be able to remove the backup device from the physical area where the computer is, in case of flood, fire, power surge, theft, or other unexpected event. It doesn't do much good to have a backup of all your important data on a device that can be destroyed by the same cup of coffee you spill on your computer!

External hard drives can be purchased from almost any computer store or online source and are generally *plug and play*. This means that you simply connect the power cord and connect the Universal Serial Bus (USB) or FireWire cable, and the hard drive is automatically ready to go. Some even come with built-in backup software you can run on a schedule. While I would really like to say that I approve of this software, as it encourages you to set up a backup schedule and backs up your data automatically, I can't. To do this, you have to leave the device on and connected all the time. You know that a thief isn't going to leave that backup device behind when he steals your PC or laptop, and a tornado or flood isn't going to spare it just because you've set it on top of your tower. So, while it's okay to use the software that comes with a backup device if you really do want to, just be careful that you disconnect the device and store it somewhere safe after the backup completes.

Other options are available for backing up data. Here are a few of them:

- Online backup services let you upload data to an Internet server that is managed by a third party. Generally this requires you to pay a monthly fee, but most of the backup tasks are covered:
  - Backups are often scheduled and automated.
  - The backup company keeps redundant copies of your data.
  - You can access your data from anywhere with Internet access.
  - Your backups are offsite.
  - You can back up every night if you desire.
- A backup server is a computer you set up and dedicate solely to backups. You can't really move a server offsite, though, which is a security problem. However, you can create redundant backups and move those offsite. You can also automate backups with a backup server. If you have a spare computer, there's lots of software available to help you turn that into a backup data server.
- CD and DVD drives are okay to use for backups, but can be a little cumbersome as a long-term solution. A single disc doesn't hold the amount of data you'll need to copy to create a full backup, so you'll have to extend the backup across multiple discs. This is only one of the headaches you'll encounter.
- Small USB flash drives are great solutions for moving data offsite and performing quick backups. They fit in the palm of your hand and can store, literally, gigabytes of data. However, it's easy to lose them and all too easy to connect them to a keychain or belt loop, reducing the security of your data. They are also not always big enough to hold a "full" backup. However, USB flash drives have lots of pros too; they
  - Plug into any USB port
  - Are plug and play, so it's easy to move data between non-networked computers
  - Can be used to back up data on multiple computers
  - Can be used to easily move your backup data offsite for safekeeping

The most important advice I can give you is to make sure you actually use your backup device. Don't just put it on your desk to impress the neighbors. Develop a system whereby you back up your data on a regular basis. I'll help you with that in the next chapter. This is especially important as you become more diligent about removing files and programs as part of your degunking routine.

Tweak System Restore Settings

This book would not be complete without mention of System Restore. System Restore is a feature of Windows 7 that creates and automatically stores information about your computer so that if something goes wrong, you can revert to a time when all was well. System Restore *points* are created automatically each day and, in many instances, before a potentially damaging piece of software, update, driver, or application is installed. You can also manually create a restore point, if you think you're about to do something risky. The System Restore interface is shown in Figure 13-11. You're probably aware of System Restore, so I'm not going to discuss how to use it. What I will discuss is how to tweak the settings.

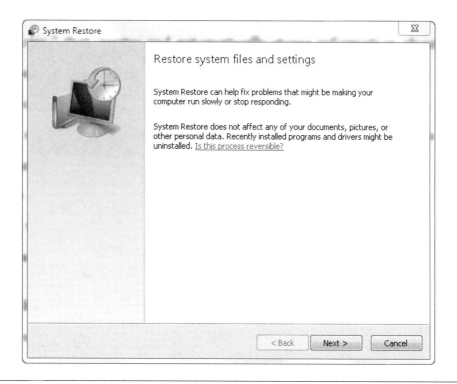

FIGURE 13-11   System Restore lets you return your computer to an earlier time when everything was working properly.

NOTE   System Restore is the perfect tool to solve minor problems with applications gone bad, downloads gone wacky, desktops gone berserk, or drivers gone crazy. It can also be useful if you are suddenly having odd computer problems, problems with applications, or problems with hardware you can't resolve quickly. System Restore can't remove viruses, though, so don't count on it for that.

For all of System Restore's good points, System Restore is a hard disk space hog. It's an important feature, mind you, and I'm not going to suggest you turn it off, but I am going to tell you how to tweak it, just in case you want to save a little (or possibly a lot of) hard drive space.

Let's check out your System Restore settings, and take a look at how much hard drive space is being used:

1. Open Control Panel and click System and Security.
2. Click System and then System Protection.
3. In the System Properties dialog box, under the System Protection tab, select your hard drive.
4. Click Configure.
5. Note, as shown in Figure 13-12, how much disk space is being used by System Restore.

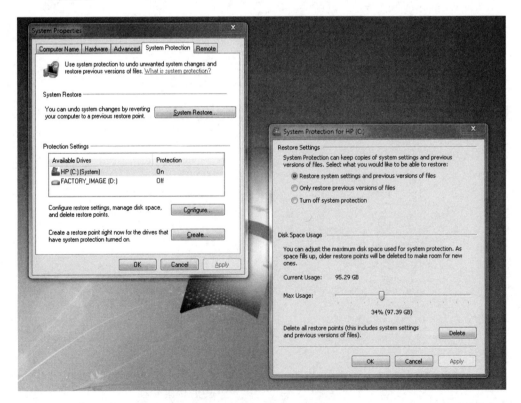

FIGURE 13-12   You may be surprised how much hard disk space is being used.

6. To reduce the amount of disk space System Restore uses, move the slider to the left. To increase it, move it to the right.

NOTE   The more space you allot to System Restore, the more restore points you'll have access to. For the most part, 1GB generally suffices, and with 1GB set aside for System Restore, you'll always have several weeks of restore points from which to choose. This will be a welcome relief if and when you need them.

7. Click OK and OK again to apply your changes.

TIP   System Restore is the first thing you should try before running more time-consuming tasks like upgrading the OS using the Windows 7 DVD.

Repair a Problem Using the Windows 7 Installation DVD

When you encounter problems so severe that you believe you're missing important system files, you can run System File Checker to repair those missing files. Often, this works to resolve the problem. You'll know you're missing system files if cryptic, alien error messages begin to appear, usually at bootup.

To run System File Checker:

1. Choose Start | All Programs | Accessories | Command Prompt.
2. Right-click Command Prompt and click Run as Administrator.
3. Type **sfc /scannow**.
4. Wait while the scan completes.
5. Restart the computer when System File Checker completes, if errors are found and resolved, even if you are not prompted to do so.

If you still see missing-file errors or your computer is no better after running the file check, you can install Windows 7 again, using the Repair option. I'm not sure what good this will do if System File Checker doesn't find any "integrity violations," but you never know. It certainly won't hurt to try; repairing or upgrading Windows 7 won't affect your data or programs. To reinstall Windows 7 and repair your current installation:

1. Log on as administrator.
2. Disable any antivirus programs.
3. Input the Windows 7 DVD.
4. Run the Setup.exe program on the DVD.
5. Choose the Repair option when prompted.

Physically Clean the Machine

I'm not going to say that if you physically clean your machine you'll get better performance, but I will say that if you do, it'll likely last longer than it would if you never clean it. For instance, you absolutely must use canned air at least a few times a year to clean the dust out of the inside of your computer case and to clean out the fan vents. That dust can cause real problems by physically settling on sensitive internal parts and causing them to gunk up (often by overheating)! Additionally, gunk in between keyboard keys can cause them to stick. You don't need a new keyboard; you only need to clean the one you have. And although you may not believe it, cat hair *can* get under that little laser eye hole on the bottom of your mouse and cause it to skip and jump. I know this firsthand. No, it was not the mouse pad!

CAUTION   The inside of your computer case is filled with dust. If you smoke, if you have cats or dogs, or if children have access to your computer, the problem is surely worse.

Keyboard

There are parts of your computer that just collect stuff—your keyboard likely has crumbs in it and your monitor has grime. You have to clean your computer just as you'd clean your house, and you have to have a starting point. Let's start with your keyboard.

CAUTION   Always turn off your PC and all components before cleaning them.

To clean your keyboard:

1. Perhaps this is going to sound silly, but pick up your keyboard, turn it upside down, and give it a couple of good shakes. What fell out? A few eraser bits, a piece of bread, cat hair, a lost hamster, paper clips, and other odds and ends? This might seem like a primitive way to clean, but it works. Use compressed air to get out those stubborn pieces, or use a vacuum cleaner with attachments.
2. Take a bit of liquid bleach cleanser on a clean, lint-free rag and gently wipe off the keys. Use Q-tips to get into the cracks if necessary, but be careful not to drip any cleaner anywhere. You want to get only enough on the rag to clean the stains; you don't want to immerse the keyboard in cleanser or let fluids dribble down between the keys onto the circuit board that holds them.

If you are cleaning a laptop keyboard, you might be able to pop up the keyboard and get under the keys to really clean the gunk out. If individual keys will pop off your keyboard (many do), you can use a small screwdriver to remove a key to get under where the grime really hides. If you use this technique, make sure you remove only one key at a time and replace it before you pop off another key. Otherwise, you could easily forget where your keys go and you'd end up with a real mess! Laptop keyboards really take a lot of "gunking" abuse because they are often used in environments that aren't always the cleanest, such as airports and hotel rooms.

> TIP   If your wireless keyboard or mouse is acting wonky and you've cleaned it, replace the batteries.

Mouse

If you have a generic, roller-ball mouse, which I surely hope you do not, flip it over, turn the backing plate, and remove it. Take out the ball. Use a Q-tip and alcohol to carefully clean the ball and the rollers inside the mouse that the ball touches. You might have to reach in there to pull out the gunk that comes off. Make sure the ball and components are completely dry, and then replace the ball and clean the outside of the mouse with cleanser.

If you have a laser mouse, look very carefully at the bottom of it, where the eye is. If you see anything in there, carefully blow it out or remove it with tweezers, being careful not to scratch the surface. If you have a wireless mouse, open the battery compartment and verify there's no gunk in there. If there is, remove it with canned air or a soft, dry cloth.

Next, consider replacing that worn-out mouse pad; it can have snags or uneven spots that cause the mouse to hang, and may shed fragments that can work their way inside the mouse.

Once you fully clean your mouse like this, you'll be amazed at how well it works.

Computer Case

If you want to clean the outside of the computer case, do so carefully. A small rag with a little dish soap usually works, but you have to be very careful not to drip any cleanser into the case, the disc drives, printer ports, display ports, or USB ports. Getting these components wet can damage or destroy them. The same holds true of the back of the computer case where all of the external hardware plugs in. Don't go near that with anything wet at all. A good dusting with a dry cloth should do, and finish out all the cracks and crannies with clean, dry Q-tips.

> TIP   For better scans, clean your scanner bed with window cleaner and wipe it until it's streak-free.

Monitor

Clean the monitor based on your manufacturer's instructions. If you have a regular CRT monitor with a glass screen, you can usually clean the screen with a glass cleaner on a clean, lint-free rag. Turn it off first, unplug it, don't spray too much cleaner on the rag, and be sure to clean all of the streaks with a dry towel. If you have an LCD (or flat) screen, use a soft, dry cotton cloth. If that doesn't work, try adding a little rubbing alcohol on the cloth to remove the stubborn stains. As with cleaning your keyboard, don't let fluid run down the display face and into the body of the monitor.

TIP CD/DVD drives can be cleaned with special CD-ROM cleaners you can purchase from a computer store.

Degunk Inside the Case

The inside of the computer case contains all of the working parts and should be cleaned at least twice a year to maintain optimal performance. Dust particles, animal hair, and cigarette smoke can get sucked into the computer via the air vents, and before you know it, these contaminants can corrode the circuitry and cause other problems. While this only really applies to desktop PCs, you can still use canned air on a laptop to disperse dust that collects by the vents.

Most experts agree that using compressed air is the best way to clean the inside of the computer case, although some prefer a vacuum. Either way, the procedure is basically the same. Here I'll detail the compressed air option:

1. Turn off the computer, unplug it, and carefully open the case. If the case opens on more than one side, open both sides. Remember, we're talking only about desktop PCs here, not laptops.
2. Position the computer so that when you blow the compressed air into it, the dust will be removed from the case, not just blown around in it. You should also be able to vacuum up what is blown out, so don't blow all of that dust underneath your desk!
3. Hold the compressed air in the upright position and use the air quickly and in short bursts to remove the gunk.

If you're a smoker, have pets, or are in a dusty environment, repeat this procedure four times a year; nonsmokers, those without pets, and those in a clean environment should repeat this procedure twice a year.

Summing Up

It seems like you can always find something else to degunk. When you're finished degunking, it seems like you have to start again, from the beginning. While this is ultimately true, once you've been through the degunking process once, subsequent degunking sessions should take far less time.

In this chapter you learned some final degunking techniques. You learned how to get rid of system pop-ups and third-party pop-ups to make the computer less annoying. You learned how to run older software, find drivers for older hardware, and troubleshoot driver issues. You learned what can be upgraded and how, and even some tips for physically cleaning your machine.

14

Back Up Precious Files

Degunking Checklist:

☑ Put safeguards in place to avoid needing your backups in the first place

☑ Learn what to back up

☑ Learn how often to back up

☑ Learn how to store backups

☑ Create a full backup with the Windows 7 Backup and Restore application

☑ Drag and drop files to a USB flash drive for redundancy and to create daily backups

☑ Understand the restore process

One of the most important tasks for a computer user to remember to do is to back up data regularly. And as you become more diligent about degunking your PC on a regular basis, you'll need a good backup strategy. After all, degunking your PC properly involves deleting documents and programs as well as moving files around on a regular basis. If you have a regular backup strategy in place, you'll feel more confident about getting rid of files and programs because you'll be able to restore them if you later decide that you need them.

CAUTION   The worst kind of degunker you can be is the "packrat degunker," which is the person who is afraid to throw anything away because they think that something valuable might be lost. Usually, this fear comes from having a lousy backup strategy!

Backing up data is especially important these days because we store everything—family videos, pictures, music, important documents, faxes, important records—all on a single hard drive. Imagine how much data could be destroyed by a single hard drive crash! A hard drive crash isn't the only thing that can happen, though; a hard drive disaster can also be caused by a house fire or flood. Imagine, every important picture, video, file, and fax would be lost in such a catastrophe.

In this chapter, you'll learn various ways to back up data and the best places to store it once it's done. I know I've talked about backing up data in previous chapters, but this chapter brings all the details together in one place so that, a year from now, when you're looking for backup advice, you won't have to search the entire book to obtain the tidbits scattered throughout.

TIP   It's not just a hard drive crash that can steal your data. A thief can too.

Make Sure Safeguards Are in Place

This entire chapter is dedicated to backing up your data. However, the best backup is one you never have to use. Before you start backing up anything, then, read and put in place the safeguards listed next. You can help prevent ever having to use your backups by keeping the following in mind and in place.

- Secure your computer and/or your home. Kensington makes computer locks to secure any computer to any desk.
- Don't leave a laptop on a car seat for a thief or the heat or cold to get to it, and if you must leave it in your car, lock your doors and put the computer in the trunk of the car.
- Secure your computers with passwords, and pick strong passwords that contain letters, numbers, and symbols. If your computer is stolen, you can safely use your backups on your new, replacement PC without fearing your data has been compromised.

Beyond those physical safeguards, verify that

- Windows Defender is running.
- Antivirus software is installed and running, and set to update regularly.
- System Restore is running on all drives that contain data. See Figure 14-1.
- Action Center is configured to look for and suggest solutions to problems it finds.
- Windows Update is set to get all updates automatically and to install all important ones.

Finally, know your options before opting to restore your computer from a backup:

- If you're having boot problems, don't opt to simply reinstall. During bootup, press F8 and choose Last Known Good. If that doesn't work, try Safe Mode and then troubleshoot the problem.
- If you're having data problems, don't restore from a backup just yet. Try System Restore.
- If you've installed a driver and the computer is acting weird, try Roll Back Driver.
- In an administrator console session, type **sfc /scannow** to replace missing system files. (To do this, choose Start | All Programs | Accessories and right-click Command Prompt. Opt to Run as administrator.)

FIGURE 14-1   Make sure System Restore is enabled; it can be used to get you out of a jam.

GunkBuster's Notebook: Perform Backups Before Deleting, Installing, Moving, and Experimenting

You know you should create a System Restore point prior to performing a risky task like installing a downloaded application from a third-party web site, installing software from a file sharing Internet site, performing virus removal tasks, or installing an unsigned driver. But you might not know that there are other circumstances under which you should also perform a backup.

Although System Restore can often restore your computer successfully if something happens, sometimes it can't. This is especially true if a procedure such as removing a virus, editing the Registry, or installing some third-party software

(Continued)

that has questionable code goes awry. You'll need a good, solid backup to recover from that. Create a backup before doing anything risky, including the following:

- Installing software you've downloaded from the Internet
- Editing the Registry
- Making changes to the BIOS
- Installing an upgrade
- Creating a dual-boot system
- Using partition-moving software to make major changes to the hard disk's configuration
- Performing a virus removal procedure
- Joining a file sharing Internet group

Learn What to Back Up and How Often

You must make sure you have good, solid backups that you can trust. You can easily get gunked up with a virus; even the most secure computers can catch a virus if you hit the wrong web site at the wrong time, or open an infected e-mail from a trusted friend. Of course, if you're poking around in the Registry, you can create your own problems just as easily. And you well know that you must always be prepared for disaster or theft. Bad things happen to good people (and good computers). Be a good Boy Scout and *be prepared*.

What and How to Back Up

So what should you back up and how should you do it? For the home user, I suggest creating a complete backup using Windows Backup and Restore and storing it on a separate hard drive first, and then following that up with various backups of important data to CDs or DVDs, iPods, iPads, external drives, flash drives, network drives, MP3 players, and/or other mediums. You can back up data you create daily to a flash drive, to create a sort of interim plan for your data between complete backups. By having a complete backup along with various others, you can be sure that you'll have the data you want should the need ever arise.

While you're in backup mode, make sure you're backing up everything you should be backing up. If you're an artist, you likely have a Fonts folder that is very important to you, and perhaps it changes regularly as you add new fonts. You may have personal folders or client folders you've created that are not part of your personal folder system or personal libraries. Some of this data might not get backed up automatically unless you specifically identify it. You may have data stored on external drives that you'd like to back up. Perhaps you created this data when you moved media you rarely use off of your computer in an earlier degunking session. The point is, take inventory and make a list of everything that needs to be backed up. Then, make a list of things you'd like to back up *twice* (family videos, medical directives, precious photos, pets' records, and similar data). You can then plan your Windows Backup and Restore strategy and another, secondary strategy.

How Often to Back Up

You should develop a backup schedule based on how much data you can stand to lose. I perform a backup to a flash drive for important data like chapters and screen shots at the end of each working day, but I make quite a few changes every day to the data stored on my hard drives and I consider my data quite valuable. I perform complete backups using Windows Backup and Restore once a week on a schedule. It's pretty carefree. I also have a library of DVDs that contains archived data (really old stuff), and an external drive to back up music, photos, videos, and so forth (sort of a backup of backups). I keep the latter because, well, you just never know if the Restore portion of Windows Backup and Restore will work in every situation, and I want to be prepared. (Oh, and I have an iPad for all of my media.) If, however, you only log on twice a week to send a few e-mails, there's certainly no need to create a backup schedule like this one. Table 14-1 briefly outlines common backup strategies.

Regardless of how much you use your computer, you should have at least one complete backup, and you should create it now. If you can install a backup device and create a schedule for it, even better. You should perform daily backups to flash drives or external drives as you deem necessary. I think, for most people, backing up important data like family photos and such should be redundant.

TABLE 14-1   Backup Schedules for Different Users

If you are a...	Perform a backup of data recently added or changed...	Perform a complete backup with Windows Backup and Restore...
Casual user who only turns on the computer twice a week to e-mail a friend	Once every two weeks or anytime anything is created that cannot be lost	Four times a year
Home user and access the computer daily	Two or three times a week or anytime anything is created that cannot be lost	Six times a year
Home user and digital media enthusiast or if you work from home	Once a day, at the end of each day	Once a week or twice a month
Home user and run a home-based business	Once a day, at the end of each day	Once a week

Where to Store Backups

As you know, a spilled soda that lands on your computer and then spills over onto your backup device will destroy both, so placing your external hard drive (with your backups on it) on top of your tower doesn't make much sense. In the same vein, a lightning strike that gets by your surge protector will likely destroy anything that's plugged into it, so even having the backup device in the same room can offer up problems. A fire that destroys your home will also destroy the backup on a networked computer in the same house. Thus, if you can store your backups to an external drive that you can take offsite, do so. If you can store it to a network drive, do so. If you can store your data "in the cloud" on Internet servers in some other state or country, do so. Remote storage solves all of the problems that have to do with your backups being destroyed or stolen the same time your computer is. If you can't take it offsite, at least put your data on a drive that you can leave in another room.

CAUTION   Whatever you do, don't save your backups on the same computer where the data resides!

Use the Windows 7 Backup and Restore Application

You'll be a better degunker if you're comfortable with your backups. As noted earlier, one of the best ways to get started is to use the Backup and Restore application that comes with Windows 7. It offers an easy way to back up your data regularly. If the need ever arises you can pick and choose what to restore. It's a pretty nifty application.

NOTE   To open Backup and Restore, either search for it from the Start Search window or follow this path: Start | All Programs | Maintenance.

Using Windows Backup and Restore does not require you to have any special equipment, but it does require you to have some place to save the backup file. This can be a second hard drive, a USB flash drive, an iPod, or network drive. (You'll have to have Windows 7 Professional or Ultimate to back up to a network drive.) You can burn backups to DVDs, too. Beyond that, you can use Backup and Restore to create a new, full backup anytime, create a system image of your computer, or create a system repair disc. You'll learn more about all of this here.

Create a Complete Backup

So what's the next step, and how do you decide what to back up? That depends on how you've been saving your data and where. If you've taken my advice and moved all of your data into your personal folders, Public folders, and system libraries, you don't have much to worry about. You can tell Windows Backup and Restore to decide what to back up for you. This is shown in Figure 14-2.

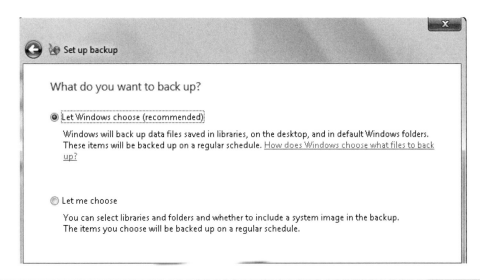

FIGURE 14-2   If you have been a diligent degunker and you know your data is in system folders, you can choose this option in Backup and Restore.

If you don't think that Windows is going to get that odd Clients folder on your C: drive, an obscure Fonts folder created by your image editing program, or data you have created or saved in quiet corners of the computer that aren't system default areas, you'll have to tell Windows what to do. I actually prefer this option, as it gives me more control, so I'll suggest you opt for it.

Walking you through each step for setting up a backup isn't imperative here. It's a wizard after all, and you can't go wrong. You need to connect a backup device, and you need to start the Backup and Restore program, but that's about it. However, during the wizard process, consider the following options carefully as you set up that first, complete backup:

- If possible, store your backups on an external drive. Connect the drive before continuing. Often, flash drives aren't big enough to hold a backup you create here, and if you opt for CDs or DVDs, you may have to span the backup across them. Get an external drive or use a network drive for best results.
- When setting up your first backup using the Backup and Restore wizard, seriously consider choosing manually the files and folders to back up. That way, you can be sure of what you're backing up.
- If you opt to manually select what to back up, browse each available tree (shown in Figure 14-3). Select everything you want. (If you have created a folder on the C: drive, for instance, under C:\, locate the folder and check it.)
- Set the backup utility to run on a schedule, weekly, monthly, or what suits your needs. When the backup is scheduled to run, make sure the backup device is connected and turned on.

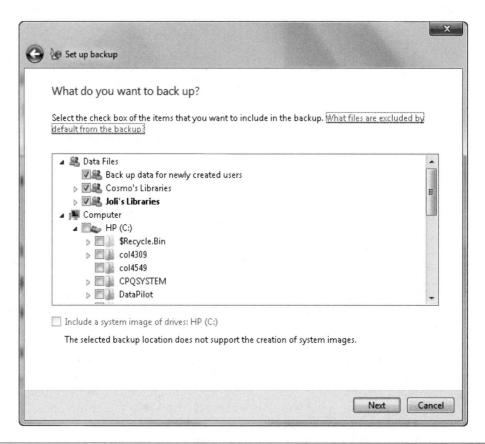

FIGURE 14-3 When you opt to select files manually, you select what you want to back up.

TIP   If you ever need to restore any data, connect your backup device or insert backup media, open Backup and Restore, and click Restore My Files. There you'll find options to select what backup to pull from and what files to restore.

Create a System Image and Repair Disc

Once you've completed your first backup, return to Backup and Restore and decide if/ when other backups are in order. You really should create a system image even if you think you'll never use it, an option shown in Figure 14-4. A system image is a copy of your hard drive. It's like a photograph. If you opt to restore from the system image, you can't pick what to restore and what not to; you can only restore the entire image. I suggest creating a system image two times a year, and whenever you make a major change like installing a service pack.

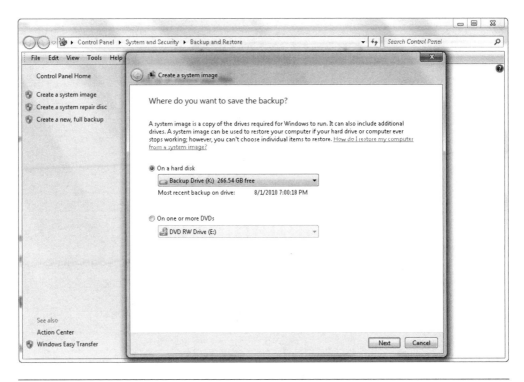

FIGURE 14-4   Creating a system image is an option from Backup and Restore.

You should also create a system repair disc. You can use this disc to boot the computer if you have problems with startup. This option is available in Backup and Restore under Create a System Repair Disc. You'll only need to do this once.

TIP   If you ever need to restore from a system image, open Backup and Restore, click Recover system settings on your computer. This option is at the bottom of the Backup and Restore window. Next, click Advanced Recovery Methods. Opt to recover using a system image.

Drag and Drop Files to a USB Flash Drive

You can back up files to a USB flash drive quite easily. This is a good daily backup option for quickly saving data you've recently changed. It can also serve as a solution for backing up data in between scheduled backups. This is a very common use for USB flash drives.

FIGURE 14-5   You can easily drag and drop to back up data or to create redundant
backups of data.

You can use the USB flash drive option to configure redundant backups, too. You
can use one large USB drive for backing up photos, another for videos, and another for
documents and other data. You can then easily store these drives in a safe deposit box
or at your parent's or children's house. Additionally, if you only have a few specific
folders to back up or if you don't have another device to save a backup to, you can use
the USB drive to manually back up that data as well.

The best way to set up your screen for backing up data to a flash drive is the
split-screen method. Open a window for your flash drive on the left, and a window
for your personal folders on the right. Then, just drag and drop files between them.
See Figure 14-5.

While we're on the subject of backing up small amounts of data to an external
drive, consider backing up oddly placed data. One example is data you don't think
about very much. Internet Explorer data includes cookies and favorites, for instance.
To back up this data, open Internet Explorer, press the ALT key to show the menu
bar, click File, and click Import and Export. Choose Export to a File and then choose
Favorites, Feeds, and/or Cookies, as desired. See Figure 14-6. (You can try a similar
approach to your e-mail program or other web browsers, among other things.)

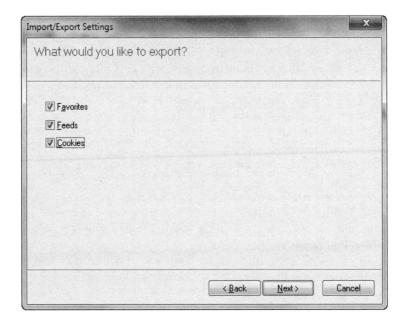

FIGURE 14-6   It's often easy to back up data from applications, like Internet Explorer.

Understand How to Restore Your Computer

If you lose a folder of data (or perhaps even a single file), and that data is not in the Recycle Bin, but it is on a USB drive, external drive, network drive, CD or DVD, iPad, iPod, MP3 player, or the like, you can easily restore the data by connecting the backup media and dragging the data back to the computer where it belongs. That's one reason I like this option for backing up, and especially for redundant backups. It's simple and you never have to sweat that it'll work. There are no wizards, no applications to go through, and no fear that a program will throw up some dreaded "can't find backup" message or "backup is corrupt." That just doesn't happen with data you drag and drop.

If that data isn't stored via drag and drop, but you instead have the data backed up with Windows Backup and Restore, you'll have to work through the Restore wizard to restore the data. I hope I haven't scared you; the majority of the time this works just fine. But I do hear horror stories...that's why you can't depend on one type and kind of backup.

NOTE   Most external drives come with a built-in backup program. You can use that in place of Windows Backup and Restore, in addition to it, or not at all.

To restore your computer using Windows Backup and Restore:

1. Connect the device or insert the media where the backup you want to use is saved.
2. If required, plug in and turn on the device; if it's a networked computer, make sure you can connect to it and it is available (turned on).
3. Open Windows Backup and Restore. Remember, you can find it in Start | All Programs | Maintenance.
4. Click Restore My Files.
5. Add files to restore. You can do this by clicking any of the following (I'll click Browse for Folders, as it's the easiest option to configure):
   a. Search
   b. Browse for files
   c. Browse for folders
6. If you click Browse for Folders, locate the folder to restore and click Add Folder. See Figure 14-7.
7. Continue adding folders in this manner (or add files as desired using other options) until all of the data you want to add is included.
8. Click Next.
9. Choose In the Original Location or In the Following Location. If you choose the latter, click Browse to state the location.
10. Click Restore.

TIP   If you've lost data, check the Recycle Bin. If you can find it there, right-click it to restore it.

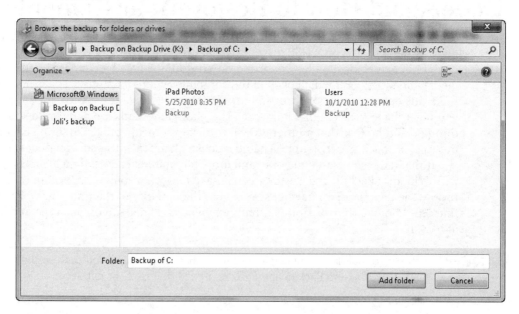

FIGURE 14-7   One way to restore data is to select entire folders to restore. This is easiest.

Summing Up

Good backups promote good degunking habits. If you know you have a backup of your important data, you're more likely to experiment with the degunking techniques introduced in this book. Besides that, though, it's important to keep up-to-date backups for the pictures, videos, personal documents, and other data stored on your computer, because losing all of this data could be potentially devastating. Windows 7 comes with the Backup and Restore application just for this purpose and offers personalized backups. You can schedule the utility to run at regular intervals. You can also drag and drop files to a portable device, burn CDs or DVDs, and store data on network drives to create additional backups. I suggest you create your own redundant backup strategy that includes full and regular backups by Windows Backup and Restore in conjunction with backups you create manually to portable or network drives. Once the backups are created, you should store them in a safe place, out of harm's way, in case they are ever needed.

A

Buy and Degunk a New PC

Degunking Checklist:

☑ Know when to buy a new PC

☑ Prepare a new PC

☑ Degunk a new PC

Sometimes, you just can't degunk an old PC, because no matter how hard you try, 1GB of RAM or 80GB of hard drive space just isn't enough, even with ReadyBoost and an external drive. It could be that the processor isn't fast enough to stream media or perform the task of rendering photos in Photoshop. Perhaps it's just noisy; the constant grinding of the hard drive or the whirring of an overworked fan can drive you nuts. These sounds also represent the eventual demise of some part of the PC, a sort of heads-up that you're going to need a new computer soon.

NOTE   There will be a time when your computer will pass on to the big computer graveyard in the sky.

The majority of the time you *can* degunk a computer, though, and get another few years out of it. That's what you've learned in this book. I hope that you've done all of that, and your computer is running along at breakneck speed. However, you well know that computers don't last forever, and sometimes, degunking just doesn't give you all of the results you need. 1GB of RAM, for instance, just won't cut it, and there's only so much you can do to improve performance if you can't add more.

In this appendix, you'll learn how to know when you need a new PC, how to prepare your new PC for use, and how to degunk a new PC to get the best performance possible.

How, When, and Why to Buy a New PC

Although I'll stress that this is a measure of last resort, you might have reached
the limits of what degunking can do for you if you have encountered the following
situations:

- You've removed all the extra files and programs from your system but it still takes
  forever to start up and runs too slowly.
- Because of all the media you want to store on your computer, or the media you
  want to record or download regularly, you have limited free hard disk space. You
  may even have to delete recorded TV to make room for more before you get to
  watch the programs you've already recorded.
- Your system crashes a lot, you can't figure out why, and you've already tried
  reinstalling the system with a clean install and updating all drivers. (This often
  indicates an intermittent connection somewhere on the motherboard.)
- You find that you need to shut down your computer fairly often and restart it
  simply to make it run a little better, and calls to tech support don't yield results
  because the computer has been out of warranty for far too long.
- You've tried running newer releases of major software packages and they're
  unusably slow.
- You've tried adding a second monitor but your computer can't handle the extra
  load and the new monitor has a noticeable delay in response time.
- You have no slots for additional RAM, and ReadyBoost isn't cutting it.
- You've considered adding a DVD-RW drive but find that you don't have an extra bay
  or (in case you do have an extra bay) that adding the drive is not cost effective.
- You don't have a built-in TV tuner, and you want to add one, but the hard drive is
  already making sickening sounds and you'd rather not make that investment now
  if the computer's going to die in six months.
- Your computer just isn't repairable because you've spilled coffee on it, it's been
  dropped, or a power surge has damaged the motherboard.

TIP   You might be able to put off buying a new computer for a while by installing
upgrades to your existing one, such as replacing a dying or too small hard drive.
Sometimes this is more reasonable than buying a whole new computer—especially
if you follow the backup instructions in Chapter 14.

So, what's a valiant degunker to do? If you are in this situation, and you know
you need a new computer, don't look to me to tell you what computer to buy, where
to buy it, or what company is good or bad. You can talk to the salesperson about all of
that. I do have some advice, though (imagine that!):

- Get the best new computer you can afford. Don't buy refurbished.
- Shop around and compare prices.
- Read online reviews of each of the computers you're considering.

- If possible, call tech support and see if they answer the phone quickly and if you can understand the person you get on the line.
- Don't buy an extended warranty, but do return the PC if you notice any problems during the initial breaking in period.
- During the first 30 days, turn on and off the computer regularly and look for any issues.
- Remember that you can still use your monitor, keyboard, mouse, printer, scanner, and other hardware. You don't have to buy a "package" with this stuff if you don't need it.
- Get more hard drive space than you think you'll *ever* need.
- Get at least 2GB of RAM, but if you can afford it, get as much as your system will support.
- *And most importantly:* Get a computer that comes with a Windows 7 DVD. A real one. It'd be great if this was accompanied by a "driver disc" or an "applications disc," but you must have a Windows 7 DVD. Don't buy a computer with a "recovery disc." Recovery discs only allow you to reinstall the computer to the condition it was in when you purchased it. This is not good, as you'll see later in this appendix when you start to degunk your new computer.

Prepare and Degunk a New PC

If you purchased a new PC, you can be sure it's filled with stuff you don't want. You'll find trialware, software, music programs, image editing programs, games, programs from the manufacturer that will automatically get updates for all of this gunk, and more. I call it all *crapware*. If you're totally into degunking, I heartily suggest you take a look at all of it for a couple of days, and then seriously consider reinstalling Windows 7 on the PC with the Windows 7 DVD and choosing to install it 'clean.'" If you do this, your PC will be pristine, with only Windows 7 on it and nothing else. Of course, to do this you must have purchased a computer that comes with a Windows 7 DVD, a driver disc, and preferably an applications disc, but if you're serious about starting off fresh, degunked, and neat and clean, this is the way to go.

There's one caveat to this strategy. If the computer came with software you actually want, say Microsoft Office, you'll need some way to reinstall it and activate it. If this is the situation you find yourself in, make sure before you reinstall clean, that you have those discs and activation numbers available.

What happens now depends on what you do with the advice in the previous paragraph. If you opt to install Windows 7 clean, and only have Windows 7 on your PC, you'll need to get a few things like an e-mail program, image editing program, and PDF reader. I'll tell you where to get all of that for free. You also need to transfer your personal data, reinstall printers and scanners, reinstall the software you want to use, and reconfigure your settings, but you have to do that with any new computer. If you opt not to reinstall Windows 7 clean, you'll first need to uninstall all of the crapware you don't want, and then assess what's left. At that time, you can decide what additional programs you need, install all of your existing hardware and software, and transfer your personal data.

What to Do Now if You Installed Windows 7 Clean

If you took my advice and purchased a new PC with a real Windows 7 DVD, *and* you reinstalled the system with the DVD, *and* you installed all of the drivers from the driver disc, *and* you reinstalled the programs you really want, you're awesome and you're ready to go! This is the ultimate way to start with a new PC; no gunk!

Now you'll need to do a few things. You need to configure your connection to the Internet. You need to reinstall any software you own and use regularly, including antivirus software, office software, and image editing software (think McAfee, Microsoft Office, and Photoshop, for instance). You need to install hardware you use regularly, including printers, cameras, scanners, and TV tuners, and you should do this one piece of hardware at a time. You need to connect your computer to your home network, and join it.

With all of that done, you should assess what you have. This may take a few days to really get right. Do you need an e-mail program? Consider the free Microsoft Live Mail. Are you missing an instant messaging program? Consider the free Windows Live Messenger, Yahoo! Messenger, or something similar. Are you in need of an image editing program? Consider the free Windows Live Photo Gallery. Here are a few other things to consider getting, but only if you'll use them:

- Adobe Reader for reading PDF files
- Skype for making Internet phone calls
- Audible, iTunes, Zune, or other proprietary media software
- Calendar syncing software, if you use a mobile or online calendar
- Cell phone syncing software
- Microsoft PowerPoint Viewer, if you do not have Microsoft Office installed
- Netflix for Media Center
- QuickTime for viewing videos
- Social connectors for Internet Explorer
- An alternate web browser like Firefox or Chrome
- Microsoft Security Essentials for free antivirus protection

What to Do Now if You Want to Degunk Your New PC Manually

New PCs these days come with all sorts of gunk preinstalled, including free trials from Internet service providers, free trials of software, and installed software you don't want and don't need. You could have more than a few gigabytes of gunk on there that you'll never use! It's not just that, though; these programs may start and run in the background when you boot the computer. Gunk! They may be constantly checking for updates, providing annoying pop-ups, and using system resources and bandwidth. Gunk!

Here are some examples of what you can expect to find on a new PC from a major retailer or PC manufacturer; while reading through this list, try to decide whether or not you'd use or appreciate this software:

- A free trial of Microsoft Office or Norton AntiVirus. Note that this will expire in 60 or 90 days, after which you'll be prompted regularly to buy it.
- A free trial for online service companies that offer Internet access for a fee.
- Software that will produce unexpected desktop pop-ups from the manufacturer, prompting you to upgrade your warranty, register, get updates, or visit its web site.
- Proprietary software from the manufacturer that you won't use, such as media music services, media installers, photo upload software, and "experience" or "instructional" software.
- Third-party software you may not be interested in, including mapping software, encyclopedias, music software, DVD burning software, games, and image editing software.
- Bundled office software that you won't need if you already use Microsoft Office or opt for something like OpenOffice.
- Multiple CD and DVD burning software applications.
- Third-party software that will often time-out 30 to 60 days after you first use it.

You need to get rid of what you won't need or won't be using right away. Don't let your brand-new PC become bogged down before you ever get the chance to gunk it up yourself! But, how do you know what to keep, what you need, and what you can safely delete? It isn't that complicated, really. Let's start with the free trials.

Free Short-Term Trials

On almost any new PC, you can expect to find a free trial of something. It may be a free trial for an Internet service provider, which you can access from the desktop, or it may be free trial software for an application, which you can access from the All Programs menu. Free trial versions of applications are "hookware," in that you can use them for a very limited time (sometimes only 30 days) and then must buy the full version. Don't get hooked! Of course, this is gunk, but how do you get rid of it? Can you? Should you? Will you mess up your new PC if you do? Those are all tough questions, and not too many people know the answers. However, it's a safe bet that uninstalling this gunk from Control Panel will take care of it, and quickly.

TIP   You're not going to want the majority of the crapware and hookware installed on your new PC. Don't be afraid; don't be a packrat. Get rid of it!

Icons on the Desktop

You may know that right-clicking any desktop icon and choosing Delete will remove the icon from your Desktop, and you can do that to get rid of the gunk there, but what you may not know is that it will not remove the actual gunk from your PC. This deletes the icon only. It won't delete the actual files from your PC.

It's the files that take up hard drive space, not the icon. To delete the actual files, visit Control Panel. If the icon is still on the desktop when you're done, right-click to delete it. Scour the All Programs menu for instances of it too, and right-click to delete those, if they exist.

TIP   Before manually deleting any files, you should create a restore point in System Restore. System Restore is available from Start | All Programs | Accessories | System Tools.

Software in the All Programs Menu

If you see free trials and unwanted software in the All Programs menu, or if you open an application and it states that it is a free trial of the application, you'll have to decide whether you want to pony up the extra money to get the full version or delete it from your PC altogether. Of course, you're here to delete stuff, so I'll assume that's what you want to do.

As with the desktop, right-clicking any item in the All Programs menu and choosing Delete will only remove it from the list; it won't remove the gunk from your PC. The actual files will still be on there somewhere. And, if you delete the application from the list now, you'll likely never notice it again and it will never get uninstalled. You often have two ways to go here: Sometimes in the All Programs list you'll see an "uninstall" option. You can use this option to uninstall the unwanted program. If you don't find an uninstall option, or even if you do, you can always turn to Control Panel. Control Panel offers an option to uninstall programs you no longer want, and it's easy to use. Figure A-1 shows some items I consider crapware, along with an uninstall option.

CAUTION   If you're ever prompted, while uninstalling anything, to delete files that may be shared with other applications, always choose No To All. You do not want to delete shared files. Doing so could cause bootup error messages or problems with other applications.

I suggest, as noted before, that you create a System Restore point prior to uninstalling programs or deleting files. That way, if something goes wrong, you can always revert

FIGURE A-1   Look at this crapware!

to the prior system setup. I also suggest that you reboot immediately after deleting programs and that, when you're finished with the tasks here, you use Disk Cleanup to clean up the computer.

Software from the Manufacturer, Third-Party Software, and Duplicate Software

The process for getting rid of software from the PC's manufacturer or from a third party is the same as getting rid of free trial applications. It's best done through Control Panel. This is especially true of software installed by the PC manufacturer. To see what's installed on your PC, browse through the All Programs menu and look for your PC manufacturer's name.

When it comes to uninstalling this kind of software, it's hard to know what you can and can't uninstall. It seems quite logical you'd need to leave intact anything the manufacturer installed. That's simply not true. The operating system contains the files needed to run the PC, and additional files added by the manufacturer are almost always unnecessary.

Here's a quick "for instance": My Sony Vaio has lots of media applications. A quick search on Google informs me that one of those applications is for turning my PC into a server so that networked computers can access media files. I'm not going to do that, and besides, I'd create a homegroup anyway; thus, this software isn't necessary. Additionally, I found several other Sony items, including programs meant to check for updates, a handful of games, and several support files. Again, unwanted. You can safely delete such additional files once you know you do not want to use their respective applications. (Again, though, create a System Restore point, just to be on the safe side, and google anything you're not sure about.)

GunkBuster's Notebook: Duplicate Applications

Just because something came preinstalled on your new PC is no reason to keep or use it. Likewise, there's no reason not to uninstall applications you don't want to use or programs for which you have equivalents. Don't keep it just because you think you "paid" for it; that's not a good enough reason.

Here's an example of duplication. I prefer Microsoft Office for writing, Microsoft Excel for creating spreadsheets, and Microsoft Access for my databases. Just because my new PCs come with other office software doesn't mean I need to change, and it doesn't mean I shouldn't uninstall the program. If I'm not going to use it, it's just gunk.

You'll have to take inventory of what you already have, too. If you use some version of Photoshop CS and your new PC came with a similar program or a trial for one, you should uninstall it. If your new PC came with Quicken but you use QuickBooks, uninstall the former. *Don't let someone else gunk up your brand-new PC.*

Where to Go from Here

If you've opted to manually degunk your new PC instead of reinstalling it clean with Windows 7 only, and you've decided to keep some programs and delete others, you'll now need to assess what you have left. Give yourself a couple of days to figure out exactly what you're missing. You may need a PDF reader, iTunes, an e-mail program, or other items. Return to the section "What to Do Now if You Installed Windows 7 Clean" to see what you need to do now. Briefly:

- You need to configure your connection to the Internet.
- You need to reinstall any software you own and use regularly, including antivirus software, office software, and image editing software (think McAfee, Microsoft Office, and Photoshop, for instance).
- You need to install hardware you use regularly, including printers, cameras, scanners, and TV tuners, and you should do this one piece of hardware at a time.
- You need to connect your computer to your home network, and join it.
- You must take inventory to define what you still need to get. This may take a few days to really get right. You may need to obtain an e-mail program, a PDF reader, Skype, iTunes, QuickTime, Microsoft Security Essentials, and other software.

Options for Transferring Your Personal Data

Once you have your computer in order, degunked of unwanted software, trialware, hookware, and crapware, and you've installed your personal hardware and software, connected to the Internet, and joined your home network, it's time to consider how you'll transfer your personal data. You have two options for doing this: you can use Windows Easy Transfer to transfer your data automatically or you can transfer the data manually.

Using Windows Easy Transfer

Windows Easy Transfer lets you automatically transfer the following: user accounts, documents, music, pictures, e-mail, Internet favorites, videos, *and more*. When it's complete, you'll see a complete report of what was transferred, programs you might want to install, and links to programs you might want to download. So why didn't I mention it sooner? Because I don't want you to use it!

Here's why.

To use Windows Easy Transfer, you need to network the two computers before you use it: the old one and the new one. This requires additional hardware like a null modem cable. If you already have a home network set up, this won't be a problem, but for newbies, this might seem like a lot of work. That's not the bad part, though.

The bad part is that you'll transfer gunk! Lots and lots of gunk! On top of that you'll miss out on that "new computer" feel. You won't be able to start over, and wipe the slate clean of the gunk you have now. I personally prefer to spend the time configuring the computer and transferring data the long way. Then I know exactly what's on it and where it's stored, and there are no possibilities of bringing on residual problems carried over from the previous malfunctioning or gunked up computer. Besides, one of the best ways to decide if the software, icons, and files you have now are gunk or not, is don't move them, period. You'll probably find you don't need them in the long run. (If you decide later you need the data, you can always transfer it from backups.)

The upside of Windows Easy Transfer is, of course, the amount of effort required to set up your new computer. You get to keep your Internet settings, including Favorites and cookies; you get to keep your screen savers, desktop background, and other personal settings; and you get to keep your connections to the Internet and other networks without having to reconfigure them. You can automatically transfer documents, pictures, videos, and music. This saves quite a bit of time. In addition, you can decide exactly what gets transferred. You don't have to transfer the My Pictures folder if you don't want to, and you have similar options with other folders and settings. I still don't like it, though, and suggest you steer clear.

Manually Transferring Data

If you've taken my advice about not using Windows Easy Transfer, your only option is to transfer data manually. You'll use your backups to do this. By now you should have decent backups. Hopefully, you have exceptional backups. Now, you may be able to use the backups you created in Windows Backup and Restore to restore your important data to your PC. That's one way, but it's eerily similar to Windows Easy Transfer. It may be too easy to transfer your gunk over to your new PC.

Thus, I suggest you manually copy data from backups you created to flash drives and DVDs to your new PC. This allows you to be selective about what you transfer. Select only the pictures you want to access from your new PC, and put the rest on an external drive for redundant backup. Move only the music you listen to, and put the rest on a media server (or network drive), or put all of it in the Public Music folder. Move only the videos you still care about. (Perhaps you want to keep the longer version of the video you took of your scenic helicopter ride over the Hoover Dam but don't need the takeoff or landing.) If your list of Internet favorites is organized, export it from Internet Explorer and import it onto your new computer. If it's not organized, don't export it! Just start over. The same is true of other areas too: cookies, e-mail, calendar data, and so on. You get the idea. By handpicking data to move, you won't transfer any gunk from your old PC to your new one.

Summing Up

If your PC's performance is just about as good as it's going to get, if you have ongoing problems that can't be solved, if the computer hangs just as you're really getting used to that new video game, or if the computer has 1GB of RAM and no slots to add extra memory, you might have to consider a new computer. If that's the case, keep in mind that there are tools available to help you make the transition, that new computers come with their own gunk, and that you have to put aside time to get your new computer running efficiently.

Index